American Religions

An Illustrated History

American Religions

An Illustrated History

J. Gordon Melton

A B C ⬥ C L I O

Santa Barbara, California   Denver, Colorado   Oxford, England

Library of Congress Cataloging-in-Publication Data

Melton, J. Gordon.
  American religions : an illustrated history / J. Gordon Melton.
    p. cm.
Includes bibliographical references and index.
  ISBN 1-57607-222-3 (alk. paper) — ISBN 1-57607-377-7 (e-book)
  1. United States—Religion. 2. Religious pluralism—United
States—History. I. Title.
  BL2525 .M47 2000
  200'.973--dc21

00-011924

06 05 03 02 01 00   10 9 8 7 6 5 4 3 2 1

This book is also available on the World Wide Web as an e-book.
Visit www.abc-clio.com for details.

ABC-CLIO, Inc.
130 Cremona Drive, P.O. Box 1911
Santa Barbara, California 93116-1911

This book is printed on acid-free paper.
Manufactured in the United States of America

To June and Zlatko

Contents

American Religions

An Illustrated History

Introduction

As the twenty-first century begins, the United States has emerged as not only the most powerful nation on earth, but also by far the most religiously diverse nation ever. Several thousand distinct religious communities live side-by-side in relative harmony, and in any urban area it is not unusual to see a Catholic church down the street from a Buddhist temple and sharing the block with a Jewish synagogue. Not far away may be a Shi'a Muslim mosque, a Hindu temple, or an occult/New Age bookstore; while walking the streets, one could find some Latter-Day Saint missionaries and a team of Jehovah's Witnesses. Quietly worshiping in nearby apartments might be a coven of neopagan Wiccans or a Christian commune.

To some extent, the United States is a Protestant nation, and the combined membership of the several Baptist, Episcopal, Lutheran, Holiness, Methodist, Pentecostal, Presbyterian, and other Protestant churches still collectively constitutes around half of the American public. But whereas at one time they had a dominating presence among America's religious, they now share the landscape with a thousand competing religious communities that represent the spectrum of the world's religions. A variety of images have been used to express this diversity, among the best being that of a large mosaic, in which a beautiful picture has been created from bits of tile. In the finished picture, each piece of tile retains its individuality completely. Some colors dominate, but all of the pieces are necessary to the completed product. But it is the duty of the art historian to step back and see the total picture that has been created by the coming together in the shared space of the diverse elements.

American Religions: An Illustrated History is a brief summary of how we have arrived at this most interesting development in the human drama. The story begins at the end of the fifteenth century when Europeans discovered the continent and made their initial contacts with the more than 500 different peoples that inhabited it. There was already great diversity among the Native Americans, and the Europeans injected the different varieties of Christianity and Judaism. Here our story really begins and unfolds as the new settlers conquered the land, pushed aside its original inhabitants, and created a new society that we like to think of as the greatest nation on earth. Any account of the mosaic necessarily requires both a perspective and a considerable amount of interpretation.

Some who lived a century ago, and who predicted the demise of religion in the wake of scientific advance and rampant secularization, would marvel that in the twenty-first century we are still writing about religion. Their prophecies proved highly inaccurate, and religion remains a thriving concern in the United States and wherever free societies exist. It has a problem only where the state has used its power to try to control and suppress it. It is also the case that within the spectrum of religious options, one not only can choose many kinds of religion, but can affiliate with groups that advocate a purely secular, non-religious philosophical alternative. One can also choose a level of participation from the occasional visit to a worship service to full-time commitment to the religious life in an ordered community or spiritually oriented commune.

The brevity of this volume means that we are able only to hit the high points of the story and to touch upon the most prominent themes that emerge in the American mosaic. In selecting the stories to pursue, some hard choices had to be made, and I apologize to those who are mentioned only in passing or not at all. Also, space has not allowed the inclusion of a discussion on many of those questions that have been raised by the very pluralistic religious climate in which we live, not the least being the very definition of religion itself. The encounter with such diverse religious bodies as the United Methodist Church, the American Humanist Association, the Lao Buddhist Sangha of the U.S.A., and the Church of Scientology calls into question older and more simplistic definitions of religion.

Over the past twenty years, however, it has been my job to write and regularly update the *Encyclopedia of American Religions* (6th edition, 1999), to live on an almost daily basis with religious diversity, and to make choices about which communities go into the *Encyclopedia*. Working on the *Encyclopedia* has made me aware of the continuing importance of the different primary religious communities that we have often referred to as denominations or sects. They provide the basic structure of our story. If we were writing a novel instead, the larger denominations would be analogous to the major characters who appear in the first chapter, who push the action along, who are still there at the end, and who we surmise will still be there for the sequel. Other lesser characters come on the scene later and rise to importance as the story climaxes. We also take notice of some of the characters who emerge briefly as one scene succeeds another.

The plot of the story is religious diversity, and the question it pursues is how we got that way. From the beginning of the country, a great diversity of religious life could be found in North America, although each center of activity might have only one operative religion in place. It was certainly not the intent of the Europeans who arrived in the sixteenth century to create a pluralistic culture, and each generation has elevated spokespersons decrying the religious chaos they observed around them. This book attempts to provide the reader with some perspective on that seeming chaos.

As the name implies, this is also an illustrated volume, and considerable time has been spent gathering a number of pictures to complement the text. There are some instructive maps, portraits of major figures, scenes of religious people in action (many taken from contemporary sources), and reproductions of interesting artifacts. In addition there are important documents, appearing as sidebars, chosen for their importance in marking significant directions taken by those pushing the larger story along. With the treaty of Tordesillas, the Spanish tried to assert initial hegemony over North America. By 1944, the Supreme Court was dealing with the expanding implications of religious liberty.

Finally, *American Religions: An Illustrated History* is an introductory text, and thus I have attached at the end a list of books for further reading on the issues raised in each chapter. These are by no means the only ones I could have chosen, American religious history having been a vital discipline during the last decades of the twentieth century. However, I did choose from volumes that I know, that are fairly accessible, and that provide a more expanded coverage of the themes developed in each chapter. At the beginning of the Bibliography the reader will also find a list of other books on American religions in which my learned colleagues have offered more extended discussions of the overall American mosaic. I recommend any of them as follow-up reading that will supplement this volume. I have also listed a few prominent reference books that may be consulted on particular individuals or movements discussed in the text.

J. Gordon Melton
June 2000

CHAPTER 1

The First American Religions

The history of American religions really begins with the arrival of the Europeans in the New World. They brought their writing and record keeping, the stuff from which history is constructed. There is certainly a story to be told prior to 1492, but it is an account developed by anthropologists, archaeologists, linguists, and other scientists. They have put together a prehistory of Native Americans from the initial movement of people from Asia across the Bering Strait through their spreading out over a vast continent and their development of numerous groupings, cultures, and languages. Over the millennia since they first arrived, there certainly was a history, a succession of events that led to the development of the more than 500 different peoples. That history would include relationships developed, political alliances broken, discoveries made, and wars fought. Along with heroes who emerged, there must have been prophets and religious prodigies who moved people spiritually, new revelations that changed communities for a generation and longer, and new teachings that became established among different peoples. However, the record of their accomplishments and defeats has been almost entirely lost to us, and we have only the broad outlines that can be surmised from the artifacts that remain.

We do know that people probably came into North America in several waves, some separated by only a few years and others by centuries between ice ages. Analysis of languages suggests that various groups settled in different parts of the continent and then over centuries spread out to surrounding territories, eventually encountering a people who spoke a distinctly different language. To communicate, the different groups developed a sign language.

As groups settled in different regions of the country, they integrated with the land and their immediate environment. They developed a holistic culture that differs radically from the dominant modern Western culture in that it made none of the distinctions so basic to modern life. The world was not divided into sacred and secular, nor was social life compartmentalized into realms such as economic, political, social, and religious. One was born into a people and taught its way. Many of the elements of the way were crucial for the continuance and well-being of the people as a whole, and one's individual identity was thoroughly integrated into the identity of one's community. The well-being of the individual was inseparable from that of the group. Native Americans' societies were smaller and more intimate than most contemporary societies, especially as compared to the modern urban context, and families and kinship groups played a more significant role. One was born not only into a people but into a clan and/or an extended family, each of which included a set of obligations and regulations by which one was expected to abide.

The life of the community was also tied to the land from which the people gathered the basic materials by which they lived—their food, clothing, and housing. As might be expected, their perception of their environment played a large part in their vision of the world and their understanding of the sacred. Among the most noticeable differences among the distinct world-views found among Native Americans are those that can be traced to dominating elements of the environment (desert, woodlands, grassy plains, imposing mountains) and the major source of the food supply (fishing, farming, hunting).

In such a world, the sense of the sacred permeated every aspect of life. While a few things can be cited as primarily or even exclusively religious, such as the vision quest, overwhelmingly, every action, every ritual, every relationship had both sacred and secular aspects intricately mixed. European Americans, who live with the gap between natural and supernatural, mundane and miraculous, spiritual and material, still have a difficult time understanding and describing cultures in which no such distinctions are made. In Native American life, there is a sense of a spiritual power, but it finds expression in ordinary tasks and is focused in aspects of nature that westerners have long since relegated to a realm of molecules and atoms.

To Native Americans, the world was both sacred and alive; it was permeated with spiritual power and inhabited with an array of spiritual entities. Individuals were surrounded not only by the spirits of ancestors, but also by the spirits of nature, of woods and sky, personifications of those who shared the environment from the bear to the peyote button. Common tasks, such as killing an animal for food and clothing, might be accompanied with words and actions referencing the belief in the personhood of the animal and its complex relationship with the hunter.

The sacred environment that permeates the day-to-day life finds expression in myth, in ritual, in behavior patterns, and in ideas. It also requires the presence of individuals who specialize in contact with the spirit world, men and women who often combine roles as religious leader, teacher, and/or physician. Yet, if one examines this aspect of the community, the religious practitioner, the boundary between the religious and not-religious remains fuzzy at best. The ritual leader may double as clan chief; the worker of magic may also be sought in times of illness. A myth provides both spiritual insight and mundane guidance. A ritual may be quite appropriately and fruitfully examined from a religious or an economic perspective, each yielding complementary and valuable insights.

As do members of most nonliterary cultures, Native Americans had a much different sense of time than did the Europeans who moved into their world in the sixteenth century. Native Americans' memory of the past tended to be limited to that of immediate ancestors and then jumped to the mythical past of the first beings. Native American world-views tend to resonate more with those of the Western mystics who emphasized their immediate appropriation of the world beyond and took little notice of the transitory occurrences of daily existence or the passing illusions of the historical process, although an occasional extraordinary event might be elevated into mythic truth.

Having noted basic characteristics of Native American approaches to the world, it is next to be noted how that basic approach led to so many different cultures and variations in the spiritual life. These variations and differences from community to community have often become symbolized in some of the distinctive artifacts in which tribes invest spiritual significance. One thinks immediately of the totem poles of the people of the Northwest upon which the artists carve the images of ancestors back to the original ancestors, usually a particular animal from which an individual family sprung. Among the Navaho of the Southwest, healing rites culminate with the preparation of a picture made of sand. Through ritual, it is "brought to life," and then the person seeking healing sits within. The sweat lodge, in which, along with a sweat bath, religious teachings, prayer, and intimate communion are shared, has spread from the plains people like the Lakota, Crow, and Ojibwa throughout the Native American world.

Work now continues on assembling the information that has been accumulated on the various Native American peoples concerning their spiritual visions and religious teachings. This work, bolstered by the new appreciation of indigenous people worldwide, will go far in changing the images that developed among Europeans soon after they became aware of the existence of North America and still dominate pubic opinions of the "primitive" nature of Native American life and religion.

FIRST CONTACT

Some twenty years after Columbus landed in the Caribbean in 1492, the Spanish began the further exploration and conquest of the new land granted to them by papal decree. Over the next generation, a surprisingly large number of Native Americans from California to Florida had their initial contact

Early ethnologists created the first records of Native American rituals.

with the Spanish, often with disastrous results. When Ponce de León tried to land on the coast of Florida in 1513, the residents treated him as an invader and repulsed his attempts to land. His second attempt, in the wake of years of Spanish raiders collecting slaves, occasioned his death in battle as he tried to set up a colony.

In 1528, Pánfilo de Narváez landed at Tampa Bay with a small army but was finally defeated by the residents. His superior arms did not compensate for their thorough knowledge of the land. They forced the Spanish out to sea in hastily constructed boats in which they began a valiant effort to reach Mexico by sailing along the Gulf coast. Their journey ended on Galveston Island. In 1540, a youthful Francisco Vásquez de Coronado left Mexico to explore what is now the southwestern United States. He traveled from Arizona to what is now the state of Kansas, frequently engaging in pitched battles, and leaving a trail of carnage and ill will behind him. About the same time, de Soto cut an even more bloody path through the southeastern states from Georgia to Arkansas. His expedition came to an end with his death and his men fighting

The legendary Pocahontas facilitated communication between Native Americans and the first Europeans.

a running battle as they headed to the Gulf down the Mississippi River. De Soto's last act had been an unprovoked attack on a village whose inhabitants were massacred. In 1842, Juan Rodríguez Cabrillo sailed up the coast of California as far north as Oregon. Unlike Coronado and de Soto, he did not present a hostile front and found the people he encountered friendly.

In 1565, the Spanish made yet another attempt to colonize Florida. The previous year, French Protestants had set up a small settlement at the mouth of the St. Johns River. However, the new Spanish colonists started their life in Florida by wiping out the French settlement. They then established a fort (later to become St. Augustine, Florida) and a line of settlements tying it to Tampa Bay across the peninsula and then pushed northward into Georgia. Within a few years, all of these settlements were destroyed or abandoned, as was an outpost they tried to establish on Chesapeake Bay.

During the first century of the European presence on the American continent, the signs indicative of its future were most inauspicious. They did not improve in the next century. In 1595, Spanish authorities in Mexico laid out a serious plan for the colonization of what is now New Mexico. Three years later, a party of 130 soldiers and their support contingent headed north through the Rio Grande Valley. By this time, the Native Americans had learned that they could expect little of a positive nature from those approaching their land. Those unfortunate enough to come under the rule of Don Juan de Oñate, the new governor, experienced one of the more horrible periods of colonial rule.

The Acoma, among the first to accept the Spanish among them, suffered the most. After the Acoma had refused a double taxation, a small contingent of Spanish soldiers attempted to seize the supplies they had previously demanded. The refusal led to a skirmish during which all the soldiers were killed. Oñate turned his troops against the Acoma village. He killed 800 and took 500 women and children and 80 surviving males as prisoners. The female children were turned over to the Franciscans. The others were sentenced to twenty years as slaves. As an additional penalty, the 80 men had one foot cut off. Oñate ravaged the land over the next decade as he attempted to establish Spanish authority. It is little consolation that he was finally forced out and convicted for crimes he committed against the New Mexico population.

ENGLISH TERRITORIES

Ignoring the papal gift of North America to the Spanish, the British began to explore the possibilities of colonization in 1584 when Sir Walter Raleigh tried to set up a colony along the coast of North Carolina. The several attempts failed as colonists based their life on what they were given by the natives and what they brought from England rather than developing their own means of livelihood. Of more long-term importance, however, Raleigh initiated the larger British program of colonization by encouraging Richard Hakluyt to approach Queen Elizabeth with a document arguing for a venture in the New World. Drawing on an understanding of the residents of the New World as they had been popularized in England, Hakluyt suggested that one goal of colonization would be the conversion and civilizing of the millions of souls now residing there. Having only minimal knowledge of Native Americans, he drew images of alien cultures from the Bible and suggested that they were living in falsehood and darkness, worshiping idols, and destined for hell. Then, drawing on the witchcraft trials that were proceeding across Europe, he accused them of devil worship and child sacrifice. He concluded that they needed to be brought the true knowledge and worship of God.

Serious colonization by both the British and the Dutch began early in the next century. While there were a few exchanges of arrows and musket balls, the desire of the colonists to trade with the residents rather than conquer them and the colonists' choice of rather sparsely settled sites for settlement led to initial friendly relationships. That changed as the century progressed, the number of British steadily increased, and their desire for land grew. Through the sixteenth and seventeenth centuries, several patterns of interaction determined relation-

Sequoya created a written script for the Cherokee language.

Totem poles identified the family history in the mythological past among Native Americans in the Northwest.

ships between the European settlers and the native resident population. At first, settlers developed friendly relationships with their Native American neighbors. However, these soon soured as either the settlers became dependent on their neighbors or the population grew to the point that the original residents were being pushed off their land. War followed and while the natives might win battles, they almost never won the war.

During the eighteenth century especially, as European settlements pushed inland and additional peoples were encountered, European political tensions were transferred to North America, where the Spanish, French, and English were rivals for colonial hegemony. European generals played on older rivalries and enlisted the locals in their armies and used their knowledge of the land to plan troop movements. Major decisions were made about blocks of land in North America by such events as the Treaty of Paris and the Louisiana Purchase.

Following the American Revolution and the rapid movement of settlers from the Atlantic coast into the western lands, treaties guaranteeing land to different groups were broken as the increased population demanded space to homestead and develop. War was followed by an initial treaty, and often a series of treaties, each of which was in turn broken. Finally, the westward juggernaut led to the complete confiscation of the land, the total tribal displacement to reservations, and occasionally even the subsequent movement of reservations. In this process, some Native peoples were totally destroyed, many others significantly reduced in numbers.

The movement of Europeans onto the land placed Native American religions under both direct and indirect attack. Native Americans became the object of a massive effort by most of the Christian churches to convert them. Spanish missions began in the early 1500s and French and English efforts soon followed. The sustained missionary drive through the nineteenth century by the various Christian denominations led to the conversion of most Native Americans and the complete disappearance of a large percentage of the Native American religions.

Native religions also came under indirect attack from the destruction of the holistic culture of which they were an integral part. Once people were removed from their traditional homeland and forced to change their occupation, for example, from hunting or fishing to farming or business, the ability to sustain the older spiritual world-view was undercut. More often than not, neither those causing the process nor those experiencing it comprehended the process until much too late to reverse it.

As their spiritual life was being challenged and destroyed, the great majority of Native Americans attempted to hold to traditional perspectives. This effort involved at the very least the development of their perspective in light of the new challenges now impinging upon them. Beginning with their initial contact with Europeans and especially with Christian ministers, those who kept their traditional religion were forced to recast it in light of the changing world. The most wrenching changes occurred among those who were totally displaced from their traditional homes. Native peoples also reacted in other ways. First, they responded to a succession of religious leaders, some operating among one set of closely related peoples but often attempting to speak to the common dilemma of native people. Beginning with Popé in New Mexico, prophetic figures have created numerous pan-Native American movements that more-or-less militantly opposed the encroachments of Christianity (and the associated European American culture). Finally, many Native Americans, both individually and as groups, converted to Christianity. The new Christians then initiated the long process of developing an indigenous form of that faith and assuming leadership roles within the larger Christian community.

NATIVE MOVEMENTS

Seventeenth-century Spanish priests, like Hakluyt, considered the former religion of their new converts to be little more than witchcraft. In 1680, two generations of Spanish rule and the Christianizing of the residents of New Mexico was challenged by Popé, a medicine man who had previously been

The Roman Catholic Church established a mission among Native Americans in the Taos area of New Mexico in the seventeenth century.

publicly whipped and driven from the Spanish-controlled settlement at San Juan for practicing witchcraft. He retreated to Taos and there proceeded to organize the pueblos and the neighboring Apaches. Suddenly, the warriors of the coalition he had created revolted and killed the soldiers and other settlers. They also killed the priests and burned the churches to the ground. They next besieged Santa Fe. They demanded the release of all the slaves and the abandonment of New Mexico by the Spanish. With the fall of Santa Fe, Popé emerged as the most successful Native American leader of the era, and New Mexico remained under native control for the next two decades.

Some years later, in 1762, there appeared in what is now Ohio, a man known only as the Delaware Prophet. He had been away from his people on a personal quest to gain acquaintance with the "Master of Life." When the Prophet was granted an audience, the Master of Life assured him that the land, now being fought over by the British and French, was indeed for the Native American. He complained that the people had become dependent on the French, and they must reform. They must give up all the things adopted since the arrival of the white men, especially alcohol and polygamy. The Master of Life also taught a prayer that was to be shared with all. The appearance of the Delaware Prophet occurred just before the Treaty of Paris, by which the French (whom the Native Americans preferred) relinquished their North American territory to the English.

The words of the Prophet found their way to Chief Pontiac, who combined in his person both the secular role as chief of the Ottawa and a sacred status as a priest. A person of great native ability, Pontiac decided to built a confederation of tribes to take advantage of the transition of power before the British could assume control of the region. He called the different people of the region together in April 1763 and announced to those gathered the message given to him by the Prophet. His words received an immediate response, and all of the major groups of the Great Lakes region joined with him. The war to stop the British advance raged from Michigan to New York and Virginia. Hostilities lasted for four years and were eventually fought to a draw, although following the peace, the agreed upon lines could not stop the movement of settlers west, especially after the American Revolution.

In the generations after Europeans began to settle along the North American coast, quite apart from any systematic mission to proselytize, Native Americans had to begin a process of adjustment to the presence of Christianity and react to some of its more prominent claims. Christian ministers, for example, identified figures in Native American mythologies with the Christian devil. In return, Native Americans identified various mythological figures with the Christian God or with Jesus Christ. Some have suggested that the idea of the

Master of Life or of the Great Spirit were the end result of the search for a Native American equivalent of the Christian God. In the Southeast, stories from the book of Genesis, such as the universal flood, were incorporated into their mythology. By the time ethnologists began the massive task of collecting information on the life and thought of the different Native American cultures, they often found that traditional beliefs and Christianity had been joined in a complex new synthesis.

Through most of the eighteenth century, Native American people seemed to be actors in the larger political process, able to ally themselves with the various warring governments and gaining or loosing as their allies won or lost. After the American Revolution, however, that situation changed. By the end of the eighteenth century, Americans began the movement to settle the West that would result in the relocation of almost all Native Americans west of the

This painting shows people gathered for a ghost or spirit dance ceremony.

Tenskwatawa, the brother of Tecumseh, created a prophetic movement that tied Native people together against United States encroachment onto their traditional homeland.

Mississippi River. The policy gained official status following the Louisiana Purchase (1803). The following year, some nine years after the Shawano (or Shawnee) and other groups had already lost their homeland in Ohio, there appeared among them a young man primarily known for his drunkenness who claimed that he had talked to the Master of Life. The young man said that he had a revelation for those who wished to return to the good times prior to the coming of the white man. It included the requirement that they give up drunkenness and live communally. He changed his name to Tenskwatawa, "the Open Door," and established his authority with further trance experiences and revelations. In 1808, he built a town on Tippecanoe Creek in Indiana and called his new converts to come and join him there.

As the movement around Tenskwatawa grew, his brother Tecumseh emerged with a plan to unite the Native Americans along the western frontier in opposition to further expansion of the United States. Building on Tenskwatawa's revelations, he told his audiences that all of the land belonged to all of the native people and no one group could give any of it away. The two traveled widely spreading their spiritual/political message. After trying to negotiate with William Henry Harrison, then the governor of Indiana, in 1810 Tecumseh set out on a tour south along the western frontier. His arguments calling his allies to action were bolstered first by the appearance of a bright comet in the sky and then a massive earthquake from the New Madrid fault along the Mississippi River in Missouri. While Tecumseh was away, in 1811, Harrison attacked and burned the Prophet's town in what became famous as the Battle of Tippecanoe. The battle merely initiated the war that Tecumseh was planning, and hostilities flowed into the War of 1812 between the United States and Britain. Within a short time after the British defeat, Tecumseh died (1813), and the United States reestablished control of the Northwest. The confederacy died with Tecumseh, and further removals of the Native Americans to the Far West resumed.

Among the people directly affected by the defeat of Tecumseh and Tenskwatawa were the Kickapoo, traditionally residents of Illinois. In 1819, they ceded their land and planned a move to Missouri. However, several years later it was noticed that they had not moved and that in fact a man named Kanakuk had emerged among them as a prophet. It appears that he continued themes first enunciated by Tenskwatawa (as the Kickapoo had been part of

The sweat house, such as this one used by the Lakota, was a popular tool in the spiritual life of Native people in the Western United States.

Kanakuk, a Native American prophet who opposed his people's removal to a reservation in the west.

John Smohalla, here shown with an associate, Louis Yowaluch, created the Shaker religion among Native Americans in the Northwest.

Tecumseh's confederacy). He and his followers remained in Illinois, and his influence spread among neighboring tribes. Interestingly enough, because his followers gathered on Sunday, some later observers thought they had become Christians, and in fact Kanakuk had absorbed elements of Christianity into his new religion. This was most noticeable on Fridays when they gathered to make confession of their sins. During their gatherings, they used a prayer stick, a flat

KANAKUK'S VISION

My father, the Great Spirit has placed us all on this earth; he has given to our nation a piece of land. Why do you want to take it away and give us so much trouble? We ought to live in peace and happiness among ourselves and with you. We have heard of some trouble about our land. I have come down to see you and have all explained.

My father, the Great Spirit appeared to me; he saw my heart was in sorrow about our land; he told me not to give up the business, but go to my Great Father and he would listen to me. My father, when I talked to the Great Spirit, I saw the chiefs holding the land fast. He told me the life of our children was short and that the earth would sink...

My father, you call all the redskins your children. When we have children, we treat them well. That is the reason I make this long talk to get you to take pity on us and let us remain where we are.

My father, I wish after my talk is over you would write to my Great Father, the president, that we have a desire to remain a little longer where we now are. I have explained to you that we have thrown all our badness away and keep the good path. I wish our Great Father could hear that. I will now talk to my Great Father, the president.

My Great Father, I don't know if you are the right chief, because I have heard some things go wrong. I wish you to reflect on our situation and let me know. I want to talk to you mildly and in peace, so that we may understand each other. When I saw the Great Spirit, he told me to throw all our bad acts away. We did so. Some of our chiefs said the land belonged to us, the Kickapoos; but this is not what the Great Spirit told me—the lands belong to him. The Great Spirit told me that no people owned the lands—that all was his, and not to forget to tell the white people that when we went into council. When I saw the Great Spirit, he told me, Mention all this to your Great Father. He will take pity on your situation and let you remain on the lands where you are for some years, when you will be able to get through all the bad places . . . , and where you will get to a clear piece of land where you will all live happy. When I talked to the Great Spirit, he told me to make my warriors throw their tomahawks in the bad place. I did so, and every night and morning I raise my hands to the Great Spirit and pray to him to give us success. I expect, my father, that God has put me in a good way—that our children shall see their sisters and brothers and our women see their children. They will grow up and travel and see their totems. The Great Spirit told me, "Our old men had totems. They were good and had many totems. Now you have scarcely any. If you follow my advice, you will soon have totems again." Say this to my Great Father for me....

My father, every time we eat we raise our hands to the Great Spirit to give us success.

My father, we are sitting by each other here to tell the truth. If you write anything wrong, the Great Spirit will know it. If I say anything not true, the Great Spirit will hear it.

My father, you know how to write and can take down what is said for your satisfaction. I can not; all I do is through the Great Spirit for the benefit of my women and children.

My father, everything belongs to the Great Spirit. If he chooses to make the earth shake, or turn it over, all the skins, white and red, can not stop it. I have done. I trust to the Great Spirit.

Showing some influence from Christianity, the Smohalla movement met in church buildings.

piece of wood upon which was written a prayer, which they chanted. The religion appears to have survived into 1888, when it was revived among the Potawatomi and Kickapoo then living in Kansas and Wisconsin, and subsequently spread to Oklahoma.

In the 1870s, a new prophet appeared among the native peoples in Oregon and Washington. His name was Smohalla (1815?–1907). He had become a medicine man and warrior among his people, the Wanapan, but in the 1850s had had a fight and been left for dead. He survived, however, and to everyone's surprise reappeared among his people several years later claiming that he had had traveled to the Spirit World and had brought back a message for his people. He said that the day was approaching when life as it was before the whites came would return. He also introduced some new rituals and dances, and through the 1860s his movement known as the Washani or Dreamers religion spread through the immediate region and eastward to Montana. It became a matter of concern in the 1870s when the authorities began efforts to move several of the tribes in Oregon. More important, however, the new religion spread to the Nez Percé. In 1877, the Nez Percé under

Chief Joseph went to war to prevent further encroachment upon his people's land. Chief Joseph won fame for his effort in the brief war against overwhelming odds, but he was finally forced to surrender. His defeat dealt the Dreamers religion a serious blow, although it survived in the Northwest for another generation.

The various efforts of prophets to unite Native Americans against the encroachments of the whites culminated in the visions of Wovoka (1856–1932), a Paiute medicine man. His father had been a dreamer, a man who found in his dreams the substance of revelations. Thus it was that, when Wovoka was a child, his dreams were taken seriously and he was trained to pay attention to them. The substance of his dreams as a young adult in his twenties outlined the practice of the Spirit Dance (popularly referred to as the Ghost

This painting shows participants in the sun dance ceremony.

PORCUPINE'S VISIT TO WOVOKA

The Fish-eaters near Pyramid lake told me that Christ had appeared on earth again. They said Christ knew he was coming; that eleven of his children were also coming from a far land. It appeared that Christ had sent for me to go there, and that was why unconsciously I took my journey. It had been fore-ordained. Christ had summoned myself and others from all heathen tribes, from two to three or four from each of fifteen or sixteen different tribes. There were more different languages than I ever heard before and I did not understand any of them. They told me when I got there that my great father was there also, but did not know who he was. The people assembled called a council, and the chief's son went to see the Great Father [messiah], who sent word to us to remain fourteen days in that camp and that he would come to see us. He sent me a small package of something white to eat that I did not know the name of. There were a great many people in the council, and this white food was divided among them. The food was a big white nut. Then I went to the agency at Walker lake and they told us Christ would be there in two days. . . . on the third morning, hundreds of people gathered at this place. They cleared off a place near the agency in the form of a circus ring and we all gathered there. . . . Just before sundown I saw a great many people, mostly Indians, coming dressed in white men's clothes. The Christ was with them. They all formed in this ring around it. They put up sheets all around the circle, as they had no tents. Just after dark some of the Indians told me that the Christ [Father] was arrived. I . . . finally saw him sitting on one side of the ring. They all started toward him to see him. They made a big fire to throw light on him. I never looked around, but went forward, and when I saw him I bent my head. I had always thought the Great Father was a white man, but this man looked like an Indian. He sat there a long time and nobody went up to speak to him. He sat with his head bowed all the time. After awhile he rose and said he was very glad to see his children. "I have sent for you and am glad to see you. I am going to talk to you after awhile about your relatives who are dead and gone. My children, I want you to listen to all I have to say to you. I will teach you, too, how to dance a dance, and I want you to dance it. Get ready for your dance and then, when the dance is over, I will talk to you." He was dressed in a white coat with stripes. The rest of his dress was a white man's except that he had on a pair of moccasins. Then he commenced our dance, everybody joining in, the Christ singing while we danced. We danced till late in the night, when he told us we had danced enough.

The next morning, after breakfast was over, we went into the circle and spread canvas over it on the ground, the Christ standing in the midst of us. He told us he was going away that day, but would be back that next morning and talk to us.

In the night when I first saw him I thought he was an Indian, but the next day when I could see better he looked different. He was not so dark as an Indian, nor so light as a white man. He had no beard or whiskers, but very heavy eyebrows. He was a good-looking man. We were crowded up very close. We had been told that nobody was to talk, and even if we whispered the Christ would know it. I had heard that Christ had been crucified, and I looked to see, and I saw a scar on his wrist and one on his face, and he seemed to be the man. I could not see his feet. He would talk to us all day.

That evening we all assembled again to see him depart. When we were assembled, he began to sing, and he commenced to tremble all over, violently for a while, and then sat down. We danced all that night, the Christ lying down beside us apparently dead.

The next morning when we went to eat breakfast, the Christ was with us. After breakfast four heralds went around and called out that the Christ was back with us and wanted to talk with us. The circle was prepared again. The people assembled, and Christ came among us and sat down. He said he wanted to talk to us again and for us to listen. He said: "I am the man who made everything you see around you. I am not lying to you, my children. I made this earth and everything on it. I have been to heaven and seen your dead friends and have seen my own father and mother. In the beginning, after God made the earth, they sent me back to teach the people, and when I came back on earth the people were afraid of me and treated me badly. This is what they did to me [showing his scars]. I did not try to defend myself. I found my children were bad, so went back to heaven and left them. I told them that in so many hundred years I would come back to see my children. At the end of this time I was sent back to try to teach them. My father told me the earth was getting old and worn out, and the people getting bad, and that I was to renew everything as it used to be, and make it better."

He told us also that all our dead were to be resurrected; that they were all to come back to earth, and that as the earth was too small for them and us, he would do away with heaven, and make the earth itself large enough to contain us all; that we must tell all the people we meet about these things. He spoke to us about fighting, and said that was bad, and we must keep from it; that the earth was to be all good hereafter, and we must all be friends with one another. He said that in the fall of the year the youth of all the good people would be renewed, so that nobody would be more than 40 years old, and that if they behaved themselves well after this the youth of everyone would be renewed in the spring. He said if we were all good he would send people among us who could heal all our wounds and sickness by mere touch, and that we would live forever. He told us not to quarrel, or fight, nor strike each other, nor shoot one another; that the whites and Indians were to be all one people. He said if any man disobeyed what he ordered, his tribe would be wiped from the face of the earth; that we must believe everything he said, and that we must not doubt him, or say he lied; that if we did, he would know it; that he would know our thoughts and actions, in no matter what part of the world we might be.

When I heard this from the Christ, and came back home to tell it to my people, I thought they would listen. Where I went to there were lots of white people, but I never had one of them say an unkind word to me. I thought all of your people knew all of this I have told you of, but it seems you do not.

Sitting Bull, Lakota chief and spiritual leader.

Dance), by which the group of dancers communicated with the spirits of their ancestors. The goal of dancing would be the liberation of the people from the whites, a theme that continued from Wovoka's father's dreams. A total eclipse of the sun on January 1, 1889, seemed to put heavenly authority on Wovoka 's work. At the time, he was in the midst of a three-day bout with high fever, during which some of his more important revelations were received.

The spread of the Spirit Dance over the next year sent a wave of fear through the federal government, which was charged with keeping the peace in the western states. Among the first reactions appears to have been the decision to assassinate Sitting Bull (1831–1890), whose combined role of medicine man and chief was seen as blocking the "civilization" of the Lakota. The more horrendous result was the massacre at Wounded Knee at which a number of Spirit Dance adherents were killed. Part of the costume for the dance was a shirt that leaders told the dancers would make them invulnerable to bullets. Wounded Knee also killed the Spirit Dance movement even though Wokova denied any connection with the idea of the bulletproof shirts.

The Spirit Dance was the last significant pan-Native American movement that attempted to unite people around the idea of removing the whites from North America. The European invaders were here to stay, and in the future, a different type of movement would arise. The first of these was the peyote religion. Meanwhile, the Christian churches were making significant inroads in their drive to Christianize Native Americans.

THE CHRISTIAN MISSION

The Christian church was brought into the life of the Native American almost from the beginning of the European arrival. In 1492, it was the pope himself who gave the Spanish a green light to enter North America. Catholic priests accompanied Columbus on his second voyage. They established the first missions for the conversion of the native population, and their efforts to align their converts with the new political leadership experienced some success. The priests also experienced the cruel treatment of the Spanish authorities in their single-minded drive for wealth to ship back to Spain. As they were frequently forced to do over the next centuries, in 1515, the priests sent one of their number, Bartolomé de Las Casas, to Spain to inform the king of what was occurring and ask his intervention. For Las Casas, the battle to protect the conquered peoples would become a lifelong endeavor.

Everywhere the Spanish went during the sixteenth century, Christian priests accompanied them. Among the first were the Jesuits, formed to oppose the Protestant Reformation and zealous in their desire to expand the church in the face of its losses to Martin Luther and his colleagues. Early arrivals also

included the Franciscans, the order founded by the gentle Saint Francis. However, the expansive efforts through the seventeenth century had only limited results. The mission in New Mexico was largely wiped out by Popé's revolt, and gains elsewhere were later lost as Spain turned land over to other countries. The most substantial work was begun in 1869 in California with the founding of the San Diego Mission. Over the next several decades, a string of twenty-one missions were located next to villages along the California coast north to the present-day San Rafael. The prosperity of the missions is attributed to the peaceful nature of the California native population, the abundance of natural resources, and the small number of secular Europeans constantly interfering in mission work. An estimated 100,000 converted to Catholicism.

Catholics, happy to get out of uncomfortable conditions in England, also settled in Maryland in 1634. Among their number was Father Andrew White (1579–1656) who led in the establishment of a string of missions among the Native Americans of Maryland and among the Potomac in Virginia. His most substantial work was with the Piscataway, whose language he reduced to writing and for whom he prepared a grammar, dictionary, and catechism. When Anglicans took over the government, the mission system was broken up and White arrested and deported. However, a congregation made up of descendants of his original converts remains to this day.

Samuel Occom, an eighteenth-century missionary to Native Americans.

Some Protestants shared the desire to convert the native population, and in 1640 John Eliot, the Congregational minister at Roxbury, Massachusetts, accepted the responsibility of leading the effort to convert the natives. He learned the local dialect and began preaching to the several local groups. Converts were encouraged to found Christian villages, and Eliot helped build churches and several schools. He encouraged leaders at the villages to become teachers and preachers and to that end helped found the Indian college at Harvard. He translated the Bible into Algonquin (the first translation into a Native American language). In 1674, there were 1,100 "Praying Indians," as his converts were called, living in fourteen Christian villages. Unfortunately, like White, Eliot lived to see his work largely destroyed. The following year, King Philip's War began and most of Eliot's people were forced to choose sides. The work never recovered.

Moravians, German Pietists who settled in North Carolina and Pennsylvania, began to work among Indians as early as 1635. In spite of distrustful English-speaking neighbors, they built a mission of some 500 members by 1748 in Pennsylvania. They also shared the experience of White and Eliot, as their work was destroyed during the French and Indian Wars of the next decade. Although primary attention of Christian ministers during the eighteenth cen-

A baptismal ceremony among Native American converts, performed by an unidentified Methodist missionary.

tury was toward the unchurched settlers, other missionary efforts directed to the Native American community began during the Great Awakening of the 1740s. While locally successful, these efforts did not have the lasting results that had been expected, although several prominent converts, such as Samuel Occom (1732–1792), a Mohegan, later became Christian ministers.

A new era in Christian efforts to convert Native Americans began following the American Revolution. In 1796, the Presbyterian, Baptist, and Dutch Reformed Churches of New York united to found the New York Missionary Society specifically for the evangelization of Native Americans. Its efforts received a boost from the 1801 Plan of Union, in which the Presbyterians and Congregationalists joined efforts nationally to plant churches in the West. One product of that union was the American Board of Commissioners for Foreign Missions, which included the Native American "nations" among its concerns. Through the first decades of the nineteenth century, a variety of denominations launched efforts, many built around an individual minister who felt called to establish an "Indian" mission.

John Stewart (d.1823), an African American, began the first Methodist mission among the Wyandotte in Ohio. With the assistance of another black man, Jonathan Pointer, who served as his translator, Stewart established a large mission in the upper Sandusky area. Four Wyandotte chiefs, Between-the-Logs, Mononcue, Hicks, and Scuteash became well-known Methodist leaders. After only six years, Stewart came down with tuberculosis, and in 1821, James Finley was appointed to carry on his work, which prospered until the Wyandotte removal to Kansas.

Various efforts began among Native Americans in the Southeast, especially after the passing of the so-called "Civilization Bill" that supplied money for the creation of Native American schools. Churches could apply for money to support a school that would be placed next to a church. The Methodists initiated work by sending William Stevenson to Arkansas in 1819. A few years later, the American Board sent Cyrus Kinsbury and Samuel Worcester to northern Georgia. Their expanding work was then totally disrupted in 1828 when Andrew Jackson passed the Indian Removal Bill that called for the southeastern tribes to relocate west of the Mississippi. One by one, the tribes prepared themselves for the inevitable, except the Cherokee. Several of the missionaries, including Worcester, were arrested for protesting the attempted removal, and Worcester and another colleague, Elizur Butler, went to jail after refusing the pardon the authorities offered. The case of *Worcester v. Georgia* went to the Supreme Court, where Justice John Marshall declared that the state of Georgia did not have the right to extend its authority over the lands of what amounted to a separate nation. However, Jackson and Georgia officials combined efforts to undermine the decision, and eventually even Worcester began cooperating with the move to Oklahoma.

Two significant boosts to the effort to convert the Native American peoples to Christianity occurred later in the century. First, in the 1850s, the Church of Jesus Christ of Latter-day Saints established itself in the West, and Brigham Young led in the founding of more than 300 Mormon communities that stretched from Idaho to Arizona and southern California. The Book of Mormon, the church's sacred text presented its own history of ancient Native Americans, and church members offered the book to them as an accurate account of their origin. The church initiated a mission among the Indians soon after its founding in 1830, but once settled in the West, the church opened multiple missions at various native villages.

Second, in 1870, U.S. President Ulysses S. Grant inaugurated what was termed the "Peace Policy" toward the Native Americans, who by this time were almost totally located in the West. He advocated a program designed to bring them into American society and educate their children. He also pledged to

fulfill the treaty obligations as they then existed. In this effort, he called upon the churches to assist him in support of the policy and to ameliorate the problems created by previous government actions. Over the next fifty years, the Roman Catholic Church built the largest single mission and claimed more than 200,000 Native American members. Methodists had led the way among Protestants. As early as 1844, it had organized a separate Indian Mission Conference with almost 3,000 members in Oklahoma and Kansas. It vigorously responded to Grant's request as did the Episcopalians and Presbyterians.

Through the twentieth century, Christian churches have been established on almost every reservation. During most of this period, the Native American missions were seen in much the same way as foreign missions. However, after World War II views of missionary work changed radically. Most important, American denominations were called upon to drop racial stereotypes and complete the process of developing indigenous leadership. Increasingly, denominations turned Native American congregations over to Native American pastors and ceased recruiting missionaries for work on the reservations. During the 1960s, in the wake of the civil rights movement, denominations moved to fully integrate Native American work into the ongoing life of the church. As the twenty-first century begins, the majority of Native Americans are Christians, and predominantly Native American congregations can now be found in

Once established in the West, the Church of Jesus Christ of Latter-day Saints erected churches, like this one on the Cataba Reservation, among many Native peoples.

Originating in the nineteenth century, the Sun Dance is a Pan–Native American movement promoting the spiritual health and strength of participants. It has experienced a rebirth in recent decades.

denominations across the spectrum from Roman Catholic to Pentecostal and Mormon. Interestingly, very few new exclusively Native American denominations have arisen.

THE REBIRTH OF NATIVE AMERICAN RELIGION

During the twentieth century, while Christianity permeated the Native American community, innovative religious impulses originating within the Native American community arose and spread. These new movements differed in that they accepted the presence of the white culture as a permanent fact of life in North America and no longer pursued dreams of a past that could not return. Among the first of these new movements was the Native American Church. The church emerged as the use of the peyote cactus, a natural source of a psychedelic substance, spread north from Mexico. As early as 1870, peyote was introduced to the Mescalero Apache and, in the wake of Wounded Knee, to the Kiowa, Comanche, and Caddo. It use was opposed by both the government and church leaders. In 1906, a loose association of peyote users was founded in Oklahoma. Three years later, it adopted the name Union Church. Then in 1914, Jonathan Koshiway, the son of a former Latter-Day Saint missionary, led in the founding of the First Born Church of Christ, integrating Christian themes with native teachings and the use of peyote.

Russell Means, prominent advocate for traditional Native American values.

In 1918, the Native American Church was formally incorporated as a means of resisting government attempts to outlaw peyote. It eventually absorbed Koshiway's church. Over the rest of the century the church has fought a running battle with the authorities. In 1966, when federal law outlawed most psychedelic substances, peyote and the Native American Church were specifically excluded. As a generation of whites learned of the church, they attempted to affiliate as a means of covering their own drug use. So many non–Native Americans asked to join its rituals, in fact, that the church's legal status was threatened, and gradually through the 1980s it withdrew contact with the non-Indian community. It now claims more than 200,000 members.

The widespread positive attention given the Native American Church in the 1970s heralded a significant change in the consideration of the white community toward Native American religion. Heretofore, little value had been placed on Native American spirituality or religious practice. Ethnological accounts had been written, but whites rarely tried to appropriate material from Indian worship or to adopt Indian ways. However, beginning in the 1960s with the discovery of the widespread use of psychedelic substances by the indigenous peoples of Central and South America, a new appreciation of Indian culture and religion began.

One key event in this reappraisal was the emergence of Michael Harner from the forests of South America in the 1960s both to teach about American shamanism and to introduce others to the shamanic life. Harner's 1980 work *The Way of the Shaman* struck a responsive chord among a generation already familiar with the psychedelic experience, and he created the Foundation of Shamanic Studies to institutionalize the integration of shamanism into the religious life. His teaching activity emerged in the context of the series of best-selling books of Carlos Castaneda, an anthropologist who claimed to have done fieldwork among the Yaqui people of northern Mexico. At about the same time, Native Americans emerged claiming their readiness to teach outsiders their traditional spirituality in ways that did not involve illegal substances. Leading the way was Chippewa medicine man Vincent LaDuke, publicly known as Sun Bear (1929–1992). Sun Bear founded the Bear Tribe and began to invite the general public to join its ceremonies.

Harner, Castaneda, and Sun Bear provided the foundation stones of a popular neoshamanic movement that led to many Americans adopting a form of Native American spirituality. Native American religious teachings, rituals, and sacred religious artifacts were accumulated by people who otherwise have little connection with Native American peoples. Native American leaders view as a mixed blessing the sudden emergence of Native American teachers claiming status as religious practitioners but teaching outside the Native American community. They watched with apprehension the growth of neoshamanic groups claiming to advocate traditional Native American spirituality. While welcoming the new positive evaluation of Native American religiosity that appeared in the 1970s, as well as the support it offered in attempts to preserve traditional ways among Native American peoples, many saw the appropriation of their teachings by whites (not to mention its exportation to Europe, where an interest in Native American religion has appeared) as merely the continuation in a new form of the larger community's subjugation of native peoples. Native American leaders are now confronting the meaning of the integration of their traditional ways into the new pluralistic culture that has become the overarching reality of contemporary American religious life.

CHAPTER 2

Pioneers and the Coming of Christianity

When the European sailors who came to the New World with Columbus touched land, holding the first Christian worship service in the New World was a high priority.

By the beginning of the seventeenth century, the minds of the more adventurous throughout Europe were filled with images of the New World that had been discovered across the Atlantic. Although the existence of this world had been known for more than a century, the number of people who had ventured to its shores remained quite small. Part of the reason for this lack of attention was due to the actions of the Roman pontiff in 1493 and 1494. Portugal and Spain took the lead in what would become the massive European effort to explore the many lands around the world.

In the 1480s, Portuguese sailors, traveling down the coast of Africa, reached the mouth of the Congo in 1484 and rounded the Cape of Good Hope four years later. Portugal also assumed possession of the Azores and Cape Verde Islands. When the Spanish-funded Christopher Columbus (1451–1506) discovered America, immediate competition for the yet to be discovered lands north and south of the several islands Columbus located on his first voyage threatened to destroy the peace of the Iberian Peninsula. Thus, in 1493, the pope stepped in and offered a solution for his Catholic subjects. In several encyclicals (letters), he drew an imaginary line north and south 100 leagues (some 263 miles) east of the Azores. All of the lands east of that line would belong to Portugal and all to the west (and at the time none knew their extent) would belong to Spain.

A year later, on June 7, 1494, the two countries signed the Treaty of Tordesillas, by which they formally accepted the pope's suggested division, although by that time they had moved the line a further 270 leagues to the west. Unknown to both parties, this second line crossed the westernmost part of South America, which subsequently fell under Portuguese control. A century later, Brazilian affairs would intrude upon American history, a fact we will return to later. Meanwhile, Spain would focus its efforts upon exploring its new possessions.

The initial landing on what is now the United States occurred in 1513, when Juan Ponce de León discovered Florida and began his fabled quest for the Fountain of Youth. From their initial outpost on the peninsula, the Spanish explored the coast northward to present-day Maryland and westward to Texas. More important than the failure to find the Fountain of Youth, they failed to

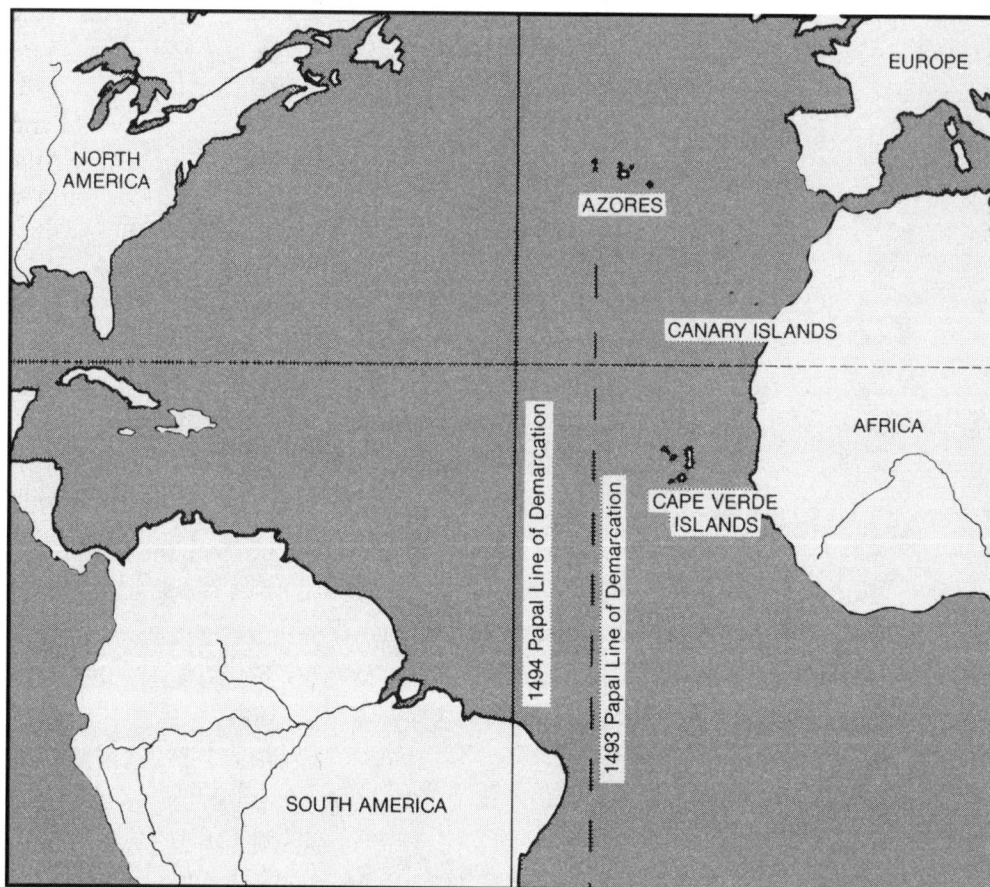

discover gold or anything like the cultures of Mexico and Central America. Spain laid claim to Florida, and the king of Spain appointed Ponce de León (c.1460– 1521) the first governor. He also charged him with the task of introducing the indigenous population to Roman Catholicism.

Florida was a low priority on the church's mission list, and it was not until 1549 that a Dominican priest was sent to convert the residents. He landed at Tampa Bay and was immediately killed. This first Christian martyr was a victim of natives who had themselves previously experienced the brutality of the Spanish conquerors. Then in 1565, Pedro Menédez de Avilés, the new governor of Florida, established St. Augustine, the first permanent settlement in Florida and now the oldest city in the United States. The following year, he invited the Jesuits into his domain. Meanwhile, Dominicans established work farther north on St. Catherine's Island (now Georgia). Their mission would be the center of a revolt that was harshly put down in 1598.

While Spain was dealing somewhat unsuccessfully with attempts to colonize Florida, far to the west, colonists initiated a more successful push north-

THE TREATY OF TORDESILLAS
June 7, 1494

...Whereas a certain controversy exists between the said lords, their constituents, as to what lands, of all those discovered in the ocean sea up to the present day, the date of this treaty, pertain to each one of the said parts respectively; therefore, for the sake of peace and concord, and for the preservation of the relationship and love of the said King of Portugal for the said King and Queen of Castile, Aragon, etc. it being the pleasure of their Highnesses, they . . . covenanted and agreed that a boundary or straight line be determined and drawn north and south, from pole to pole, on the said ocean sea, from the Arctic to the Antarctic pole. This boundary or line shall be drawn straight, as aforesaid, at a distant of three hundred and seventy leagues west of the Cape Verde Islands, being calculated by degrees. . . . And all lands, both islands and mainlands, found and discovered already, or to be found and discovered hereafter, by the said King of Portugal and by his vessels on this side of the said line and bound determined as above, toward the east, in either north or south latitude, on the eastern side of the said bound, provided the said bound is not crossed, shall belong to and remain in the possession of, and pertain forever to, the said King of Portugal and his successors. And all other lands, both islands and mainlands, found or to be found hereafter, . . . by the said King and Queen of Castile, Aragon, etc. and by their vessels, on the western side of the said bound, determined as above, after having passed the said bound toward the west, in either its north or south latitude, shall belong to . . . the said King and Queen of Castile, Leon, etc. and to their successors.

Item, the said representatives promise and affirm., that from this date no ships shall be dispatched—namely as follows: the said King and Queen of Castile, Leon, Aragon etc. for this part of the bound . . . which pertains to the said King of Portugal . . . nor the said King of Portugal to the other side of the said bound which pertains to the said King and Queen of Castile, Aragon, etc.—for the purpose of discovering and seeking any mainlands or islands, or for the purpose of trade, barter, or conquest of any kind. But should it come to pass that the said ships of the said King and Queen of Castile . . . on sailing thus on this side of the said bound, should discover any mainlands or islands in the region pertaining, as abovesaid, to the said King of Portugal, such mainlands or islands shall belong forever to the said King of Portugal and his heirs, and their Highnesses shall order them to be surrendered to him immediately. And if the said ships of the said King of Portugal discover any islands or mainlands in the regions of the said King and Queen of Castile . . . all such lands shall belong to and remain forever in the possession of the said King and Queen of Castile . . . and their heirs, and the said King of Portugal shall cause such lands to be surrendered immediately. . . .

And by this present agreement, they . . . entreat our most Holy Father that his Holiness be pleased to confirm and approve this said agreement, according to what is set forth therein; and that he order his bulls in regard to it to be issued to the parties or to whichever of the parties may solicit them with the tenor of this agreement incorporated therein, and that he lay his censures upon those who shall violate or oppose it at any time whatsoever. . . .

ward from Spain's established centers in Mexico. As early as 1540, Francisco Vásquez de Coronado (1510–1554) was commissioned to explore the Southwest, but it would be a half century later before anyone would follow up on his many discoveries. In the 1590s, a push began along the Rio Grande into New Mexico. In 1598, the Spanish established San Juan de Caballeros, the first European settlement in the American Southwest, and nine years later moved on to Santa Fe. Franciscan monks accompanied the Spanish expeditions and established several missions along the river. They soon found themselves in conflict with the governor, Don Juan de Oñate, over the harsh treatment of the native population. As early as 1598, the village of Acoma had reacted to Spanish intrusions by killing a dozen Spanish soldiers. Subsequently, the Spanish moved upon the residents and cut off a foot of every male over twenty-five years of age. Christianizing the land was slowed once the Indians identified the monks with the coming of Spanish rule and saw the authorities ignore any attempt by the Franciscans to ameliorate the Indians' condition but thrived after Oñate was replaced in 1609. By 1630, there were 50 priests at work, and they reported some 60,000 baptized converts.

REFORM AND DISUNION

As the Spanish established themselves in various North American outposts, leaders in other countries were beginning to see the wealth flowing into Spain from its American ventures. They were somewhat distracted from immediate competition by the great sixteenth-century upheaval called the Protestant Reformation. For several centuries, the Roman Catholic Church had experienced calls for internal reformation, but most responses had been superficial. The catalyst that brought together the forces demanding change was the building of St. Peter's, a massive cathedral that required vast financial resources. The pope, the head of the Roman Catholic Church, initiated fund-raising efforts across Europe. His efforts met particular resistance in German-speaking lands to the north, where an Augustinian monk, Martin Luther, emerged as the champion of a reform movement that received the backing of enough of the rulers of the many German states to split the church. The history of what was to occur in the New World cannot be understood apart from the divisions created with the Reformation.

Through the Middle Ages, the Roman Catholic Church had gained hegemony across Europe from Spain to Poland, from Italy to Ireland. In each country it dominated, it marked off the land into parishes and in every parish located a church. One or more priests were assigned to each parish to conduct worship and see to the needs of the people. Parishes were grouped into a diocese, over which a bishop presided. The more prominent of the dioceses were

Much of American history was determined by the Protestant Reformation, launched by German theologian Martin Luther.

termed archdioceses and their leaders archbishops. The diocese remains the basic unit of Catholicism, and its authority is established in and passed through the bishops, who are seen as being in a lineage of consecration to their office that goes back to the original twelve apostles gathered around Jesus.

In the centuries after the fall of Rome, the church emerged as the most effective international organization operating across Europe, and the bishop of Rome, the pope, became the leading authority in the religious realm. His authority was extended following the eighth-century reforms carried out by Pope Gregory. The pope had an additional power base as the secular ruler of the Papal States, a national state covering central Italy. The work of the church was extended by the many ordered communities that carried out special tasks. The most important were the Dominicans (famous for their work with the Inquisition), the Benedictines, the Franciscans, and the Jesuits.

Having thoroughly integrated itself into the European social structure, the Roman Catholic Church developed a total system of belief and practice that oversaw and blessed the lives of its members from their birth to their death. Soon after birth, a child was brought into the church by the sacrament of baptism. Around the age of puberty, young people went through an indoctrination program—centered upon learning the answers to a set of questions (the catechism)—and through the sacrament of confirmation were welcomed into the church as full members. Immediately after confirmation, they went through the process that would be repeated frequently throughout their lives, confession of their sins to a priest, the pronouncing of forgiveness for their sins, and performance of a penance. After confession, they were ready to receive the Eucharist, the sacramental body (bread) and blood (wine) of Christ.

The process of confession, penance, and reception of the Eucharist were the means offered to assist Christians to lead a holy life and prepare themselves for heaven. The average Christian remained a sinner all his or her life and at the end of that life, needed to spend a period of extended penance in an intermediate state called purgatory. By performing good acts, above and beyond the call of duty, one could balance the consequences of sin and shorten time in purgatory. In addition, the saints, the most holy of Christians, had by their holy lives built up a storehouse of goodness that Christians could draw upon. The church had access to that storehouse and could dispense it to designated people. At the end of one's life, the priest heard the final confession of the believer and offered the final rites that carried the believer into the life to come.

By the second decade of the sixteenth century, Catholic Europe was being challenged by Islam. The Muslim Ottoman Empire had captured Constantinople in 1453 and, over the next sixty years, moved up the Danube and overran Belgrade and Budapest. By 1520, Muslims stood at the gates of Vienna, the last barrier keeping them from overrunning central Europe. Meanwhile, in the German state of Saxony, a young theological professor and Augustinian monk was undergoing a profound religious experience.

As a young monk, Martin Luther (1483–1546) went in search of salvation but found little solace in all of the church's resources. A sense of the forgiveness of his sin eluded him. In his years of Bible study, after joining the faculty of the university at Wittenberg in 1511, he concluded that the dynamics of Christian living as he had pursued them were wrong. He had believed God a harsh taskmaster whom he was trying to placate with good works and acts of piety. He finally concluded that, quite apart from his efforts at goodness, he should first accept God's grace and forgiveness on faith. In doing that he found the release he had sought; God had pronounced him righteous, and he was justified.

This simple insight theoretically challenged much of the structure of the medieval church but had the immediate effect of setting Luther against the fund-raising campaign for St. Peter's. A Dominican, John Tetzel, came to Germany to sell indulgences. Indulgences were a means by which the church offered people the benefits of the beneficences accumulated by the saints. Tetzel suggested that the mere purchase of an indulgence could free the buyer (or a loved one) from time they were destined to spend in purgatory. Luther believed the selling of indulgences a perversion of the faith, and as a good academic, in 1517, he called for a debate by posting a set of theses for discussion, 95 in all, on the door of the Wittenberg church.

To defend his 95 theses, Luther was forced to assert the authority of the Bible over that of the church and the ability of members to read and interpret the Bible in the face of the common interpretation being offered by church leaders. Thus, two further guiding principles of the Reformation joined justification by faith: *sola Scriptura* (the authority of Scripture) and the priesthood of believers, the idea that baptism makes all believers equal (and hence going to a priest to confess one's sins is unnecessary). Among the important implications of Luther's mature position is that the entire sacramental system is not biblical and not needed. He abolished it, retaining only baptism and the Eucharist.

The Protestant ideals, pronounced at a time when German princes were asserting their independence and both rulers and citizens alike were less than enthusiastic about sending money to Italy, gained widespread acceptance through the German-speaking lands. A second strong reform leader soon appeared in the person of Ulrich Zwingli (1484–1531) in Zürich, Switzerland. As Zürich's parish priest, he began to espouse Luther's position but then took it one step further. Luther had basically believed that as long as something in the church did not contradict the Scripture, for example, statues of Jesus and the saints, it could remain. Zwingli took the more stringent position that anything not supported by Scripture must be removed. He could, for example, find no Scripture to support the presence of many items commonly found in the churches of the day and had all tapestries, pictures, crucifixes, and even candles taken away. He also refused to wear clerical robes. Most important, he could find no basis for the Eucharistic mass and disavowed the "magical" theology upon which it was based. He believed that the Lord's Supper was merely a memorial meal and refuted the idea that Christ was really present in the elements of bread and wine. The belief concerning the "real Presence" became the crucial idea separating Zwingli and Luther.

Zwingli's approach to reform left him open to the pull of even more radical voices, those who wanted to push the Reformation in Zürich to its logical conclusion. Some prominent lay leaders, including Conrad Grebal (1498–1526) and Feliz Manz (1498–1527), looked to create a church in conformity with what they saw in the Bible. For example, they raised the issue of baptism. They found no practice of infant baptism in Scripture and called for its abandonment.

Reacting to the Zürich city council's backing of Zwingli on this issue, Grebal and some of his supporters baptized one George Blayrock. That act signaled the beginning of the Anabaptist free church movement, a more radical populist position that bypassed official structures altogether and was uniformly attacked and suppressed by Catholics, Lutherans and Zwinglians alike.

The decentralized Radical Reformation spread through the German-speaking lands and created a context in which many key ideas originally articulated by Luther could be given a popular antiauthoritarian twist. The most radical theological wing of the movement was represented by the apocalypticists, who argued that the end of the world was imminent. One of their number, Melchior Hofmann, believed that Christ would appear in 1534. Arrested, he languished his last year in prison, believing that his arrest was a sign of the approaching end. Unfortunately for the entire movement, one of his converts, Jan Matthias, became the reform leader in Munster. Killed in battle, Matthias was succeeded by Jan Brockelson, who proceeded to introduce communalism and polygamy and ruled through daily revelations. He even had himself crowned as a new King David. After a lengthy siege, Munster fell to Catholic forces, and Brockelson and other leaders were tortured and executed as a warning to any others who might be tempted to copy their example.

The activities of the likes of Jan Brockelson only heightened the persecution that the radical reformers were already facing. It also led Menno Simons (1492–1559), a Roman Catholic priest in Holland who had converted to the Anabaptist position, to purge the radicals from that segment of the movement in which he was working and to re-create the Anabaptists as the Mennonites.

While the reform movement spread through Germany and Switzerland, it also gained some support throughout the French-speaking world. French Protestants found an early champion in the person of John Calvin (1509–1564), who in 1536 completed the first Protestant systematic theology, the *Institutes of the Christian Religion*, the classic statement of the Reformed position. He worked at Paris, Geneva, and Strassburg before becoming established at Geneva in 1541. Here, he attempted to create a city run strictly by the principles he had articulated in the *Institutes*. Integral to Calvin's reform was the abolishment of the office of bishop and the placement of authority in the hands of elders—the ministers, or teaching elders, and the laymen, or ruling elders. The Greek biblical word for elder is "presbyter," and when not called Reformed, Calvinist churches are frequently referred to as Presbyterian churches.

The generation following the Reformation rearranged the religious map of Europe, albeit at the cost of thousands of lives. Catholics fought Lutherans and Calvinists, and all three groups attempted to suppress the Anabaptists.

Protestant reformer John Calvin originated the theological perspective shared by the Reformed, Presbyterian, Congregational, and Baptist churches.

PROMPTE   ET SINCERE

IOHANNES · CALVINVS ·
ANNO · ÆTATIS ·53·
·B·

Some semblance of peace was finally reached in 1555 when the Lutherans and the Catholics signed a peace treaty at Augsburg. However, simultaneously, the Roman Catholic bishops were in the midst of the two-decade-long deliberations (1545–1563) known as the Council of Trent that responded to the Protestants by initiating a number of reforms within the Roman Catholic Church and creating a strategy to counter the spread of Protestantism. Through the last half of the century, the church was especially effective in turning back Protestant gains in Poland and Hungary, retained Catholic support in large segments of the German-speaking world, and stopped the further spread of Protestantism into southern Europe.

In the last half of the century, the relatively small Protestant community in France experienced increasing persecutions that culminated in the massacre of thousands of Protestants in Paris on August 24, 1572, St. Bartholomew's Day. Within weeks some 20,000 across the country were killed. After the massacre, Protestants continued to face periodic persecution until the Edict of Nantes in

1598. The Spanish rulers in Holland followed a similar program of persecution of Protestants and Anabaptists culminating in the reign of the Duke of Alva (1567–1573), the bloodiest the small nation had ever experienced. But while French Protestant strength was broken in France, the violence in Holland led to revolt, and Protestants led by William of Orange finally forced the Spanish out. The modern country of the Netherlands became independent in 1581. Along the road to independence, in 1577, William issued the decree of tolerance for Anabaptists, a keystone document in the history of religious freedom. The Netherlands became the fountainhead of religious tolerance in the next century.

THE SEVENTEENTH-CENTURY MOVE TO AMERICA—THE CASE OF ENGLAND

At the end of the sixteenth century, Catholic Europe had been divided. Northern Germany and Scandinavia had become Lutheran. Much of Switzerland and the Netherlands had become Protestant in the Calvinist or Reformed tradition, and minority Reformed Protestant communities could be found in France (the Huguenots) and Hungary. Permeating the German-speaking world, but increasingly concentrated in the Netherlands, were the Anabaptists. During the ensuing century, these religious rivalries aligned with national rivalries in the competition for space in America.

One cannot understand the American story apart from the rearrangement of religious loyalties in the sixteenth century in continental Europe. However, as significant as those events were, what occurred in England is doubly so. Like Germany, England began the century staunchly in the Catholic camp. King Henry VIII ascended to the throne in 1509, and as Luther's writing began to circulate in his land, Henry, who fancied himself a theologian, wrote a Catholic response. A grateful pope bestowed upon him the title of "Defender of the Faith." However, within a few years, he faced a crucial personal problem, the desire to establish his family as rulers of England, that would lead him to break with Rome. His attack upon Roman authority would increase when he ran into financial problems and saw a wealthy ecclesiastical institution as the immediate solution.

Henry's problem initially manifested in his wife's not bearing a son who survived. Henry's solution to his problem was to divorce her and marry a woman who, he hoped, would bear a son. In the process, he had to suppress clergy opposition to divorce and weaken their allegiance to papal authority. In 1533, the pope threatened excommunication. Henry responded by having the Parliament declare him supreme in the land, stop the payment of money to Rome, and stop the pope from nominating people to fill British ecclesiastical positions. At this point, although he had significantly challenged the pope's authority, Henry had made no move to alter doctrine in any way. Through the remaining decade of his reign, however, he invited Protestants into high positions of his government and vacillated between Protestant and Catholic positions.

Henry died in 1547. The Council of Regency, appointed to advise his son, the young King Edward VI, was dominated by the Protestants who had found their way to court in the previous decade. Archbishop of Canterbury Thomas Cranmer, the highest official in the British church, was decidedly Protestant in outlook and took the lead in introducing Protestant practices. To bolster his position, he invited a number of Calvinists from the continent to teach and preach. The Protestant era was brief, however, as Edward died after a mere five years on the throne (1553). His sister Mary, the daughter of Catherine of Aragon, succeeded him. A firm Catholic, she had Cranmer imprisoned and launched a program to return England to Catholicism. Her execution of a number of Protestant leaders earned her the title of "Bloody Mary." But her rule was as brief as her brother's, and in 1558, she passed away and left England to her younger sister, Elizabeth.

In her decades on the throne, Elizabeth would earn the approbation of history as the model modern ruler. Casting aside ideological allegiances of her siblings, she emerged as the rational pragmatist, making decisions for what she saw was the good of England. On the religious front, she faced strong communities of both Protestants and Catholics. She began a delicate balancing act to find some common middle ground. Her solution, known as the *via media*, resulted in the emergence of the contemporary Anglican tradition. The revamped Church of England retained many aspects of the former Roman Catholicism while introducing many Protestant doctrinal perspectives. In assuming this unique position, neither truly Protestant nor fully Catholic, the Church of England moved steadily toward a closer identification with the Protestant community. Through Elizabeth's reign, successive plots to reestablish Roman Catholicism were discovered, and finally an invasion was attempted by the Spanish Armada, partially financed by the pope, in 1588. The devastation of the Spanish fleet would have immense repercussions on Spain's ability to hang on to its possessions in the New World, and with Roman Catholicism pushed aside for the moment in England, it would be time for the different forms of Protestantism to vie for supremacy.

PURITANISM

The establishment of the *via media*, the middle way between Protestantism and Roman Catholicism, by no means ended the struggle for the soul of

Britain, and supporters of both positions tried to move the church in their direction. A Roman Catholic minority remained in England, although it lost much popular sympathy after the attack of the Spanish Armada in 1588. The diversity of the Protestant camp would coalesce around a call for the further purification of the Church of England. Among the first successes of the Puritans was the translation of a new edition of the Bible, whose publication they ensured by dedicating it to England's new monarch, James I.

Those Puritans who felt at home in the structure of the Church of England merely called for a doctrinal adjustment (along the lines of John Calvin) and the further Protestantizing of the Prayer Book, the volume that contained the material read in the various worship services. More radical Puritans additionally called for the removal of the bishops and the replacement of the episcopal form of church governance with the presbyterial system as defined by John Calvin in his *Institutes*. Presbyterian advocates had succeeded in gaining control of the Church in Scotland, and many Puritans hoped for similar success in England.

Still more radical were the Independents, later to be known as Baptists. They called for a complete break of the church away from the state and a reorganization of the Christian community around autonomous congregations made up of converted believers. The Independents became focused on their dropping of infant baptism, an act regularly afforded each child in both Catholic and Protestant countries signifying the child's entrance into the Christian community and pressing the image of union of church and culture. The Church of England was an inclusive church, filled with people of all degrees of faith. The Independent congregation was an exclusive church consisting of only the faithful.

Arising between the Independents and the Presbyterians (both of whom shared a Calvinist doctrinal position) were the Congregationalists. Like the Independents, they placed the authority for church governance in the hands of local congregations. However, they had no problem with the idea of an established church; they merely wanted it to be a congregational establishment.

Once she set the *via media* in place, Elizabeth I was rarely hesitant to move against prominent opponents on either side. She removed pastors who would not wear the required vestments for Sunday worship and arrested writers who advocated the Presbyterian and Independent positions. Toward the close of her reign, several Puritans were executed for their disloyal actions. The Independent leader Robert Browne (1550–1633) moved with his followers to Holland, at the time the most religiously tolerant country in Europe.

Puritanism survived into the height of the Anglican establishment during the reign of Charles I (1625–1649). While some Puritans left for America, oth-

ers bided their time. Charles's policy gradually cost him popular support, a fact signaled by his dismissal of Parliament in 1629 and his attempt to rule alone. His course of action led first to a revolt in Scotland and then one in England when he attempted to raise taxes to put down the Scots. Parliament rose up in 1645 and took control of the country. They abolished the episcopacy and the Prayer Book and instituted Presbyterianism. They also called the leading Presbyterian clergy and scholars to an assembly that met at Westminster. That assembly drafted the series of documents that came to define the Presbyterian Church.

After Charles was beheaded in 1649, Oliver Cromwell (1599–1658) rose to power as the political leader of the Protestant cause. He granted religious freedom to all except the Anglicans and Roman Catholics. His Protestantizing

Puritan colonists made the church building, often doubling as a fort, their initial communal structure.

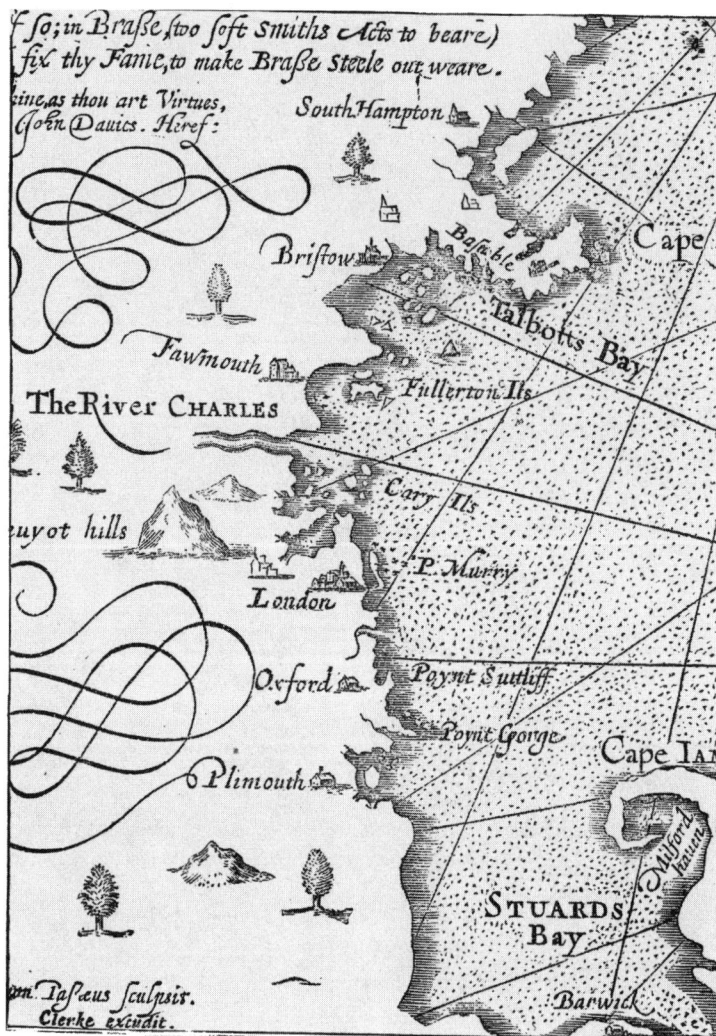

of the British church, however, was reversed after his death, when a new king reinstituted Anglicanism and even tried to favor Roman Catholicism. A generation of further struggle finally ended in the arrival of the Protestant King William of Orange and his wife, Mary. Anglicanism settled in as the established Church of England, even though toleration was accorded to all of the dissenting Protestant groups in 1689.

THE TRANSFER OF EUROPEAN RELIGION TO AMERICA

The first members and clergy of most of the different European churches that emerged out of the Reformation to arrive in the New World accompanied various expeditions during the sixteenth century, and their efforts were

Pilgrims gather for worship at Plymouth.

largely unsuccessful at establishing any permanent presence. For example, in 1564, a group of French Huguenots settled along the St. Johns River in Florida. Florida was Spanish territory, and the next year, Spanish forces obliterated the fledgling community. The first Anglican services in the New World were held in 1587 at the lost colony of Roanoke in Virginia.

Apart from St. Augustine, permanent settlement of what is now the United States would not begin until 1606 and the founding of the Jamestown colony by representatives of the London Company, a mercantile coalition operating out of the British capital. Robert Hunt (c.1568–1608) settled at the colony as the first Anglican parish priest in the New World, though he soon succumbed to the environment and died. He was succeeded by Alexander Whitaker (1585–c.1616), an Anglican with distinctly Puritan leanings, who enjoyed a long and fruitful ministry. In 1619, the legislature in the growing Virginia colony formally established the Church of England as the official church of the land. From its initial base in Virginia, through the remainder of the seventeenth century, the Church of England would spread through all of the colonies that came under British control. In those from Virginia southward,

Preparing to leave Holland for Massachusetts, the Pilgrims pause for a moment of prayer.

it would be the dominant religious force; in others like Pennsylvania and Massachusetts it would have only a token presence.

The next group to find its way to America was made up of self-exiled members of an Independent congregation that had left England in 1608 and settled in Holland, at Leyden. Here they enjoyed religious freedom but over time saw that their remaining would lead to their children's assimilation into Dutch life. Thus, they sent agents to London to negotiate a possible move to America. Finally, in 1620, a group with a contract from the Virginia Company persuaded the Leyden group to join their settlement attempt. The thirty who chose to go to the New World were but a minority of the party but provided substantial leadership, especially in the drafting of the Mayflower Compact, a plan of governance for their new colony based upon the social contract theories that had so influenced the organizational models of Independent congregations. The settlement at Plymouth was established in December 1620, and the original church set up by the Leyden Independents, now known as the Pilgrim's Church, continues as a viable congregation.

Plymouth Rock marks the spot where the Pilgrims landed in Massachusetts.

MAYFLOWER COMPACT 1620
Agreement Between the Settlers at New Plymouth : 1620

IN THE NAME OF GOD, AMEN. We, whose names are underwritten, the Loyal Subjects of our dread Sovereign Lord King *James*, by the Grace of God, of *Great Britain*, *France*, and *Ireland*, King, *Defender of the Faith*, &c. Having undertaken for the Glory of God, and Advancement of the Christian Faith, and the Honour of our King and Country, a Voyage to plant the first Colony in the northern Parts of *Virginia*; Do by these Presents, solemnly and mutually, in the Presence of God and one another, covenant and combine ourselves together into a civil Body Politick, for our better Ordering and Preservation, and Furtherance of the Ends aforesaid: And by Virtue hereof do enact, constitute, and frame, such just and equal Laws, Ordinances, Acts, Constitutions, and Officers, from time to time, as shall be thought most meet and convenient for the general Good of the Colony; unto which we promise all due Submission and Obedience. IN WITNESS whereof we have hereunto subscribed our names at *Cape-Cod* the eleventh of November, in the Reign of our Sovereign Lord King *James*, of *England*, *France*, and *Ireland*, the eighteenth, and of *Scotland* the fifty-fourth, *Anno Domini*; 1620.

Mr. John Carver, Mr. William Bradford, Mr Edward Winslow, Mr. William Brewster. Isaac Allerton, Myles Standish, John Alden, John Turner, Francis Eaton, James Chilton, John Craxton, John Billington, Joses Fletcher, John Goodman, Mr. Samuel Fuller, Mr. Christopher Martin, Mr. William Mullins, Mr. William White, Mr. Richard Warren, John Howland, Mr. Steven Hopkins, Digery Priest, Thomas Williams, Gilbert Winslow, Edmund Margesson, Peter Brown, Richard Britteridge George Soule, Edward Tilly, John Tilly, Francis Cooke, Thomas Rogers, Thomas Tinker, John Ridgdale, Edward Fuller, Richard Clark, Richard Gardiner, Mr. John Allerton, Thomas English, Edward Doten, Edward Liester.

John Winthrop was the first governor of the Puritan-dominated Massachusetts Bay Colony.

In 1628, John White, a Puritan minister, took the lead in forming the New England Company and in sending a group to Massachusetts, where a settlement and church were established at Salem. The following year, the New England Company was superseded by the Massachusetts Bay Company, which had received a royal charter to establish an additional colony in Massachusetts. Their urge to colonize was encouraged by the erratic actions of King Charles and the archbishop of London, William Laud, who was working for absolute conformity to Anglicanism. The initial group left in 1629 and the larger party the following year. They settled north of Plymouth and soon spread out to form a number of communities (Boston, Charlestown, Medford, etc.). They also set up a church according to the Congregational model.

The stories of the Pilgrims and Puritans have become part of the myth of American life and are often combined and confused. The Pilgrims were a small group of Separatist Protestants who came to the New World both to raise their children in an English cultural environment and to worship freely as they had chosen. The Puritans, on the other hand, came primarily to establish themselves as an economic community and to escape the persecution that they felt was soon to reach unbearable levels in England. They too wanted to worship as they had chosen, but they did not take the additional step to create a society in

which religious freedom was a reality. Like the majority party in England, the Puritans in New England believed that they were following the true way, and they had little tolerance for dissent.

The demand for conformity was amply illustrated in the cases of Roger Williams (1603–1683) and of the Quakers. Williams, a Puritan minister, arrived in Massachusetts and in 1635 assumed the pastorate of the church at Salem. Dissenting on various issues in the colony, he urged the Salem church to separate. The General Court acted promptly and banished Williams. Rather than risk deportation back to England, he fled Salem and headed south. He eventually purchased land from the native people and in 1536 founded the town of Providence, now the capital of Rhode Island. He was later joined by other Massachusetts dissidents such as Anne Hutchinson (1591–1643). The articulate Williams also founded an Independent congregation, later affiliated with the Baptists, and emerged as the true prophet of America's religious freedom.

The first Quakers arrived in Massachusetts in 1556. They were members of a new religion whose founder, George Fox (1628–1691), had received a mystical enlightenment in 1647 and begun preaching his rather unorthodox ideas about continuing revelation from the believers' inner light. A charismatic speaker, he soon attracted a following. He spoke against alcohol and various

St. David's Episcopal Church, erected near Philadelphia in 1715, was built on a site previously used by Welsh pioneers.

forms of entertainment and was a devout pacifist, at a time when the English civil war raged around him. Oliver Cromwell had him imprisoned. The Massachusetts leadership agreed with Cromwell's action and responded to the Quakers by arresting them, treating them brutally, and banishing them. A short time later the Massachusetts General Court imposed penalties on any Quakers entering the colony, including the death penalty upon any who returned after being expelled. The court hung two Quakers in 1659.

On the other end of the British religious spectrum, Roman Catholic membership had declined in England in the years after the defeat of the Spanish Armada, but in spite of laws placing them outside the religious consensus and preventing any public worship, many remained loyal to the Roman Catholic Church. As it turned out, most of the kings of England in the seventeenth century were also personally inclined to Catholicism. Thus it was that a convert to the church, George Calvert (1580–1632) was made Lord Baltimore by King James I, who also granted him a charter for a tract of land in the Americas. The charter allowed for non-Protestant churches, a provision that

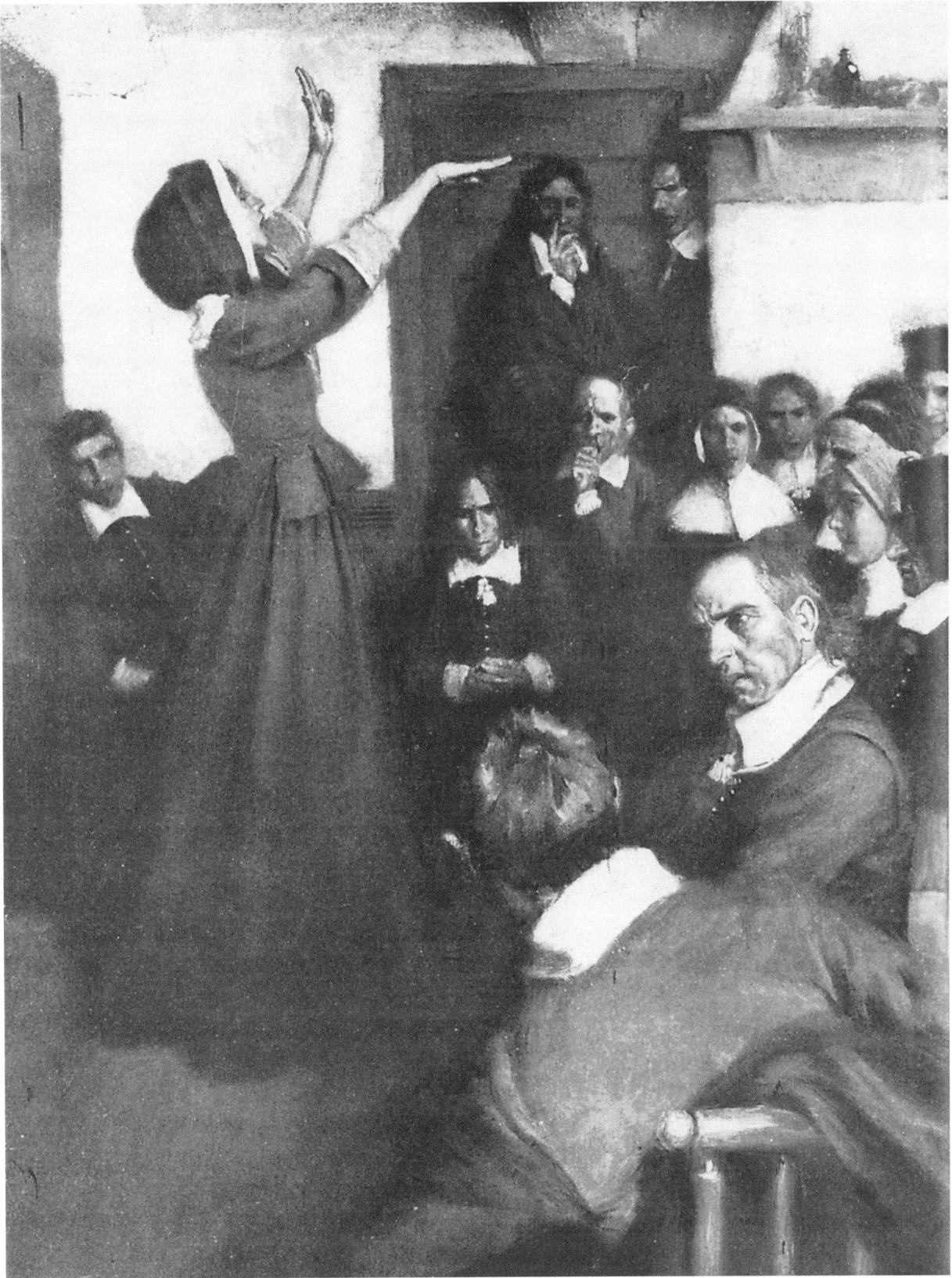

The Old Brick Church (now St. Luke's Episcopal Church) in Isle of Wight County, Virginia, is the oldest church building in the United States, dating from 1632.

allowed him to invite his co-religionists to his new colony and made Maryland the only land under the British crown where Catholics could openly worship according to their faith. To ensure the future of the colony, Lord Baltimore granted freedom to all forms of Christianity. The first group of colonists that arrived in 1634 included two Jesuits among them.

Maryland faced problems from the beginning. The charter left its boundary with Virginia undetermined, leading on several occasions to open warfare. Also, strong anti-Catholic sentiment in both England and the other colonies continually led to challenges of the charter and the freedoms that Catholics enjoyed. In the end, Maryland Anglicans marched on the capital, then located at St. Marys, and overthrew the government. In 1692, the Anglican Church was

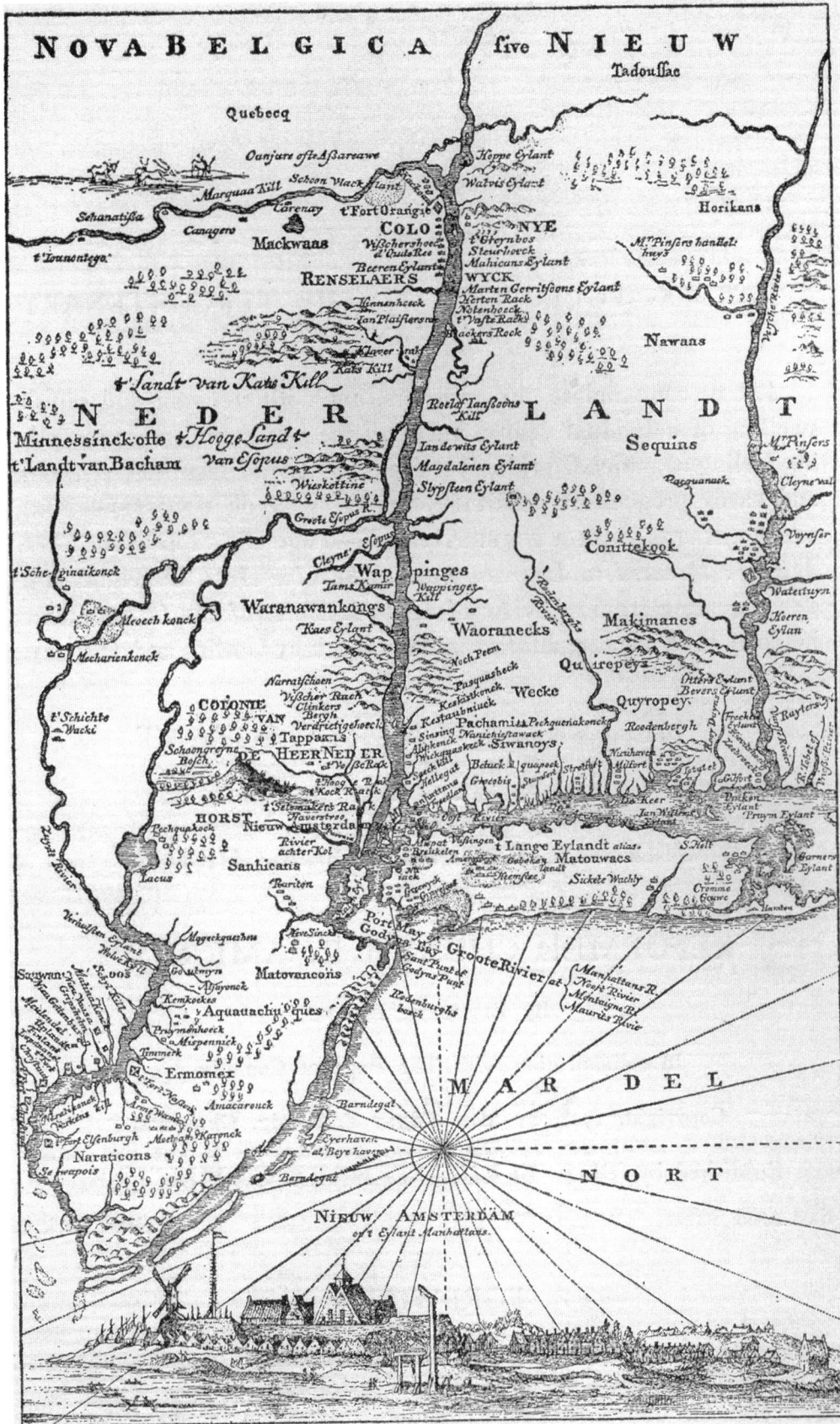

Reformed believers from Holland planted churches in New York and northward through the Hudson River Valley.

Peter Stuyvesant, the Dutch governor of New York, unsuccessfully tried to stop the multiplication of religious groups in his domain.

The Old Swedes Church survives as a remnant of the Swedish Lutheran settlement at Wilmington, Delaware.

established as the official religious body in the colony, although the new government lacked the power to suppress the large body of Catholics that now resided throughout the land.

Dutch exploration of the American coast south of New England had begun in 1609 and permanent settlement in the area around New York Bay in 1624. Two years later, a group led by Peter Minuit (1580–1638) settled on Manhattan Island. New Amsterdam soon became the center of the Dutch colonization effort. In 1628, the Reverend Jonas Michaelius (b. 1577) established the first Dutch Reformed Church, now known as the Collegiate Church of the City of New York. It was followed by others as Dutch settlements spread into what is now New York and New Jersey, especially along the Hudson River.

Farther south, in 1638, Swedes began a settlement at Fort Christina (where present-day Wilmington, Delaware, is located) on the Delaware River a settlement also under the leadership of Peter Minuit, who had had a falling out with leaders in New Amsterdam and had gone to work for some Swedish investors. In 1640, Reverend Reorus Torkillus arrived to organize the first Lutheran church in America. Lutheran growth was slow until the later part of the century, when German Lutherans began to arrive in the new colony of Pennsylvania, and remained rather loosely organized until the 1740s when Henry Muhlenberg (1711–1787) arrived and organized the Ministerium of Pennsylvania in 1748.

EVEN QUAKERS AND JEWS

The outlines of what was to be in America for many years were established as businessmen founded colonies and members of the larger Christian churches of Europe migrated to the New World. They came for all the assortment of reasons that individuals in an old settled society will abandon their homes, their extended families, and the familiar for an unknown possibility. Although some found disaster, those that survived were able to reap a rich harvest, and the Roman Catholic, Anglican (Episcopal), Congregationalist, Reformed, and Lutheran Churches they formed continue to serve key roles in the ever-changing religious community of the United States.

But our story of the origin of the unique religious community being assembled by the European settlers in what was to become America would be grossly distorted without including two additional accounts. The first begins in England as the unpopular King Charles I and the Puritan-led Parliament found themselves at loggerheads. A young George Fox (1624–1691) had a religious vision, and as everyone else was lost in the morass of civil war, he was calling people to pay attention to the Inner Light. When the dust settled, Cromwell

Quaker William Penn created the
colony of Pennsylvania as a haven
for persecuted religious groups.

New England Puritans attempted
to beat Quakerism out of its
adherents.

was sure he did not like the Society of Friends, which some called Quakers and
others labeled fanatics. And when in 1660 a new king was enthroned, old divisions still plagued the country, but people on both sides still agreed that they
did not like the Quakers.

However, in the years of Charles II's reign, the Quakers found a champion in the form of a young man, William Penn (1644–1718), who associated
with the Quakers since his meeting with Fox. As it turned out, Penn was the
son of an admiral and had an inheritance due him from the king. Concerned

with the persecution faced by his fellow religionists, he accepted a land grant in America and slowly put together the outlines of an amazing experiment. He received his charter in March 1681 and moved quickly to take possession of his new land and to invite the members of the Society of Friends and others (including members of minority religions on the European continent) to make their home in Philadelphia and the surrounding territory. A government was established, and among its first acts was a law granting liberty of conscience to its citizens, a sharp contrast to the religious laws dominating Massachusetts.

The second story goes back to the 1490s and the division of the New World between the Spanish and the Portuguese. The papal decision coincided with a wave of anti-Semitism sweeping through the Iberian Peninsula. The persecution of Jews in Spain and Portugal created a new group of citizens, the Marranos, Jews who had been publicly baptized into Catholicism but who secretly retained their Jewish faith and practiced in the privacy of their homes. In 1492, Spain expelled the remaining Jews who refused to convert to Christianity, and Portugal followed suit the following year. Many Iberian Jews found their way to the tolerant Holland. There they prospered and built an economically and culturally rich community. At the same time, many moved to Recife, a town on the northern coast of Portuguese Brazil.

In the 1630s, Holland found itself at war with Portugal, and Recife fell to the Dutch. They discovered that some Marranos who had quietly lived in

Dutch priest Menno Simons organized German and Swiss believers who later took his name as Mennonites.

Recife for more than a century had assisted their capture of the settlement. Under the new colonial rule, Jews declared their faith openly and organized the first synagogue in the Americas. Unfortunately for the Marranos, the Portuguese returned to power twenty years later, and the Jews had to give up all they had gained and again migrate. Some went to Holland, some to the Dutch island of Curaçao off the coast of Venezuela. Others came to North America. One group landed in New York, where a hostile governor, Peter Stuyvesant (c.1610–1672), allowed them to settle only when authorities in Holland ordered him to grant them space. He then procrastinated as long as he could in granting them the privilege of creating a cemetery, organizing a congregation, and finally constructing a synagogue. A second group found their way to Rhode Island, where Roger Williams, who had extended his under-

Attempting to duplicate a biblical life, the Pietist groups who flocked to Pennsylvania adopted practices such as the kiss of peace in greeting fellow believers.

More than any single individual in the seventeenth century, Roger Williams articulated the rationale for religious freedom.

standing of religious freedom far beyond Christian sectarians, welcomed them. They settled in Newport.

With the coming of the Jews to the American colonies, and the settlement of the Quakers in Pennsylvania, the main outlines of what was to become the shape and structure of American religion were largely in place. It would be a land of religious diversity with some very large religious communities, but none so large as to dominate the whole, and it would be a place where numerous smaller groups could find a haven and test the viability of their message and spirituality. In succeeding centuries, several new religious communities that had not even been conceived in the seventeenth century would attract a mass following and grow into large national bodies. But before that could happen, there was the matter of a revolution through which the American people had to pass.

The story of the Jews and Quakers in America also emphasizes the premier role of Roger Williams and William Penn as the fountainheads of American commitments to religious freedom. Although the steps that would lead to the freedoms gained in the American Revolution were many and varied, and certainly included the contribution of the Roman Catholics in Maryland, they can be traced most clearly and decisively through Rhode Island and Pennsylvania rather than Massachusetts. While Quakers and Baptists were speaking clearly for full religious freedom, Congregationalists were struggling to comprehend the meaning of toleration and only in the nineteenth century abandoned their attempts to control New England.

Touro Synagogue, Newport, Rhode Island, the site of the second-oldest Jewish congregation in America.

CHAPTER 3

The Colonial Church

America at the beginning of the eighteenth century existed as a string of settlements along the Atlantic seaboard from Boston in the north to Charleston in the south. Between the cities lay forest lands that were just beginning to be cleared and settled. Roads were created to tie the cities together, but ships remained a preferred way of travel. A fledgling sense of unity was granted by geography. The American colonies were separated by some rough terrain from the Canadian settlements along the St. Lawrence (under French control), and Montreal remained a significant sea journey. To the south, the British had to remain vigilant of Spanish encroachments from Florida. However, the colonies remained distinct entities. Each looked individually across the Atlantic for support, and each pursued distinct goals. Each colony also developed a unique religious community.

Maryland was possibly the most distinctive colony among the original British settlements. The Catholics who came to Maryland were truly a despised lot. Roman Catholicism had its last opportunity to dominate England during the reign of Mary (1553–1558). Her brief reign was too short to reestablish Roman Catholicism, and under Elizabeth, Anglicans and Protestants remembered those who died. John Foxe's *Acts and Monuments of the Christian Martyrs* became a manifesto against Catholicism around which both Anglicans and Puritans could unite. The issue was joined in the war between England and Spain, and the defeat of the Spanish Armada was widely seen as a blow against Catholicism. Hopes of British Catholics for some toleration or even favoritism from King James were dashed following discovery of a Catholic plot, with Jesuit leadership, to blow up Parliament and the king. As a result, Catholicism was officially repressed.

Through the rest of the century, the battle in England was between Puritans and Anglicans, the later finally winning out. Efforts of Charles II and James II to encourage the Catholic worship were repeatedly rebuffed by Parliament, and in the end James was forced from the throne. The Toleration Act of 1689 granted status to the several Puritan sects but specifically exempted the Catholics from its provisions. Through the eighteenth century Catholicism had to operate as an underground church.

George Calvert, the first Lord Baltimore, was a friend of James I, and his continuing support of James's successor earned him a grant of some 10 million acres along Chesapeake Bay. The aging Calvert did not pursue the colonization project, but two years after his death, his son Cecelius organized the first company of 200 people, although he remained behind in England where he was able to attend to the continuing political issues posed by the colony's existence.

Religious leadership for the colonists was placed in the hands of two Jesuits, one of whom, Father Andrew White (1579–1656), became known as the "Apostle of Maryland" because of his effectiveness in converting both some non-Catholic settlers and the native population, especially the Piscataway. White proved an accomplished linguist and produced a grammar and then a catechism for them. He was possibly the first person to develop a written form for one of the Native American languages. White's success, however, created problems at home. The idea of Jesuits working effectively in a British colony raised the ire of powerful people in Parliament, and Lord Baltimore had to appeal to Rome to have the Jesuits replaced with Franciscans. Soon, the first secular priests were also introduced to the colony.

In like measure, Baltimore moved to change the image of Maryland as a "Catholic" colony by having a Protestant residing in the colony designated as lieutenant governor. Then, in 1649, the Maryland legislature passed a toleration act that included all Christians, a work now seen as a landmark in the history of religious freedom. Baltimore's efforts were not enough. During the Commonwealth under Oliver Cromwell, Protestants seized the colony and repealed the Toleration Act. Roman Catholics were always a minority in their own colony and now those non-Catholics who were members of other churches had gained control. Then, in 1688, after James II was driven from his throne, Anglicans, a small minority in Maryland, launched a campaign to name the Church of England the established church in Maryland, as it was in England. They finally accomplished their goal in 1702.

THE CHURCH OF ENGLAND ABROAD

The establishment of the Church of England in Maryland followed the church's consolidation of power in the homeland. Its position as the established church would not again be significantly challenged. With a new century before it, the church realized that as England moved out into the world, so did its church members. The church was the established church in Virginia and the colonies to the south, but it was a very weak establishment. The great majority of colonists were not religious. Increasingly, through the seventeenth century, those immigrants who were religious were members of a host of sectarian movements and dissenting churches, from Baptists to Quakers, from

Apoſtolick Charity,

ITS
Nature and Excellence
CONSIDER'D.
IN A
DISCOURSE

Upon *Dan* 12. 3.

Preached at St. *Paul's*, at the Ordination of ſome *Proteſtant Miſſionaries* to be ſent into the *Plantations*.

To which is *Prefixt*,

A *General View* of the *Engliſh Colonies* in *America*, with reſpect to *Religion*; in order to ſhew what *Proviſion* is wanting for the *Propagation* of *Chriſtianity* in theſe Parts.

Together with *Propoſals* for the *Promoting* the ſame: And to induce ſuch of the *Clergy* of this *Kingdom*, as are Perſons of *Sobriety* and *Abilities* to accept of a *Miſſion*.

And to which is ſubjoin'd

The *Author's Circular Letter* lately ſent to the *Clergy* there.

By **Thomas Bray,** D. D.

LONDON,

Printed for *William Hawes*, at the Sign of the *Roſe* in *Ludgate* Street, 1699.

*Thomas Bray lobbied for the Church of England's
mission in North America.*

As governor of the Puritan Massachusetts Bay Colony, Sir Edmund Andros forced colonists to allow Anglican worship in Boston.

Moravians to Presbyterians. In addition, there was no bishop for America, a necessity if a strong church in the Anglican tradition was to develop.

Into this situation at the end of the century stepped one Thomas Bray (1658–1730). Bray served as the commissary for the church in Maryland for five years (1695–1700). He returned to England with both knowledge of and empathy for the Church abroad and became the leading force in the organization of two of the most important structures in the life of the Church of England: the Society for the Propagation of the Gospel in Foreign Parts (SPG) and the Society for Promoting Christian Knowledge (SPCK). The SPG began the recruitment and sending of Church of England ministers to the colonies, first to provide ministerial leadership for the scattered congregations and then to establish new ones. Along with the Maryland problem, British Anglicans had become concerned with Anglican minorities in other colonies, especially in Massachusetts, where for a century the Congregationalist establishment had prevented an Anglican parish from being founded.

The SPG had placed some 300 ministers in the colonies by the beginning of the American Revolution. They were scattered along the length and breadth

Supporters of the Church of England tried unsuccessfully through the eighteenth century to have a bishop appointed to oversee the work in the colonies.

of the land but created strong parishes in the cities (where many of the most wealthy were Anglicans) and did monumental work in the middle colonies. In the meantime, the SPCK supported the establishment of a number of theological libraries. The church never had the support of a large enough percentage of the population to create a strong establishment, but everywhere it's identification with the ruling class made it a force with which to be reckoned.

FROM NEW AMSTERDAM TO NEW YORK

The first Dutch Reformed minister arrived in New Netherlands only in 1624, some four years after the settlers arrived, a symbol of the secular interests that created and controlled the colony. The managers of the Dutch West India Company were so focused on profits that their long-term interests, which would have been served by the development of a strong colony, were swept aside. The Reformed Church thus developed largely in spite of rather than

The Reformed church members from Holland built churches, like this one in Albany, New York, throughout the Hudson River Valley.

with the support of the colonial governors. Slowly, the church was established, and the six ministers had formed twelve congregations by the time the British moved in 1664 to take over the colony. Thus, both the Dutch and the Reformed Church lost their opportunity to build a strong presence in America.

Reformed Church growth did not end with the transformation to British rule. A steady stream of immigrants continued to flow into New York and the surrounding colonies, especially New Jersey, and church membership doubled during the next generation, although it was lost amid the massive influx of people from other European centers. As it turned out, the Dutch proved to be the initial wave of the children of John Calvin to wash up on America's shores. Just to the south, large numbers of German Reformed would respond to William Penn's invitation to move to his colony and give to southeastern Pennsylvania its reputation as the home of the Pennsylvania Dutch (by which reference was made to Germans, from Deutschland, not the Dutch from Holland).

Both the Dutch and German Reformed would be overwhelmed by the influx of the Calvinists from the British Isles, the Presbyterians. While a few Presbyterians trickled into the British colonies through the seventeenth century, they constituted the main body of Puritans and were very much in the running for dominating England through most of the century. Presbyterianism had displaced Anglicanism in the 1500s in Scotland and dominated England during the Commonwealth. Presbyterian hope of regaining power persisted through the Restoration under Charles II and James II but was dashed by the Glorious Revolution that brought William and Mary to the throne. Thus it was only in the last half of the century that Presbyterians began to migrate to the Americas in any numbers.

When they did begin their move, Scots and Scotch-Irish Presbyterians flowed into New York, Pennsylvania, and New Jersey, and for a period were the dominant religious presence in those colonies. Francis Makemie (1658–1708), was commissioned by the Irish as the first Presbyterian missionary to America. He established his initial congregation, interestingly enough, in Maryland, but then for two decades roamed from New England to North Carolina establishing additional churches. He finally consolidated his work in 1706 with the formation of the Presbytery of Philadelphia. It adopted the Westminster Confession of Faith as its doctrinal standard. The following year Makemie was arrested in New York as a disturber of the peace, as he was not licensed by the Church of England, but he won the case by appealing to the Toleration Act of 1689, which, though it did not specifically extend its provisions to England's colonies, did grant toleration to Presbyterians in the homeland.

PENN'S LAND

By far the most unique of the American colonies was Pennsylvania. Penn founded Philadelphia in 1681 and launched his "Holy Experiment" by stepping beyond mere toleration to advocate both true religious freedom and a policy of equitable treatment of the native population. Penn did not just provide a haven for his fellow Quakers, but went to the Continent and actively invited those dispossessed by laws demanding religious uniformity to his new land. Germans displaced by various civil wars as well as the conflicts with the French were the single largest group to respond and initially settled what is now the Germantown section of Philadelphia. In the 1690s, Germantown became home to possibly the strangest group to surface in the New World during the colonial era, a Rosicrucian group that mixed Christian piety with a Renaissance occultism. Members of the small group cast horoscopes while they watched the heavens for Christ's return. In the early 1700s their leaders passed on and they dispersed to perpetuate German folk magic, the hex tradition, among the German communities of southeastern Pennsylvania.

The Germantown Rosicrucians were a small group that few outside the city ever encountered, but everyone knew of the Quakers, and to pious Christians, they were as strange as any would want to imagine. All of the other

Though holding Deist beliefs, the wealthy Benjamin Franklin supported the churches of Philadelphia.

groups, even the Catholics, shared a broad foundation of essential Christian affirmations that had been drawn from the Bible. Though basically operating out of Christian assumptions, the Quakers stepped out of that consensus. They believed that God had implanted within each person an inner spark (they generally called it the Inner Light) and that by paying attention to that Inner Light, individuals will know what to do and have the means to follow through. This radical individualistic approach to the religious life gave the Quakers a mystical bent, and their gathering in silence to let the Inner Light work became characteristic of their worship. They also emphasized a nonviolent life that led them to pacifism. Their pacifist assumptions caused them to be highly critical of fellow Christians who placed doctrinal orthodoxy above loving relations or moral interactions with their neighbors (including the native people).

The freedom that the Quakers gave to others to come to their land and freely practice their faith meant that gradually they lost control, although so many groups made Pennsylvania their home that no group could seize control. The colony eventually fell into the hands of several coalitions. The Quakers prospered in Philadelphia and in the end ran into trouble only when the forces

Quakers became known for their quiet worship, waiting to be moved by the Spirit.

German Pietist Johannes Kelpius led a Rosicrucian group to Pennsylvania at the end of the seventeenth century.

Conrad Beissel founded a successful eighteenth-century Pietist community at Ephrata, Pennsylvania.

of war descended upon the land and Quakers were forced to refuse the call of their country to fight.

Among the other groups that benefited the most from the existence of Pennsylvania were the descendents of the Radical Reformers. Like the Quakers, the small free churches in Europe were equally disliked by Catholic, Lutheran, and Reformed churchmen. They rejected the idea of an established church and withdrew to live quiet and simple pious lives. Like the Quakers, they tended to be pacifists. Once the boundary lines between the Protestants and the Catholics were drawn, many governments welcomed the presence of

WILLIAM PENN

PREFACE TO THE FRAME OF GOVERNMENT
OF PENNSYLVANIA (1682)

The seventeenth-century language of establishment is often overlooked by those who are concerned to locate instances of official toleration or allowance of religious liberty in colonial affairs. The Articles of Capitulation on the Reduction of New Netherland, for instance, are cited because Clause 8 allowed the Dutch the "liberty of their consciences in Divine Worship and Church Discipline." The significant implication, of course, is that a single establishment of religion seemed right and proper and that this departure from that practice was an expediential arrangement. In a similar way, while William Penn is justly celebrated for granting civil liberties to all who confessed "God as the Lord of conscience," this should not obscure the fact that such was a Quaker version of the conventional "language of establishment." Because man's "spiritual relation" was "free and mental" the church could not be "corporeal and compulsive." Yet government was said to be divinely authored—"sacred in its institution and end"—not only to restrain sin but to regulate "many other affairs," and Penn required confession of God on the part of the inhabitants and profession of Jesus Christ as Saviour on the part of the rulers. This might be contrasted with Williams' proposal that spiritual and temporal affairs be radically segregated. It is natural that we should be sympathetic toward Penn's charity in comparing him with many of his contemporaries. This does not mean, however, that the Pennsylvania experiment was more than another change rung on the medieval theme that man's double relation required coordination of his religious and civil lives.

When the great and wise God had made the world, of all his creatures it pleased him to choose man his deputy to rule it. And to fit him for so great a charge and trust he did not only qualify him with skill and power, but with integrity to use them justly. This native goodness was equally his honour and his happiness. And while he stood here all went well. There was no need of coercive or compulsive means; the precept of divine love and truth in his bosom was the guide and keeper of his innocency. But lust prevailing against duty made a lamentable breach upon it. And the law that before had no power over him took place upon him and his disobedient posterity that such as would not live conformable to the holy law within should fall under the reproof and correction of the just law without in a judicial administration.

[Saint Paul] settles the divine right of government beyond exception, and that for two ends: first, to terrify evil doers; secondly, to cherish those that do well—which gives government a life beyond corruption and makes it as durable in the world as good men shall be. So that government seems to me a part of religion itself, a thing sacred in its institution and end. For if it does not directly remove the cause it crushes the effects of evil and is as such (though a lower, yet) an emanation of the same divine power that is both author and object of pure religion. The difference [between them lies] here: the one is more free and mental, the other more corporeal and compulsive in its operations. But that is only to evil doers, government itself being otherwise as capable of kindness, goodness, and charity as a more private society. They weakly err that think there is no other use of government than correction which is the coarsest part of it. Daily experience tells us that the care and regulation of many other affairs, more soft and daily necessary, make up much of the greatest part of government and [this] must have followed the peopling of the world had Adam never fell, and [it] will continue among men, on earth, under the highest attainments they may arrive at by the coming of the blessed Second Adam, the Lord from Heaven. Thus much of government in general, as to its rise and end.

As fashion changes, the plain clothing of groups like the Amish Mennonites set them apart.

the hardworking free church people for a time, but turned on them as soon as trouble approached (or the throne changed hands).

Groups like the Mennonites and the German Brethren gratefully accepted Penn's invitation. The Mennonites had survived in Holland. Their community had slowly grown and spread back into Germany and Switzerland where they had many roots. But there was little hope for advancement for the Mennonites in Europe. Many left for Russia when Catherine the Great offered toleration for settlers who would move to the southern Steppes. A few actually found their way to New York when it was still New Amsterdam, but Penn's invitation hit a responsive chord in the largest group, and they began to migrate to Pennsylvania, to the land Penn set aside for them.

In the meantime, a new wave of pietism was sweeping through western Germany that would lead members of the next generation out of the state church into a separated life. In 1708, eight of these Brethren, as they came to be known, under the leadership of Alexander Mack, baptized each other and made a mutual covenant to follow Jesus. As this movement spread and attracted members of the state churches, the Brethren, like the Mennonites, became unwelcome in place after place. In 1719 they began to migrate to Pennsylvania. Their first church was opened in 1723 with Peter Becker serving as pastor.

Uniting these various free churches was a desire to live simply, without any ostentation. This wish led them to adopt very plain and somewhat uniform attire that over time increasingly separated them from their neighbors and their ever-evolving fashions. They became known as the "Plain People." Over time, the persecutions of the past became a distant memory; voices arose among them calling for changes in nonessentials. On matters not strictly biblical, they could make alterations that would lower the tension they still felt with their neighbors. Many chose such a course, and today a range of practice and attire exists among the Plain People. Many have adopted modern dress and drive automobiles while many still wear the uniform clothing of the eighteenth century, with a range of practice in between.

THE PURITAN COMMONWEALTH

In stark contrast to Pennsylvania's pluralistic environment, that of the founders of the Massachusetts Bay colony arose from a somewhat clear vision of what they hoped to create, a holy land dominated by God's one true church. The Puritans had developed an understanding of Christianity derived from the *Institutes*, John Calvin's restatement of the faith. Calvin's theology emphasized the sovereignty of God in his creation of the world, his giving of the law, and his establishment of a means of salvation in Christ. Under Calvin's leadership, much of the sacramental system and traditions developed by the Catholic Church over the centuries had been jettisoned. In its place, Calvin emphasized a life of faith and faithfulness. In the Calvinist system, church and state worked together, although maintaining responsibility for very separate realms. The state's job was to enforce the laws of God, thus creating an orderly society and holding the evil results of sin in check.

Those who settled Massachusetts Bay were by no means all Puritans or even religious people. But those who took the lead in the colony were. They saw the church organized as its members professed their faith and commitment to God and accepted a formal document, the church covenant. Such covenanted churches took the lead in building a Christian commonwealth, an ideal society in so far as one was possible in human life. Life was built around the church. The ministers preached the gospel, the governmental officials ordered society, and the members led a godly life. There was a single autonomous congregation in each community. Males who joined the church were recognized as freemen and thus enfranchised as voting members of the

The interior of the Old Ship Meeting House at Hingham, Massachusetts, shows the intimate simplicity in Puritan worship.

community. These church members thus chose the magistrates from among their number. Ministers had no official role in the government, but they were often consulted prior to major decisions, and government officials were expected to be in church each Sunday.

Sabbath was closely observed throughout New England. Some of the relatively plain meeting houses remain to give the modern visitor a sense of the austerity of a Sunday, especially in winter in an unheated building. Worship followed the Reformed emphasis upon orderly meetings and included a lengthy time for prayer and even lengthier time for the sermon, the format of which blended into a theological lecture. The service, which might last as long as four or more hours, would adjourn at noon for a lunch hour.

PREFACE: THE BLOODY TENET
by Roger Williams

First, That the blood of so many hundred thousand soules of *Protestants* and *Papists*, spilt in the *Wars* of *present* and *former* Ages, for their respective *Consciences*, is not *required* nor *accepted* by *Jesus Christ* the *Prince of Peace.*

Secondly, Pregnant *Scriptures* and *Arguments* are throughout the Worke proposed against the *Doctrine* of *persecution* for the *cause* of *Conscience.*

Thirdly, *Satisfactorie* Answers are given to *Scriptures*, and objections produced by Mr. *Calvin*, *Beza*, Mr. *Cotton*, and the Ministers of the New English Churches and others former and later, tending to prove the *Doctrine* of *persecution* for cause of *Conscience.*

Fourthly, The *Doctrine of persecution* for cause of *Conscience*, is proved guilty of all the *blood* of the *Soules* crying for *vengeance* under the Altar.

Fifthly, All *Civill States* with their *Officers* of *justice* in their respective *constitutions* and *administrations* are proved *essentially Civill*, and therefore not *Judges, Governours* or *Defendours* of the Spirituall or Christian State and Worship.

Sixthly, It is the will and command of *God*, that (since the coming of his Sonne the *Lord Jesus*) a *permission* of the most *Paganish, Jewish*, Turkish, or Antichristian consciences and worships, bee granted to all men in all *Nations* and *Countries*: and they are onely to bee *fought* against with that *Sword* which is only (in *Soule matters*) *able* to *conquer*, to wit, the *Sword of Gods Spirit*, the *Word of God.*

Seventhly, The *State* of the Land of *Israel*, the *Kings* and *people* thereof in *Peace & War*, is proved *figurative* and *ceremoniall*, and no *patterne* nor *president* for any *Kingdome* or *civill State* in the *world* to follow.

Eighthly, *God* requireth not an *uniformity* of *Religion* to be *inacted* and *inforced* in any *civill State*; which inforced *uniformity* (sooner or later) is the greatest occasion of *civill Warre, ravishing* of *conscience, persecution* of *Christ Jesus* in his servants, and of the *hypocrisie* and *destruction of millions of souls.*

Ninthly, In holding an inforced *uniformity* of *Religion* in a *civill state*, wee must necessarily *disclaime* our desires and hopes of the *Jewes conversion to Christ.*

Tenthly, An inforced *uniformity* of *Religion* throughout a *Nation* or *civill State*, confounds the *Civill* and *Religious*, denies the principles of Christianity and civility, and that *Jesus Christ* is come in the Flesh.

Eleventhly, The permission of other *consciences* and *worships* then a state professeth, only can (according to God) procure a firme and lasting *peace*, (good *assurance* being taken according to the *wisedome* of the *civill State* for *uniformity* of *civill obedience* from all sorts.

Twelfthly, lastly, true *civility* and *Christianity* may both flourish in a *state* or *Kingdome*, notwithstanding the *permission* of divers and contrary *consciences*, either of *Jew* or *Gentile.*

The attempt to create an ideal Puritan society was constantly frustrated by dissent. After Roger Williams had been banished, Anne Hutchinson, a woman who had had some theological training in England, began to gather people in her home to expound upon the Sunday sermons. She advocated, in the face of the predestinarian ideas of her pastor, John Cotton, the notion that one could prepare oneself to receive salvation (a notion later popularized by the Methodists). Having committed the double offense of being a female teacher and teaching heretical ideas, she was excommunicated from the church and, like Williams, banished from the colony. An even worse fate awaited Quakers, four of whom were hung between 1659 and 1661.

While devilish teaching kept appearing, the Congregationalists had to contend with an internal problem. Only a shrinking number of the children of the first generation could make a profession of a relationship with God that allowed those who had been baptized as children to be received as full adult church members and hence freemen and voters. By the time that the third generation came on the scene, the problem had reached crisis proportions. One group of ministers proposed a stopgap measure called the halfway covenant, by which people of good conduct could present their children for baptism, and hence have them raised in the church, but the parents could not receive the Lord's Supper until they made a profession of faith. Others, such as Solomon Stoddard (1643–1729), pushed for setting up a full parish system and allowing all the residents of the parish to be baptized and receive the Lord's Supper. Something similar to Stoddard's suggestion was eventually adopted, although by no means did all New Englanders avail themselves of the opportunity.

By far the greatest challenge to the New England establishment came from the internal divisions in the community. These divisions became most visible in the reaction to the popular practice of folk magic that many members of the community had brought with them from England. The church fathers believed sincerely in the existence of malevolent magic and constantly feared the presence in the community of individuals who not only practiced such magic but worshipped His Infernal Majesty as well. Witch was the name they gave to such people, and they took very seriously the biblical condemnations of such acts. Through the last half of the seventeenth century, a number of such suspected practitioners were put to death, mostly those who were also on the fringe of the community and who had previous angered their neighbors with their unbridled tongues.

The most famous incident of the prosecution of accused witches began when the daughters of the pastor at Salem Village (now Danvers) began experiencing convulsions. Asked what had happened to them, they complained of bewitchment. In fact, they and the family slave Tituba, had been working some

Cotton Mather, leading Boston minister at the time of the Salem Witchcraft trials.

The death of many accused of witchcraft at Salem Village, Massachusetts, after trials like the one depicted below, had a global impact.

Increase Mather, leading Massachusetts minister in the seventeenth century.

harmless magic, attempting to discern something about the future mates of the girls. Whatever the case, the girls accused two women in the community of practicing malevolent magic. When these women's homes were subsequently searched, some dolls of the kind used in image magic were discovered. The case might have ended there had Tituba not made a confession that she was a witch and that there were seven others in the community. The girls confirmed Tituba's charges with claims that the apparitions, or "spectres," of the accused were visiting them and causing their torment. Eventually, others were called out and convicted primarily on the additional "spectral" evidence offered by the girls.

As executions began, a community-wide debate arose over the existence of witchcraft and over putting people to death merely on the claims of spectral torment. Unfortunately some twenty people were killed before the skeptics and those such as Boston ministers Increase Mather and his son Cotton Mather, who argued against spectral evidence, united to stop the proceedings. When the community had time to reflect, it engaged in a lengthy process of public repentance. At the same time, the Salem trials contributed significantly to the ending of public witchcraft trials throughout the Western world and gave a boost to those who equated belief in magic with ignorance and superstition. Salem entered American folklore and became an incident for repeated research and debate, especially in the later twentieth century with the rise of new neo-pagan movements whose practitioners called themselves witches.

THE BAPTIST CHALLENGE

Amid all of the incidents that were continually popping up throughout New England, none would provide the long-term competition as that supplied by the Baptists. The Baptists were all the more difficult as, unlike the Quakers, they accepted the basic Calvinist theology of New England Puritanism. Their challenge was one of church order, and it drove a dagger into the very heart of the Congregationalists' vision for their society. Baptists derived from the Independent movement among the Puritans of England. They took the Congregationalists' own argument that the Christian church should be based in a pure congregation of adult believers to its logical conclusion. They jettisoned the practice of infant baptism (a mandate for which they could not find in the Bible). In its place they advocated the biblical example; the church should baptize only adults (that is, people old enough to understand what Christianity was about) and only those who profess their faith in Christ. Such congregations had no role in running the state, they said, and there was certainly no biblical basis for voters being limited to full church members.

The first Independent congregation in the American colonies was the Pilgrim congregation at Plymouth that would eventually be absorbed into the Congregational fold. The first Baptist church, however, was founded in Roger Williams's Rhode Island. After Williams helped organize the Baptists, leadership fell to the Reverend John Clarke (1609–1676), who attempted to spread the Baptist perspective through the neighboring colonies. His idea that the state should stay out of church life and that members should support the church through their voluntary contributions were radical ideas when initially expressed in the seventeenth century.

Outside Rhode Island, the Baptists had a rough path to tread. In 1652, Clarke published a report on the Baptist problems, *Ill News from New England*, but Baptists had few supporters there and his argument largely fell on deaf ears. The Baptists were stymied in organizing followers into congregations until after the passing of the British Act of Toleration in 1689. They still found New England a hostile place for another generation but in the 1740s launched an era of growth.

Baptists found a slightly more hospitable environment farther south. The Pennepack Church opened in Philadelphia in 1688, and the City of Brotherly Love would become a major Baptist center. The first Baptist association was formed there in 1707. In 1742, it adopted the London Confession of Particular Baptists (promulgated in England in 1689) as its standard of faith. At the time, the larger Reformed theological movement was feeling the effects of the teachings of Dutch theologian Jacob Arminius (1560–1609) who had reworked Reformed thinking in response to some of the more stringent statements of predestination that bordered on an absolute determinism. Arminius hoped to construct his theology in such a way as to avoid making God the author of evil or humans nothing more than automatons. His final result affirmed that Christ died for all but that salvation was efficacious only for those who responded in faith. The effect of Arminuis's position was to allow some room for free will. His position was summarized in five points by his followers soon after his death in 1609. His opinion became the subject of a synod held at Dordrecht, Holland, in 1618, at which the more conservative Calvinists asserted five counter points. Within the English-speaking world, the affirmations of the Synod of Dort are remembered by reference to the flower popularly identified with the Dutch:

T   Total predestination
U   Utter depravity
L   Limited atonement
I   Irresistible grace
P   Perseverance of the saints

Among the Baptists, the Arminian–Calvinist debate focused upon the atonement. If Christ died only for the elect, whom God had chosen, the Calvinists argued that the elect would awaken to their condition and they would find their way into their church home. This position, which the Particular Baptists adopted, did not encourage evangelism and missions. Those who adopted the Arminian position argued for a "general" or unlimited atonement. They tended to see their task as preaching the gospel to the unsaved and allowing them the opportunity to respond to God's grace. The General Baptists adopted the Arminian perspective and in the first generations carried the day.

The Baptists who arrived in the American South in the late 1600s were General Baptists. They grew slowly by immigration from the British Isles and Ireland at first, but through the eighteenth century experienced spectacular growth. Through the century, Particular Baptists (also called Regular Baptists) spread through the South, and General Baptists would found support in the North. Over the century, the Particular Baptists came to predominate, although the common assumptions about human free will that came to dominate America would lead most Baptists to a modified Calvinism, not unlike the Arminian approach in many respects.

During the eighteenth century, however, the Baptists had other issues with which to deal. For example, as revivals came to America with the Methodists, the Baptists quickly identified with the revivalist movement and grew rapidly. Not only were new converts appearing, but old church members were for the

Isaac Backus, pioneer Baptist preacher during the Great Awakening.

first time testifying to a personal experience of regeneration (later to be called a "born again" experience). Some drew the obvious conclusion that the churches had many members who lacked regeneration. Thus arose those Baptists who demanded that church membership (and baptism) be withheld from any who had not had such an experience. As these believers withdrew from their brethren, they became known as the Separatist Baptists.

The revivals also brought to the fore those preachers who relied more upon strong emotional appeals than upon either the logic of argument or a straight appeal to biblical authority. The outbursts of emotions accompanying the revivals, while quite acceptable to some, offended many who were committed to the Calvinist emphasis on orderly worship. Thus the Baptists (and other groups) began to divide into the New Lights (accepting of the emotional demonstrations) and Old Lights (the loyal opposition). The location of authority in the local church allowed the divisions to travel as far as advocates were found to spread it. During the 1700s, the Separatist movement tended to be concentrated in New England.

AWAKENING A NATION

By the end of the seventeenth century, the British had consolidated their hold on the American colonies. The Dutch had taken over the small area that had briefly been an outpost of Sweden in 1663. However, their conquest was short lived. In 1664, Charles II gave the future king of England, then James, the

Duke of York, several parcels of American land including all of Maine and all of the land that at that moment constituted New Netherlands. The Dutch colony fell without a shot. Governor Peter Stuyvesant had lost the support of the residents, and they refused to rally to his defense of the city. The commander of the expeditionary force took control and promptly changed New Amsterdam to New York, after the new owner.

By this act, the British territory now extended from South Carolina to Maine. The issues of the establishment of their power in North America shifted to disputes with the French, who controlled the territory to the north, and the Spanish, who ruled in Florida. In all of the settlement of the North American coast, the land between Charleston (South Carolina) and the mouth of the St. Johns River (in present-day Florida) appeared to have been overlooked. However, this oversight was corrected in 1732 when James Oglethorpe (1696–1785) was given the right to settle the area between the Savannah and Altamaha Rivers. Oglethorpe, a member of Parliament with the Tory party, hoped his new colony would provide England with relief with from several besetting problems, not the least of which were the overcrowded debtors prisons.

He founded Savannah in 1733, and several other settlements quickly sprang up along the coast as he moved to secure the southern boundary of the British holdings. The settlers of the new colony of Georgia brought the Anglican Church with them and, as the colony expanded, invited additional ministers to come to Georgia. One of the ministers to answer the call was a youthful John Wesley (1703–1791), the son of a minister and recent graduate of Oxford. Wesley arrived in 1735 on the same ship that brought a group of German colonists, members of a small independent pietist church with Czechoslovakian roots, the Moravians. They quickly pushed inland and settled in present-day Winston-Salem, North Carolina.

Wesley, a staunch Anglican and naïve missionary, had a disastrous experience. He had no feel for the demands of starting a new colony and attempted to reproduce a traditional rural Anglican parish. He angered his parishioners and ultimately Oglethorpe himself and left a failure, his future in doubt. His work was surely of no consequence to the future of the colony. Returning home, Wesley took his failure to heart and launched a period of intense spiritual searching that would lead to a life changing spiritual experience, one that not only would change England, but within in a few years would reach out to change the land that he had so briefly visited.

Upon his return to England, Wesley began to attend the informal meetings of what were called "religious societies." These gatherings had sprung up across England in response to the need many felt for a deeper spiritual life than that provided by the established churches. He had brought to the fore memo-

John Wesley, the founder of Methodism,
began his ministry in colonial Georgia.

ries of the conversation he had had with one of the Moravian leaders concerning his own personal relationship with God. His search climaxed in 1738 when he had what he spoke of as a "heart warming" experience. He soon began an independent religious society that would grow into a movement that unsympathetic observers would begin to call by the derisive name Methodists.

Wesley was just getting started, however, when in 1739 he got a call for help from one of his Oxford classmates, George Whitefield (1715–1779). Whitefield had been powerfully influenced by Wesley and had subsequently become an Anglican minister. Now he was preaching to whoever would listen. "Whoever" turned out to be a group of miners in Bristol. He preached in the open air near their mine, where he met them every day after their shift. But he had decided to go to America, and he asked Wesley to take responsibility for the group who came to hear him. Wesley overcame his offense at conducting religious exercises in such an uncouth setting (the consequences of which will be explored in the next chapter), and Whitefield left on his historic journey.

Whitefield landed in America a young man of only twenty-five years. His youthfulness was offset by his intense zeal for the message he preached, a strong voice, and oratorical skills hardly matched by any of his contemporaries. He also pitched his sermons at common people, the miners in Bristol never far from him. From the beginning of his American tour in Savannah in January of 1740, Whitefield drew crowds in the thousands. His voice carried clearly to all who gathered, and his message began to evoke emotional responses that led to outbreaks of behavior far outside the decorum expected of those attending church. Especially in New England, while pastors had the experience of people falling asleep during their sermons, they rarely had heard the moans of people under conviction of felt sin or the shouts of joy of someone moved by the Spirit.

Some denounced Whitefield as crude and vulgar, but they could not fault his conservative Calvinist faith. Everywhere he went, he stirred up the religious environment, and as he had no ambitions to found a new church, all of the churches received the benefits of the new life he injected into the community. And as word of his activity spread, crowds awaited him in the next town he visited. He was particularly effective in New England where a large stable religious community existed, but a community that rarely heard such a warm, vital presentation of Christianity.

Through 1740, Whitefield traveled from Savannah to Philadelphia and back to the South. After taking a ship to New England, he completed his tour in New York and New Jersey. No religious leader had made such a journey before, and for the first time, colonists from Georgia to Maine shared a single experience. Prior to Whitefield, believers in different communities had experi-

George Whitefield's preaching in the colonies is credited with promoting an early sense of unity among the Americans.

enced revivals in their spiritual life, but for the first time, the whole of the American colonies shared in a single Great Awakening. Whitefield's tour became both a spiritual and political watershed in American life.

Whitefield did not arrive as a totally new phenomenon to America. A pattern for revivals was already present. His most prominent precursor was the pastor of the Congregational church in Northampton, Massachusetts. In the mid 1720s, a youthful Jonathan Edwards had a deep experience of God working in his life. Later as a minister, he was able to communicate that experience effectively to people, even in the context of the demands of the Congregational Church. Thus it was that in the mid 1730s, a powerful revival broke out in both Edwards's congregations and in the churches in nearby towns in the Connecticut Valley. He believed that the revival was evidence of God's work with the people of New England, and in 1736, he wrote a description and defense of the revival, *A Faithful Narrative of the Surprising Work of God*, a volume widely read on both sides of the Atlantic.

Arrested, at his
trial Francis
Makemie
successfully
defended his
preaching apart
from the Church
of England.

Having read Edwards's book, Whitefield wanted to meet him. He routed himself through Northampton as he traveled from Boston to New York. The two men, so different in many ways, admired each other. After Whitefield departed for home, the task of defending what had occurred would fall on Edwards's shoulders. This he did in two books, *The Distinguishing Marks of a Work of the Spirit of God* (1741) and the more substantive *Some Thoughts Concerning the Present Revival* (1743). In the latter work, he attacked both the more extreme happenings in the revival and those who hesitated in the face of the strong emotional outbursts so common as the awakenings ran their course.

Further foundation for Whitefield's visit had been laid within the Presbyterian community. Francis Makemie had been attempting to organize all of the Presbyterian settlers from Scotland and Ireland into a church that closely resembled the Presbyterian Church they had known in the homeland. He was continually stifled by his inability to woo ministers to come to America. He tried recruiting those trained at Harvard or Yale but found they had been infected with Congregational ideals. Into this situation stepped William Tennent (1673–1746) and his son Gilbert (1703–1764), both of whom had joined the Presbyterian Church by the mid 1720s. The elder Tennent had begun to meet the educational needs of the church by tutoring young men destined for the ministry. These efforts became more and more formalized until 1735, when he erected a simple building later known as the Log College in which he held classes. His son Gilbert joined him as a second instructor.

The formalized status of the Log College precipitated a controversy among the Presbyterians as the conservative leadership moved to block the Tennents' work. Tennent had come out in support of the revivalism described by Edwards and was raising up ministers equally supportive. In 1735, the church's synod passed a resolution that any ministerial candidate whose degree did not come from one of the New England schools or from Europe would have to submit to a special examination by the synod. The resolution obviously was directed at the Log College's graduates.

The Log College graduates formed the initial base of support for Whitefield as he toured New Jersey, New York, and Pennsylvania in the fall of 1740 (and on subsequent visits). Reciprocally, George Whitefield's preaching heightened the controversy already existing in the synod and led to its split into two

Jonathan Edwards, theologian, revivalist, and college president.

Barbara Heck, pioneer of Methodism in colonial New York.

A VISIT TO JONATHAN EDWARDS
FROM THE JOURNAL OF GEORGE WHITEFIELD

Hadfield and Northampton

Saturday, October 18. At Mr. Edwards's request, I spoke to his little children, who were much affected. Preached at Hadfield, five miles from Northampton, but found myself not much strengthened. Preached at four in the afternoon to Mr. Edwards's congregation. I began with fear and trembling, but God assisted me. Few eyes were dry in the assembly. I had an affecting prospect of the glories of the upper world, and was enabled speak with some degree of pathos. It seemed as if a time of refreshing was come from the presence of the Lord.

Northampton

Sunday, October 19. Felt great satisfaction in being at the house of Mr. Edwards. A sweeter couple I have not yet seen. Their children were not dressed in silks and satins, but plain, as become the children of those Who, in all things, ought to be examples of Christian simplicity. Mrs. Edwards is adorned with a meek and quiet spirit; she talked solidly of the things of God, and seemed to be such a helpmeet for her husband, that she caused me to renew those prayers, which, for some months, I have put up to God, that He would be pleased to send me a daughter of Abraham to be my wife. Lord, I desire to have no choice of my own. Thou knowest my circumstances; Thou knowest I only desire to marry in and for Thee. Thou didst choose a Rebecca for Isaac, choose one to be a helpmeet for me, in carrying on that great work which is committed to my charge. Preached this morning, and good Mr. Edwards wept during the whole time of exercise. The people were equally affected; and, in the afternoon, the power increased yet more. Our Lord seemed to keep the good wine till the last. I have not seen four such gracious meetings together since my arrival. Oh, that my soul may be refreshed with the joyful news, that Northampton people have recovered their first love; that the Lord has revived His work in their souls, and caused them to do their first works!

Modern Princeton University grew from a small colonial Presbyterian school that trained church leaders.

Samuel Hopkins, Congregational minister and colleague of Jonathan Edwards.

John Murray,
founder of Universalism.

factions. The Tennent faction, called New Lights, grew as more and more graduates were turned out by the Log College. It would continue to function until the elder Tennent's death in 1746. Its work would then be picked up by the College of New Jersey (now known as Princeton University), founded by a cadre of Log College graduates. It would later call an aging Jonathan Edwards to be its president.

The New Light/Old Light split affected all of the older churches, although the two parties would eventually find a means to reconcile their differences. The story would be repeated, however, under different names in subsequent centuries. Older established religious communities would hold to gains of past generations as newer groups would seek to reach out to new constituencies with variations on the revivalistic techniques introduced into American religious life during the Great Awakening. The emergence of revivalism marked an important transition in the entire structure of the religious community in the West. Long centered upon congregations, buildings, and leadership supported by the secular ruling powers, religion had functioned as an arm of the state. Revivalism was a radical departure from that pattern that helped institutionalize the new denominations that had to survive by continually reviving the support of the believers they served.

AFRICAN AMERICANS

People of African descent began to arrive in the colonies from their beginnings and were quickly integrated into the life of the churches. As early as 1618, a woman known only by her new Christian name, Angela, arrived in Virginia. The following year, two Africans, indentured servants, arrived at Jamestown. After fulfilling the term of their indenture, they became the core of the large free-black community in antebellum America. There is every reason to believe that some of these individuals worked for Anglican church members, given that in 1623, before their period of servitude was completed, one of their babies was baptized and given the name Anthony. In the 1630s, Africans were present in New Netherlands, and several were baptized in the Reformed Church in 1639. Two years later an African female was baptized and accepted into full membership in the Congregational Church in Dorchester, Massachusetts. In 1669, the first African Lutheran was baptized into the congregation in New York.

Through the years, Africans also arrived as slaves, and gradually they came to outnumber the free Africans. Also, conditions began to change significantly for Africans in the 1660s, as British control of the colonies was consolidated. An important consensus was reached that conversion to Christianity did not grant freedom for slaves. Then, in 1670, Virginia disenfranchised the free-black

community and declared that all newly arriving Africans were to be slaves for life. In reaction, some slaves escaped their situation by forming isolated Maroon communities in the interior. Increasing the perception of their uniqueness, the Quakers became the only group in the colonies to protest the growth of slavery (1688), and that only after a decade of activity by John Woolman (1720–1772), the voice in the wilderness in the cause of ending slavery.

During the eighteenth century, the number of Africans grew from less than 30,000 to almost 900,000. As the great majority of white people were not church related, it can assumed that the same was the case for black people. Certainly, the perception was that Africans, both free and slave, could use both the salvation and "civilizing" benefits from Christianity. Certainly, they needed to be handed the same tools of education that were available to the white community. Thus, as early as 1704, a Frenchman in New York named Elias Noeau opened a school to teach African children the catechism. The first missionary activity specifically to the slave population was begun by Peter Böhler,

The First African American Baptist Church was erected in Savannah, Georgia.

Christopher Rush, second bishop of the African Methodist Episcopal Church.

Peter Williams, born in slavery, became a founding member of the African Methodist Episcopal Zion Church.

a German Moravian who moved to Georgia in 1738. As the eighteenth century proceeded, the records of Africans joining various churches increased as individual ministers in the older churches took it upon themselves to minister to black people in their parishes.

As the century progressed, the Baptists and then the Methodists paid the most attention to the African population and, as a result, reaped the rewards. Baptists, a miniscule group as the century began, jumped into prominence following the Great Awakening. Their unschooled preachers had their greatest effect upon people at the lower end of the economic scale, including many Africans. In the 1750s, two white Baptists, Philip Mulkey and William Murphy, influenced the slaves on the plantation of William Byrd III of Lunenburg, Virginia, and in 1758 they led in the constitution of an all-African Baptist congregation, the first known to have existed. Discontinued for a while, the church was reconstituted in 1772, and the first black Baptist preachers were ordained, three brothers, Moses, Benjamin, and Thomas Gardiner, and a fourth man known only as Farrell.

While the Baptists at Lunenberg were struggling to survive as a congregation, elsewhere in Virginia, a young slave named George was growing to manhood. Around 1773 he moved with his owner, Baptist deacon Henry Sharp, to Burke County Georgia, and shortly thereafter was converted in the Buckhead

Creek Baptist Church under the ministry of Matthew Moore. With Sharp's consent, George Lisle (c.1750–1820) was licensed to preach and began to travel to nearby plantations to conduct services. At the plantation at Silver Bluff, South Carolina, he organized the second African Baptist congregation in the colonies.

Lisle would go on to have a long career. He was given his freedom as the Revolutionary War approached. Henry Sharp identified with the British cause and died in 1778, a Tory officer. Lisle relocated to Savannah, and during the three years it was occupied by British forces, he enjoyed considerable freedom to build the Baptist movement among the city's free blacks. Sharp's family tried to reenslave him at one point, but he left with the British forces in 1782 and relocated to Jamaica. After paying off his transport with a period of indenture, he was free to resume his preaching. He created the First Baptist Church of Kingston, the initial congregation for black people on the Islands.

Before Lisle left for Jamaica, he ordained Andrew Bryan (1737–1812), who built upon Lisle's pioneering activity. The African Baptist Church in Savannah became a sign of the future. It stood as a herald of the desire for freedom and was the first of the autonomous black-led structures that had to be founded as step by step the African population won and then actualized their lives as free Americans.

FREEDOM IN THE AIR

The forces that led to the American Revolution were many and varied. England was on a learning curve concerning the management of its growing overseas empire, an empire that frequently transferred old European rivalries to new locations. Under the Treaty of Paris in 1763, British America almost doubled in size as French Canada was formally transferred to British control. At the same time, the government still treated the settlements along the Atlantic coast as thirteen distinct colonies. Questions were continually raised about the extension of British law to the colonies and the representation that the colonies would have in London. Although political and economic concerns dominate any consideration of the Revolution, revolutionary action could not have been taken had not a broad ideological foundation been laid among the public. The religious elements contributing to that foundation were quite varied.

Christian thought had for centuries enjoyed a consensus that it was the church's job to live peacefully within the state. The biblical grounding for the position was Paul's statement to the Romans, "Let every soul be subject to the higher powers, For there is no Power but of God: the powers that be are of God. Who, therefore resists the power, resists the ordinances of God." Based upon this and additional relevant passages, although Christians had been active in advising emperors and assumed strong positions on issues before legislatures, they had generally opposed revolution, even in the most extreme situations. Further, since the emergence of the state churches, their leaders had generally been a part of or, at the very least, identified with the ruling authorities.

In the West, a break with this consensus came about with the Reformation. First, Christian groups emerged that withdrew their support from the state. They did not advocate anything approaching violent revolution (in fact most were pacifist), but they did attempt to sever their connections with the ruling powers. Persecuted as cancerous entities in the larger body politic, they came to America, where at least they were tolerated.

Then in the sixteenth century in England, Henry VIII's financial and marriage problems unleashed forces that provided a platform for people with very different views of how the country and its religious life should be structured. In the attempt to solve the problem, it became obvious that no one of the three obvious solutions (Anglican, Roman Catholic, Protestant) could command majority support. The conflict was eventually settled on the battlefield in a civil war, the establishment of a commonwealth, and the eventual reestablishment of the monarchy. Many of the losers in this process fled to the New World, seeing the establishment of a society that would allow them a degree of freedom as the best option then available.

However, in the colonies, the long-term trend was for the establishment of something closely resembling the society operating in England. Had not the Revolution intervened, there is every reason to believe that the Church of England would have moved to strengthen its position as the established church in most colonies and moved into places such as Pennsylvania and Massachusetts as a strong competitor to the older churches. The continued movement of British citizens into the colonies would have ensured the Anglicans a bright future. With the growth of the SPG in the colonies, the naming of a bishop for America, essential to building a strong church, became an issue, and Protestants united in efforts to oppose it.

Crucial to Christians joining in the revolutionary enthusiasm, however, was the identification of themes of freedom in the Bible with political freedom. Such an identification began with the Great Awakening, as Baptist and other churches that had no status with the state began to create a widespread free church presence throughout the colonies. Members of the free churches were exercising their freedom every time they gathered, and they saw themselves as against those churches that were home to the ruling class.

The roughly articulated ethos of freedom within the Baptist tradition was reinforced by the emergence of Congregationalist ministers who began to articulate the same position in a more sophisticated manner. As early as 1749 (the anniversary of the execution death of King Charles I), Boston minister Jonathan Mayhew began to oppose the imposition of Anglican power in the colonies that began to open ways around Romans 13, in his *Discourse Concerning Unlimited Submission and Non-Resistance to the Higher Powers*. In the 1760s, as the British began to enact the legislation that would eventually erupt in revolution, Mayhew took the lead in developing his earlier position in a more secular environment. To an audience in 1765, for example, he chose as his text before an audience already enflamed by the Stamp Act, Galatians 5:12–13, "brethren, you have been called unto liberty."

Also entering powerfully in the leadership of the colonies in the mid-eighteenth century was a new theological perspective, radically critical of the Christian tradition and of clericalism, the temporal power exercised by the clergy in the typical established-church system. Deism, the religious expression of the Enlightenment, offered a religious perspective stripped of supernatural themes. To Deists, God was the creator of this law-abiding world just beginning to be explored by science. Like a watchmaker, God had made the world and now largely left it alone to run according to natural law. Religion should follow reason and morality, not revelation. Such a view, of course, left only a limited role for prayer and worship.

While Deism was never the religion of more than a relatively few people in colonial America, it counted among its adherents a number of key leaders including the likes of Benjamin Franklin, Thomas Jefferson, and George Washington. Jefferson, nominally an Anglican, was highly critical of clericalism. This unorthodox perspective was opposed to the imposition upon the public of a traditional orthodox form of Christianity, especially Roman Catholicism and Anglicanism, and as war with England loomed ever closer, had no biblical inhibitions against revolution.

When the anger at the prejudicial actions directed toward the American colonies boiled over, the Baptists, those Congregationalists and Presbyterians who agreed with Mayhew, and the Deists found a way to make common cause with a large number of people of no faith, to establish their independence from England. They were joined by the handful of Methodists and the small community of Roman Catholics. At the same time, many colonists, most now forgotten or ignored, opposed the Revolution. Many who were affected negatively by the various new laws still saw no justification for what amounted to treason. The Quakers, Mennonites, Brethren, and Moravians were opposed to war on any grounds. Africans were caught in the middle of the white man's war. Some sided with the Patriots, hoping that along with the colonists' talk of freedom from England, they might be included. Others fought with the British, their freedom being their wage.

Then suddenly, the war was over. The colonists had against all odds won. A bridge had been crossed and there was no going back. The religious people of the land rolled up their sleeves and began the task of creating not only a new country but a new national reality called the United States.

CHAPTER 4

Denominationalism —
Building the Post-Revolution Church

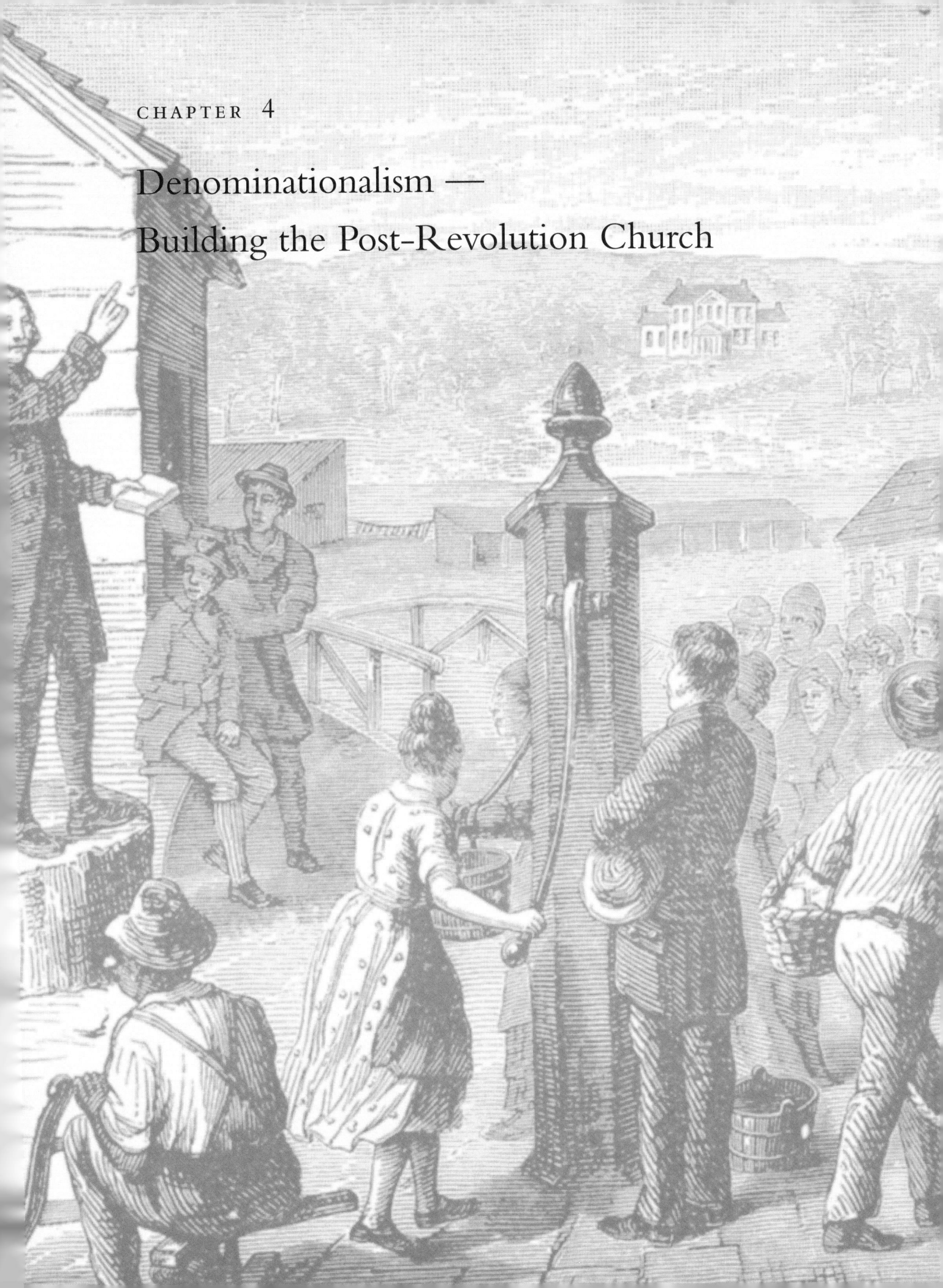

Just as the American Revolution found Americans aligned across a broad spectrum, from those who were staunch supporters of the king and Parliament to those who were ready to fight to free the colonies from England, so a similar spectrum appeared among the minority of Americans who were church related. The Anglicans were a case in point. Many of the prominent and wealthy leaders in the colonies were Anglicans who also had strong ties to the homeland, and several Anglican clergy served as chaplains for the British troops. The Church of England in America had developed considerable strength as several hundred SPG (Society for the Propagation of the Gospel in Foreign Parts) missionaries spread throughout the colonies. Anglican strength was concentrated in a band from New York City through Connecticut and from Philadelphia south through Virginia. It was also strong in South Carolina. At the same time, although their heart was not in the church, many of the most prominent American patriots (George Washington, Thomas Jefferson) were Anglican laymen, wealthy plantation owners who put everything on the line for the Revolution.

Within the churches possessing the least attachment to England, the majority favored the Revolution, and over 100 ministers (primarily Congregationalist, Reformed, and Baptist) served as chaplains in the Revolutionary forces. John Peter Gabriel Muhlenberg (1746–1801), the son of the aging Henry Muhlenberg, who had initially welded the scattered factions of Lutherans into a national organization, went even farther. He called his congregation to join the battle. Shortly after hearing of the fighting at Bunker Hill, he preached a fiery sermon supportive of the rebel cause, at the close of which he changed his clerical dress for a colonial uniform and signed up the men of his congregation into the militia. He eventually rose in the ranks to become General Muhlenberg.

On the other hand, Congregationalists such as Eli Forbes, the minister at Brookfield, Massachusetts, spoke out against the Revolution, and were joined by other pastors and laypersons, especially those who had taken the lead in dealing with England over the previous few decades. Losing their social status, and in some cases their jobs, after the Revolution, they faded into obscurity. Speaking more for the majority was the General Association of Congregational

The large Mansion house at
Oneida was the center of life in
the prosperous communal society.

Henry Melchior Muhlenberg pulled
scattered Lutherans together into
the first American Lutheran synod.

Prominent Congregationalist minister Lyman Beecher fought against the disestablishment of his church in New England.

Ministers, which in 1776 proclaimed its adherence to the Patriot cause. In their resolution they declared that the residents of the colonies faced "the sad Necessity of defending by Force and Arms those precious Privileges which our Fathers fled into the Wilderness quietly to enjoy." They waxed eloquent concerning the Tories in Massachusetts by decrying the "Detestable Parricides interspersed among us aiming to give a fatal stab to the Country which gave them birth, and hath hitherto fostered them in her indulgent Boston."

Catholics (still a small community of about 16,000) likewise expressed a spectrum of opinion on the war. In the colonies, they enjoyed privileges that were denied them in England and saw hope in the liberal policies granted to their brothers and sisters in the faith in Quebec, which had recently come under British rule. However, they also remembered the way that Anglicans had taken over Maryland and imposed a new non-Catholic establishment. One Catholic layman, Charles Carroll, emerged as a popular voice for the Patriot cause and assuaged the fears of other churchmen as to where they stood. During the War, as Washington attempted to garner support from Quebec, he ordered the army to drop their celebration of Guy Fawkes Day, the anti-Catholic holiday brought over from England. Catholics were largely perceived as supportive of the Revolution, and its success gave them a major boost in their American adventure.

The angelic communications of Swedish seer Emanuel Swedenborg inspired the Church of the New Jerusalem, the first new church to emerge in America after the Revolution.

John Humphrey Noyes founded the Perfectionist communal society at Oneida, New York.

Baptists were a major force in support of the Revolution, especially in Virginia where they were the largest body competing with the Anglicans. The Baptists had, since the founding of Rhode Island, the clearest perception of the meaning of religious freedom and quickly perceived the relationship between religious freedom and the political and economic freedoms being sought by the leaders of the Patriot cause. Isaac Backus (1724–1806), the Baptist leader from New England who had picked up the mantle of Roger Williams, supported the Revolution as a fight for freedom on all fronts. After the shooting stopped, as Massachusetts moved to reinstate the old Congregational establishment, he continued the fight for separating the government from the religious life.

Several groups found themselves caught in the middle by the outbreak of hostilities. Most traumatized were the then relatively new groups that would, because of their actions during this war, become known to future generations as the historic peace churches. Quakers, who were especially strong in Pennsylvania, along with their German pietist neighbors, the Brethren, the Mennonites, and the Moravians, had their beliefs put to the test at a time in which pacifism and cowardice were still commonly identified with one another. Even as the General Association of Congregational Ministers in Connecticut affirmed their allegiance to the Patriot cause, the Philadelphia Yearly Meeting of the Society of Friends wrestled with members who compromised their pacifist stand. The meeting let it be known that those who paid for someone to go to war in their stead or sent relatives or servants to the battlefield "by so doing manifest that they are not in religious fellowship with us."

Unwilling to support either side, Quakers were viewed as enemies by both. Some of the more heroic tales coming out of the war concern the efforts of the members of the peace churches to discern the implications of their standing back when their neighbors fought each other. Thus, as Philadelphia changed hands during the war, administrators in charge of the city took action against the Quakers as they moved about irrespective of politics, ministering to those they found in need. But both sides received an education when the Quakers showed up at Guilford Courthouse (Connecticut) to attend to the wounded of both the Continental and British armies.

The Methodists had just emerged in the colonies in the 1760s and were, as the war began, caught in the middle, but in another way. At the time, they viewed themselves as a renewal movement within the Church of England, and their leadership had distinct Tory leanings (given clear voice by Methodist founder John Wesley). However, Methodism was dedicated to one purpose, pursuing a rather focused task of delivering their message of personal relationship with God to a sinful generation. While, individually, Methodist laymen took up arms, the preachers found themselves unable to participate in the war. Following the end of hostilities, most of the preachers, like the Anglican priests, returned to England, leaving the few who had committed themselves to the new land behind to rebuild.

The obverse of the Great Seal of the United States pictures the all-seeing eye of God, a symbol popular among eighteenth-century Freemasons and Rosicrucians.

THE END OF THE WAR

The American Revolution came to an end in a series of steps that began with the surrender of General Cornwallis at Yorktown, Virginia, on October 19, 1781; the signing of the preliminary Articles of Peace the following year; and the departure of the last British troops, encamped in New York City, on November 25, 1783. In April, anticipating the withdrawal of the last units of the British Army, 7,000 loyalists sailed from New York, the last group exodus of the 100,000 that had either returned to England or migrated to Canada. The citizens of the United States now had to come to terms with what they had accomplished.

Following the declaration of peace, the Articles of Confederation that had been adopted in 1777 became the new nation's government in reality. Also, anticipating victory, efforts started during the war had already led to the reorganization of the state governments as self-governing entities. An initial economic shot in the arm to the new governments came from the confiscation of land previously owned by the British government and the fleeing loyalists. The former state establishments supportive of Anglicanism were all abandoned, although the Massachusetts government continued the favored status of the Congregational Church. Among the most important action of any state legislature through this period was the 1786 adoption of a statute on religious freedom by Virginia. The measure in effect institutionalized the voluntary system that would come to characterize American religion by providing that none could be compelled to attend or support any religious institution against their will or be discriminated against because of their professed beliefs.

During 1787, the Continental Congress met to draft a new constitution for the weakly affiliated colonies, After some months, it was ratified by the required nine states. The first national election was held on January 7, 1787, and Washington inaugurated as president on April 30. Among the first acts of the new government, on September 25, the Congress sent to the states for ratification twelve constitutional amendments including one that guaranteed freedom of religion. The wording of one of the last amendments to be approved read as follows: "Congress shall make no laws respecting an establishment of religion, or prohibiting a free exercise thereof."

Ten of the twelve amendments (including what would be listed as the First Amendment) were finally approved over the next three months and became the law of the land on December 15, 1791.

The new amendment was largely based on that older Virginia law that had been authored by Thomas Jefferson, and thus it was appropriate that he write one of the first commentaries on this very short sentence. On New Year's Day

GEORGE WASHINGTON'S LETTER
TO TOURO SYNAGOGUE

To the Hebrew Congregation of Newport, Rhode Island.

Gentlemen:—While I have received with much satisfaction your address, replete with expressions of esteem, I rejoice in the opportunity of assuring you that I shall always retain a grateful remembrance of the cordial welcome I experienced in my visit to Newport from all classes of citizens.

The reflection on the days of difficulty and danger, which are passed, is rendered the more sweet from the consciousness that they are succeeded by days of uncommon prosperity and security. If we have the wisdom to make the best use of the advantage with which we are now favored, we cannot fail under the just administration of a good government to become a great and happy people.

The citizens of the United States of America have the right to applaud themselves for having given to mankind examples of an enlarged and liberal policy worthy of imitation. All possess alike liberty of conscience and immunities of citizenship. It is now no more that toleration is spoken of as if it were by the indulgence of one class of people that another enjoyed the exercise of their inherent natural rights, for happily the Government of the United States, which gives to bigotry no sanction, to persecution no assistance, requires only that they who live under its protection should demean themselves as good citizens in giving it on all occasions their effectual support.

It would be inconsistent with the frankness of my character not to avow that I am pleased with your favorable opinion of my administration and fervent wishes of my felicity. May the children of the stock of Abraham, who dwell in this land, continue to merit and enjoy the good will of the other inhabitants, while everyone shall sit in safety under his own vine and fig-tree and there shall be none to make him afraid. May the Father of all mercies scatter light and not darkness in our paths and make us all in our several vocations useful here and, in His own due time and way, everlastingly happy.

President Thomas Jefferson helped establish the principle of the separation of church and state in American law.

of 1802, Jefferson penned a letter to the Danbury (Connecticut) Baptist Association. The key passage of that letter read

> Believing with you that religion is a matter which lies solely between man and his God, that he owes account to none other for his faith or his worship, that the legislative powers of government reach actions only, and not opinions, I contemplate with solemn reverence that act of the whole American people which declared that their legislature should "make no law respecting an establishment of religion, or prohibiting the free exercise thereof," thus building a wall of separation between church and state. Adhering to this expression of the supreme will of the nation in behalf of the rights of conscience, I shall see with sincere satisfaction the progress of those sentiments which tend to restore to man all of his natural rights, convinced he has no natural rights of opposition to his social duties.

In this commentary, Jefferson injected the famous phrase "wall of separation between church and state." Even though it is not in the constitution, jurists and legislators alike adopted the phrase as a definitive metaphor capturing the intent of the First Amendment. As written, the amendment immediately prohibited the government from setting up a state establishment of religion. States could, as Massachusetts did, have an established religion, although most chose not to do so. Eventually, all the states added a clause similar to the First Amendment to their own constituting documents. As the amendment would be tested in the courts over the years, the implications of its two clauses, one preventing establishments and the other guaranteeing free exercise, would be drawn out in great detail. For the moment, however, the churches were put on a somewhat equal footing, and the future loomed before them.

ANGLICANS AND METHODISTS

Most of the fifteen denominations that had appeared in America prior to the Revolution had developed their own organization and were prepared to move forward as autonomous units. The two major exceptions were the Anglicans and the Methodists. The Church of England is an episcopal church, that is, a church built around the leadership of bishops who are believed to have their authority through a lineage that could be traced generation by generation back to Christ's original twelve Apostles. All of England had been divided into a network of dioceses in such a manner that a bishop was in charge of all of the churches in the land. In spite of the hundreds of parishes that operated throughout the colonies, no bishop had ever been sent, although a commissary operating under the bishop of London had been appointed with some limited episcopal powers.

The Church of England in Canada was greatly strengthened by the war, and in 1787, a bishop was finally sent to oversee its parishes. In contrast, the Anglicans in the United States were devastated by the war. The church was stripped of its favored status, most of its clergy returned to their home in England, and the parishes had to find a new means of financial support. Many of its members became Methodists. The price of breaking with Rome two centuries earlier had been the declaration of the ruler of England as the church's "supreme governor." The presence of the king in the church's structure created a problem of loyalty for American Anglicans and also a significant obstacle in replacing the clergy lost during the war. Prior to the war, all of the church's clergy had been trained in England, and no alternative structure had emerged in America.

The first step in reorganizing the church was made by Samuel Seabury (1729–1796), a Church of England priest in Connecticut who had been an uncompromising Tory during the war but decided to remain in the new nation after the war. He initially gained the endorsement of the ten priests who had also stayed behind in Connecticut, and in 1783, he traveled to England for the purpose of being consecrated as the bishop for the Anglicans in America. The British bishops turned him down, since he could not swear allegiance to the king. At that point, he operated on an alternative plan that required a side trip to Scotland, where a small schismatic Anglican church existed. This church was headed by the so-called nonjuring bishops who had refused to acknowledge the authority of William and Mary after they assumed the British throne in 1688. These bishops agreed to consecrate him.

Upon his return to the United States, the new bishop offered himself as the ensign around which a new American Anglican church could rally. Unfortunately, Seabury had rushed ahead of the rest of the church members, who resented the action of the Connecticut clergy in assuming authority without consultation with their brethren to the south. Many who had met him also disliked Seabury's rather acerbic leadership style. In his stead, the majority of the clergy looked to William White (1748–1836), the pastor of the influential Christ Church in Philadelphia. White lacked the political baggage of Seabury, as he had actually served as the chaplain for the Continental Congress that had met in Philadelphia to draw up the Declaration of Independence.

White moved to organize the first General Convention of what was to become the Protestant Episcopal Church in the United States of America. It met in Philadelphia in 1785. He also opened formal negotiations with the Church of England that led to Parliament's making changes that would

Many presidents have worshipped at the Episcopal church of St. Johns, Lafayette Square, located across the street from the White House.

As their bishop, William White led the remnants of the Church of England in the United States to form the Protestant Episcopal Church.

allow for the designation of American bishops. Then, in 1787, he and Samuel Provoost (1742–1815) traveled to London where they were consecrated on February 4. The church had an uphill struggle during its first generation as it rebuilt its community of clergy and established a means of training them. However, during its second generation, it began to flourish and establish itself as the church serving many of America's wealthiest families.

As White went about the business of creating the new Episcopal Church, he also had to contend with the problem of the Methodists. Growing out of the deep religious experience of John Wesley (1703–1791), an Anglican clergyman, the Methodists had spread across England and Ireland beginning in the 1740s. They emerged in America in the 1760s as Methodist gatherings (societies) were founded in Virginia, New York, Baltimore, and Philadelphia. As a whole, the Methodists were Anglicans who attended Sunday services at the Anglican church (where they would partake of the sacraments), but their real allegiance was to their smaller midweek gatherings and to the Methodist preachers who came to town. The preachers were unordained and confined their work to speaking and exhorting people to adopt the precepts of holy living that gave the group its name.

Following the war, most of the preachers sent by Wesley to lead the work in America returned to England like their Anglican counterparts. But, of importance, one remained, Francis Asbury (1745–1816). As soon as the war was over, he and preachers who had been recruited from the American membership prevailed on Wesley to acknowledge the need for an American Methodism independent of the Church of England and to assume some authority to ordain ministers for it. From his reading of church history, Wesley found the precedents he needed to act; in 1784, he ordained two men, Thomas Vasey (1742–1826) and Richard Whatcoat (1736–1806) and then "set apart" the Reverend Thomas Coke (1747–1810), another Church of England priest who had identified with the Methodists, as a "superintendent" for the American work. Wesley intended Coke to share authority with Asbury.

While Wesley had managed the movement he had founded in a somewhat authoritative manner, the post-Revolution American brethren were not ready to simply take Wesley's instructions and were determined to hold a conference of the preachers and take a vote on the instructions that Wesley had sent. That conference was held at Lovely Lane Chapel in Baltimore during Christmas week of 1784. They elected Asbury as their superintendent and on three successive days, Asbury was ordained a deacon, an elder, and a superintendent. Coke returned to England but three years later returned to the States with another communication. Wesley called for the establishment of a General Conference as an ultimate legislative structure and for Whatcoat to also be

John Wesley, founder of Methodism.

America as it appeared to Episcopalians in the 1840s.

Francis Asbury rode the length and breadth of the land to establish Methodism as the nation's largest church through the first half of the nineteenth century.

named a superintendent. At this point, the Americans truly showed their independence. While agreeing to the General Conference structure, they refused to elect Whatcoat to the designated office. Also, by this time, Samuel Seabury had been consecrated as an Anglican bishop, and the conference, against Wesley's wishes, substituted the title "bishop" for superintendent.

While Coke returned to the United States periodically for several years, his mission became the spreading of Methodism around the world. The building of the American church fell on the shoulders of the new Bishop Asbury. From the Christmas conference until his death in 1816, he would travel the length and breath of the land, and through the early decades of the nineteenth century, the Methodist Episcopal Church would become the largest church in the country.

The Methodist secret was in its deployment of dedicated ministers. With Asbury as their example, the preachers were given the task of riding their assigned territory establishing preaching points (and locating a place to sleep overnight) that they then visited regularly (every few weeks). At each preaching point, a group was organized and over time a church constructed. Together, these preaching points and churches constituted a circuit. Preachers were regularly assigned to different circuits, and as the country expanded westward, new circuits were systematically created. The Methodist circuit rider became one of the most familiar sights to new residents of the frontier. As the preaching points grew into churches, Methodism spread through the countryside as did no other denomination. As larger churches emerged, a more settled pastorate assumed the place of the pioneer preachers, and a new generation of circuit riders was deployed into newly opening lands to the west.

Henry Boehm led the spread of Methodist revivalism within the American German-speaking community.

The camp meeting was among the most popular structures for spreading Christianity on the frontier.

Methodist circuit riders traveled the countryside and preached wherever they could draw an audience.

BAPTISTS

If the Methodist circuit rider was the most visible image of the new churches coming to dominate the religious life of the frontier, the Baptist farmer/preacher was certainly his close rival. Unlike the mobile circuit rider, the average Baptist preacher was himself (women were yet to become preachers) a pioneer and likely a farmer or tradesman. Like the circuit rider, he was not formally trained but picked up his education from reading the Bible and a few select books. He had some native skills, such as oratory, and learned to construct and deliver sermons by listening to other preachers. Once settled into a new home, the preacher was immediately available for Sunday services and revival meetings. The number of Baptist preachers proliferated side by side with the Methodist circuit riders, and by the end of the nineteenth century would outnumber them. But together, they became the religious leaders most often encountered by settlers as the country grew westward.

In many ways, the Baptists stood in stark contrast to the Methodists with their planned deployment of circuit riders. While Methodism grew from the top down, the Baptists were a complete grass-roots organization that started with independent preachers scattered randomly around the country, forming independent churches where they could. When several churches appeared in the same area, they affiliated in a loosely organized association. Churches in a state or large area might form a more encompassing convention or association of churches, and individual churches might also associate with one of the several national Baptist organizations.

The organization of Baptist associations proceeded slowly, and the creation of the first national organization came only in 1814, twenty years after the Methodists'. Its organization can be traced to events in 1806, when some students at Williams College in Massachusetts (a Congregational Church school) began to act on their previous conversations and prayer about the need for foreign missions. Their spreading concerns led in 1810 to the formation of the Board of Commissioners of Foreign Missions (supported by Congregationalists and Presbyterians) and the commissioning of the first missionaries, Luther Rice, Adoniram Judson, and Samuel Mills. Judson and Mills left for India in 1812. During the long voyage, Judson, who expected to meet the British Baptist William Carey in India, prepared himself to refute the unique Baptist doctrines, especially the view that the immersion of adult believers was the correct form of baptism. However, his long hours of Bible study led in the opposite direction, and he concluded the Baptists were, in fact, correct. Thus, when they arrived in India, Judson and his wife were rebaptized. Rice arrived shortly thereafter, and he too became a Baptist. They both resigned from the

American Board, and Rice returned home to raise money for what had inadvertently become the first American Baptist mission.

Rice arrived in the United States planning to return to the mission field as soon as support was found. Instead, he stayed in the States, attended college, and dedicated the rest of his life to promoting the missionary cause. Touring the country, he encouraged the formation of missionary societies in local churches. He also began to formulate a plan for coordinated national action through the formation of state missionary conventions and then a national convention. The first General Missionary Convention of the Baptist Denomination in the United States met in 1814. It appointed a board to garner support from Baptists around the country. Meeting every three years, the Triennial Convention, as it came to be called, inspired additional national efforts to extend the ministry of the local churches, including the American Baptist Tract Society (1824, later the American Baptist Publication Society) and the American Baptist Home Missionary Society (1832).

The establishment of these societies would greatly benefit the Baptist cause in the United States, but it would also reveal some deep disagreements within the movement. At the time of the formation of the Triennial Convention, two models for organization were presented. One, the convention

Baptists frequently conducted their baptisms in ponds set aside as baptismal pools.

model, saw the work as that of the congregations, who would send representatives to the convention meetings and directly support its program. For many, the convention appeared to take on the trapping of a denominational structure that would compromise the autonomy of the local congregations. They preferred the model of a society, an independent organization that would be supported by those individuals who agreed with its program. In the end, the society model was chosen, and thus the additional societies were founded to keep the Triennial Convention focused upon its primary task. The primary support for the convention model was in the South and for the society model in the North.

While the majority of Baptists fought over the nature of national organization, others decried the very idea as an unbiblical innovation. In their understanding, the Baptists were a Bible-based movement that attempted to conform to the New Testament model both in belief and practice. The movement, they observed, had grown tremendously through the eighteenth century without the need of missionary organizations or any other organizations above the local church, such as Bible publication societies and theological schools. As the influence of the national societies grew, the movement in opposition arose. In 1827, the Kehukee Baptist Association in North Carolina adopted a series of statements affirming their desire to have nothing to do with missionary societies, Bible societies, and theological seminaries and not to countenance their representatives in their member churches. Those churches opposed to the association's stand withdrew, and other associations began to line up either for or against the position. In Baltimore, in 1832, Baptists meeting at the Black Rock Church issued a widely circulated statement favorable to the Kehukee position. As antimissionary sentiment spread through the Baptists, and lines of fellowship were reorganized along mission/antimission lines, a new antimission denomination, the Primitive Baptists, emerged, its main strength being in the South.

THE GROWING NATION

The new nation formed after the Revolution claimed as its own all of the land from the Atlantic to the Mississippi River and south of Canada, the only exception being Florida (which was ceded to the United States in 1819). In 1803, Napoleon, abandoning plans for an American Empire, sold the Louisiana territory to the United States. The United States thus came into possession of a huge area of sparsely populated land, and those unable to find their place in the East began the trek to the West that would dominate American life for the century. Religiously speaking, the new territory was no man's land, and no church or religious groups had prior claims to hegemony. And as settlers, primarily from the older families in the East or fresh from Europe, poured

Congregationalist Charles Finney was the leading voice for revivalism in the mid-nineteenth century.

into the area and pushed the native population aside, religious life would be redefined.

Prior to the Revolution, settlement had been largely confined to the coast regions and inland along the major river systems. The Congregationalists and Presbyterians had the most impressive followings and a high level of agreement theologically. Although by no means the largest churches in the new nation, the two groups had and were to continue to have an influence far beyond their numbers.

In 1636, the Congregational clergy, many of them trained at Cambridge University and determined to keep education alive in the new world, established Harvard College, at Cambridge, Massachusetts. This first institution of higher learning in what is now the United States heralded a string of church-sponsored colleges. Its rival Yale traces its beginnings to 1701. The Great Awakening spurred the development of Presbyterian education, first through the Log College and then in 1746 with the founding of the College of New Jersey, now Princeton University. The determination of the Congrega-tionalists and Presbyterians to maintain a college-educated ministry, very unlike that of the Methodists and Baptists, meant that the development of an American theology largely fell into their hands and that a disproportionate number of the nation's leaders were drawn from their ranks. However, when the nation began its rapid growth following the Revolution, it meant that they were the least

Timothy Dwight, a theologian at Yale University, arose as a powerful advocate of a post-Revolutionary spiritual awakening.

equipped to seize the opportunity provided by the frontier, and they lagged behind in moving into the West.

In part because of their emphasis on education, in each generation the Congregationalists produced a score of outstanding ministers who took the lead in articulating the issues of the day. Cotton Mather emerged as the leading minister at the time of the Salem witch trials, and as the voice of the Boston ministers, he interceded with the governor to stop the proceedings just as the body count was about to explode. As the Great Awakening moved across the land in the 1740s, Charles Chauncy arose to speak against the domination of the religious life by mere feelings and champion the cause of standards by which to judge the revivals. Chauncy was the first of a long line of New England ministers who opposed the enthusiasm unleashed at the revivals that were fast becoming a standard part of the American religious scene.

SAVING THE FRONTIER

Almost immediately after the new nation was constituted, settlers began to push westward. The great majority of Americans were unchurched, the colonies having been settled by those Europeans who had the least ties to the homeland and to the institutions that gave structure to a social life. The pioneers pushing westward also included those for whom even the life on the East

Coast had proved less than favorable and who sought another chance to make it. The older churches did not have a history that informed them on the best methods of dealing with this new situation. In contrast, the Methodists and Baptists were more open to learning from the frontier and adapting to it. They were also quite willing to go to where people were and create churches rather than to wait until enough church members had assembled in one place and then draw them together as a congregation (the standard pattern for Anglicans, Presbyterians, and Congregationalists). However, it would be in a Presbyterian setting that the religious life of the frontier would be changed.

In the summer of 1800, James McGready (1758–1817) was the pastor of three Presbyterian churches in south central Kentucky. He encouraged his people to pray for a revival of religious faith in the area and at one point in June held a combined communion service and extended preaching/prayer meeting that lasted for several days. Toward the end of the meeting, they were joined by two Methodist circuit riders, whose preaching led to an emotional outburst among the people. McGready described it as a Pentecostal experience (referring to the events described in the Bible, Acts chapter 2, concerning the first Christian Pentecost and the coming of the Holy Spirit). At the end of July, when McGready was planning a similar service, hundreds came prepared to camp out until a similar thing occurred again. This is now seen as the first of thousands of camp meetings that were to characterize nineteenth-century religion in the South and Midwest. People came expectant, and the emotional release in the atmosphere of lively preaching was intense and expressive. People swooned, cried out, shouted, and acted out their feeling in various bodily motions. Many found their entrance into the religious life.

Camp meetings became such useful tools for spreading religion that ministers began to plan them well in advance, the optimal time being midsummer between the planting season and the harvest. They were usually interdenominational affairs, although as groups grew in strength, those denominations most committed to winning the West for Christianity were able to hold their own camp meetings.

The camp meetings were designed to entertain, grab attention, and eventually convert the attendees. They manifested the divergent visions of Christian society that determined the actions of the newer free churches as opposed to the transplanted older state churches. The older churches operated as institutions focusing the religious in what was viewed as basically a Christian society. They spoke the word and offered the sacraments. They understood that many were irreligious but knew that all had been baptized and that most would turn to God sooner or later. The free churches had a much different vision. They saw the world as primarily home to sinners, lost and disconnected from God.

Their mission was saving as many as possible from the sinful world and bringing them to a saving faith. Their vision seemed verified in the United States, where even in the cities, the outward acknowledgment of the church was at a minimum; it was all but absent on the frontier.

Thus it was that during the early nineteenth century, evangelism became the consuming passion of church leaders. Some, such as Peter Cartwright (1785–1872), became known for their success in having people respond to their oratory and in their longevity as evangelists. Cartwright wandered through Tennessee and Kentucky and then Illinois for sixty-five years.

While Jonathan Edwards had done much to legitimize the revivals and the emotional outbursts that accompanied them, as a whole, they were seen as spontaneous affairs. No one knew when and where a revival might occur. That changed somewhat with the coming of Charles Grandison Finney (1792–1875). After his conversion in 1821, he studied for the Presbyterian ministry and began preaching in upstate New York in 1824. Revivals broke out in response to his preaching, and he became a student of revivalism, especially that of Jonathan Edwards and John Wesley. As he read the older accounts of revivals and observed what was occurring around him, he began to introduce a variety of new practices, such as the protracted meeting, special preaching services that had a beginning date but no announced ending, or allowing women to lead prayer in public. These were termed "new measures" and defended as being both immensely useful in assisting revival and not contrary to the Bible. His lectures, later collected and published in 1835 as *Revivals of Religion*, constituted the first of many "how to" books on conducting revivals to follow.

Finney emerged as the dominant figure in revivalism, especially in the northeast and took his "new measures" successfully into cities such as Boston, New York, and Philadelphia, where in many cases the larger churches were manned by ministers staunchly opposed to his innovations. Finney also wedded his revivalism to the great social crusades of the era, and he attempted to recruit the new converts to Christianity into the causes of temperance and abolition.

THE AFRICAN AMERICAN FACTOR

The number of Africans coming to America increased decade by decade. At the beginning of the nineteenth century, there were more than 800,000. At the beginning of the Civil War in 1860, there were almost 4 million. They were a unique people on the American landscape, as the great majority had come to the United States against their will. Some, especially those who came as indentured servants, had found a place in the culture, and even in the cities of the Deep South, large communities of free black people thrived. On the other

"God our Father; Christ our Redeemer;
Man our Brother."

THE BUDGET

FOR 1884

RICHARD ALLEN,
FIRST BISHOP OF THE A. M. E. CHURCH.

COMPILED AND EDITED BY
REV. B. W. ARNETT, D. D
FINANCIAL SECRETARY.

*Richard Allen, the founder
of the African Methodist
Episcopal Church.*

St. Paul's AME
Church in Waco,
Texas, an early
prominent
congregational
center.

From the *LIFE EXPERIENCE AND GOSPEL LABORS OF RT. REV. RICHARD ALLEN*

A number of us usually attended St. George's church in Fourth street; and when the colored people began to get numerous in attending the church, they moved us from the seats we usually sat on, and placed us around the wall, and on Sabbath morning we went to church and the sexton stood at the door, and told us to go in the gallery. He told us to go, and we would see where to sit. We expected to take the seats over the ones we formerly occupied below, not knowing any better. We took those seats. Meeting had begun, and they were nearly done singing, and just as we got to the seats, the elder said, "Let us pray." We had not been long upon our knees before I heard considerable scuffling and low talking. I raised my head up and saw one of the trustees, H—M—, having hold of the Rev. Absalom Jones, pulling him up off of his knees, and saying, "You must get up—you must not kneel here." Mr. Jones replied, "Wait until prayer is over." Mr. H——— M——— said "No, you must get up now, or I will call for aid and force you away." Mr. Jones said, "Wait until prayer is over, and I will get up and trouble you no more." With that he beckoned to one of the other trustees, Mr. L——— S——— to come to his assistance. He came, and went to William White to pull him up. By this time prayer was over, and we all went out of the church in a body, and they were no more plagued with us in the church. This raised a great excitement and inquiry among the citizens, in so much that I believe they were ashamed of their conduct. But my dear Lord was with us, and we were filled with fresh vigor to get a house erected to worship God in. Seeing our forlorn and distressed situation, many of the hearts of our citizens were moved to urge us forward; notwithstanding we had subscribed largely towards finishing St. George's church, in building the gallery and laying new floors, and just as the house was made comfortable, we were turned out from enjoying the comforts of worshipping therein. We then hired a store-room, and held worship by ourselves. Here we were pursued with threats of being disowned, and read publicly out of meeting if we did continue worship in the place we had hired; but we believed the Lord would be our friend. We got subscription papers out to raise money to build the house of the Lord. By this time we had waited on Dr. Rush and Mr. Robert Ralston, and told them of our distressing situation. We considered it a blessing that the Lord had put it into our hearts to wait upon those gentlemen. They pitied our situation, and subscribed largely towards the church, and were very friendly towards us, and advised us how to go on. We appointed Mr. Ralston our treasurer. Dr. Rush did much for us in public by his influence. I hope the name of Dr. Benjamin Rush and Robert Ralston will never be forgotten among us. They were the first two gentlemen who espoused the cause of the oppressed, and aided us in building the house of the Lord for the poor Africans to worship in. Here was the beginning and rise of the first African church in America.

hand, those Africans, in both North and South, who were not slaves constantly felt the impact of discriminatory laws.

Through the eighteenth century, people of African descent joined different denominations but seemed to particularly favor the Methodists and Baptists. The Methodists welcomed black members from the beginning, and the congregations in New York and Philadelphia developed a particularly strong black constituency. In the wake of the first Baptist church in Savannah, additional Baptist churches appeared, but it would be 1834 before the first Black Baptist Association would be formed, in Ohio.

In the freedom-centered atmosphere of the post-Revolution period, independent black congregations began to appear. A revolt against white racism among Black Methodists in Philadelphia in 1787 set the stage for the emergence of the African Methodist Episcopal (AME) Church, and a similar revolt in New York City led to the formation of the African Methodist Episcopal Zion Church. Both denominations spread through the free states during the first half of the nineteenth century. Richard Allen (1760–1831), the leader of the Philadelphia Methodists, was able to stay on cordial terms with Methodist bishop Francis Asbury, who dedicated Allen's new church building (1794), ordained him as a deacon (1799), and eventually consecrated him as the bishop of the new denomination (1816). The AME Church is the oldest continuously existing institution in the African American community. Black congregations in other denominations would also soon appear, although African constituencies in most denominations remained small.

In the South, both Methodist and Baptist preachers paid attention to the slave population and attempted to include them in their ministrations. Slaves were often allowed to attend camp meetings and participate in their emotive atmosphere. Black members were welcomed at most churches but were given segregated seating either in a slave gallery, in the back of the sanctuary, or outside the building. Preachers visiting plantations most often held separate meetings for the whites and blacks.

In 1829, William Capers (1790–1854), a white minister with the Methodists, was appointed as a missionary to plantation-bound slaves. His work launched a significant effort to evangelize the slaves and eventuated in many identifying themselves with the church. However, the efforts to evangelize blacks, both slave and free, were negatively affected by the rebellion by slave preacher Nat Turner (1800–1831) in 1831. Some sixty white people were killed before Turner and his followers were stopped. Consideration of Turner's religious training and the potential of church meetings as an opportunity for conspiracy was in the mind of those who the following year passed a new set of repressive slave laws. These laws severely limited preachers' access to slaves and led to the closing of black churches.

THE MORAL DILEMMA OF SLAVERY

The presence of a growing slave community and the growing knowledge of the horrors inflicted upon slaves created a moral dilemma that permeated every area of American life. Three positions soon found popular support, both inside and outside the church. Anchored in the South were the defenders of slavery. Christians built their defense upon what they believed was the civilizing role of Christianity. Africans were followers of a primitive polytheistic faith, and their exposure to Christianity, even as slaves, would be uplifting. The Bible pictured slavery as part of human society, and it did not argue for freeing slaves when given the opportunity. The Christian position (drawn from such passages as Paul's letter to Philemon) was one of treating slaves kindly.

Standing against the defenders of slavery were the abolitionists, who demanded the immediate freeing of the slaves as ultimately the only moral course. They argued that the implication of the gospel was that each individual was a child of God and of infinite worth. As such, it was un-Christian to inflict slavery upon anyone. A Quaker, John Woolman (1720–1772), stood at the fountainhead of abolitionist thought. Almost single-handedly, he persuaded the Friends to remove themselves from any attachment to slavery. His efforts would inspire others to speak and act in the abolitionist cause.

Standing between the two positions were a large number of people, in both the North and the South, who were antislavery but also antiabolitionist; that is, they opposed slavery but saw it coming to an end in stages over a period of time. Antislavery people tended to fear the abolitionists as fanatical and that the sudden abolition of slavery would cause a social disaster. Some antislavery people also pursued a scheme of returning black people to Africa. The antislavery position tended to dominate the churches in the North and allowed them to continue working with southern leaders who supported slavery.

The slavery issue continually intruded upon the deliberations at national church gatherings, as it was attached to a variety of issues (much as homosexuality has repeatedly arisen in the assemblies of the major denominations through the last decades of the twentieth century). Among the Baptists, Presbyterians, and Methodists, new incidents and issues sparked the next debate, and the continued rancor eventually precipitated division. The issue among the Methodists, for example, reached a crisis when Georgia Bishop James O. Andrew (1794–1871) inherited some slaves. Georgia did not at that time allow manumission. The 1844 debate over his situation set the stage for the Methodist Episcopal Church, then the largest religious body in the States, to divide. They would not reunite until 1939. About the same time, the Baptists disagreed over the sending of a slaveholder to the foreign mission field. The Northern Baptists felt that the sending of a slaveholder would make them

Harriet Tubman
(left), abolitionist
leader in the
underground
railroad and
member of the
African Methodist
Episcopal
Zion Church.

responsible for something they could not in good conscience sanction. The Southern Baptist Convention and the Northern Baptists (now the American Baptist Churches in the U.S.A.) have moved in divergent directions ever since and show no signs of reuniting. The Presbyterians were able to remain a single ecclesiastical unit until the war started, but after the first shots were fired and the Confederacy was proclaimed, the southern presbyteries withdrew and formed a separated church body.

The presence of slavery and the agricultural life it supported served to set the South apart as a distinctive part of the United States. Actions by those who wished to abolish the institution increasingly alienated southerners from their neighbors to the north, and the break in the several large denominations merely served as a visible manifestation of a division that ran through almost every institution, religious or secular. The division became determinative for the growth of the nation westward, as new states tended to be added in pairs, one slave and one free. As the North continued to push its objections, the South eventually attempted to separate in order to preserve its social system, complete with that increasingly unpalatable element. The separation drew the nation into bloody war.

Sojourner Truth, reformer and abolitionist and member
of the African Methodist Episcopal Zion Church.

NEW FORMS OF RELIGIOUS LIFE

The relatively free atmosphere of the American colonies allowed a number of religious radicals to conduct experiments with very different religious options. Beginning with Plockhoy's Commonwealth (1663) and the Labadist community (1683), a variety of communal groups came and went. They were as a whole short-lived affairs, although the Woman in the Wilderness community that settled in Germantown, Pennsylvania, in 1693 did have a broad impact on the German and Scandinavian communities through a generation and then injected a magical element into the Pennsylvania Dutch community of southeastern Pennsylvania. Islam actually came into the country during the eighteenth century, brought by a few slaves who were Muslims, although their continuity with the present Muslim community is doubtful.

It was during the nineteenth century that a variety of new and different religious communities that would have a broad impact on the culture would arise. The first of these began in upstate New York, the so called "burned-over" district. In the years after the opening of the Erie Canal, the area had been flooded with settlers and with evangelists who attempted to light the fires of revival. So intense and persistent were their efforts that cynical commentators began to suggest that the areas had been burned over, exhausted by the competing religious groups attempting to claim prospective members.

For many, like Joseph Smith, Jr. (1805–1844), the problem became the inability to choose between the competing sects, each sure that it alone possessed the gospel truth. This sensitive young man took his concern to God in prayer and was rewarded with a series of visions of God the Father and his son, Jesus Christ, and various angelic personages. Along the way, he was told where a manuscript was, purporting to be an ancient account of the Hebrews who had come to the Americas in Old Testament times. Smith was also given the means of translating the manuscript, claimed by Smith to have been originally written on gold plates. The result was the Book of Mormon, a volume that in published form resembled the Bible and was touted as an additional testament.

In 1830, Smith founded the Church of Jesus Christ of Latter-day Saints based upon his belief that the endtime was near and that he had a responsibility of establishing the apostolic church anew, its having disappeared many centuries before. His job would be to gather the Saints and build the earthly center of Christ's kingdom. The gathering of the Saints placed the Mormons in high tension with their neighbors, and the Mormons were driven from Ohio to Missouri and finally to rural Illinois. There in 1845, Smith was assassinated. The majority of Mormons disappeared into the Far West, and many Americans believed that the fifteen-year odyssey with the Mormons had finally

Popular Reformed minister T. DeWitt Talmage was among the host of anti-Mormon voices at the end of the nineteenth century.

come to an end. In fact, the interaction of the Mormons with America was just beginning. In 1852, when Smith's successor, Brigham Young (1801–1877), who led the Mormons to Utah, openly announced the practice of polygamy as a way of life in the church, he launched a controversy that would carry into the next century. But for the moment, polygamy would have to wait; the matter of slavery, took precedence.

The famous burned-over district would also give birth to another new religious movement, Spiritualism. The very first group to come into the new nation following the Revolutionary War was the Church of the New Jerusalem, a small group built around the angelic revelations of Emanuel Swedenborg (1688–1772), a Swedish seer who claimed to have been given the true spiritual understanding of the Bible. Swedenborgianism spread through the northern states at about the same time that magnetists, healers who followed the theories and practice initiated by Austrian healer Franz Anton Mesmer (1733–1815), began to tour the country giving demonstrations of healing and of what would come to be called hypnotism. Mesmeric demonstrations would provide popular entertainment through the first half of the nineteenth century.

Both Swedenborgianism and the magnetist movement set the stage for the occurrences in a home in Hydesville, New York, in 1848. Young Kate Fox

Joseph Smith, Jr., and several colleagues organized the Church of Jesus Christ of Latter-day Saints in 1830. This portrait shows Smith as head of the Mormon militia shortly before his death.

JOSEPH SMITH'S FIRST VISION

After I had retired to the place where I had previously designed to go, having looked around me, and finding myself alone, I kneeled down and began to offer up the desires of my heart to God. I had scarcely done so, when immediately I was seized upon by some power which entirely overcame me, and had such an astonishing influence over me as to bind my tongue so that I could not speak. Thick darkness gathered around me, and it seemed to me for a time as if I were doomed to sudden destruction.

But exerting all my power to call upon God to deliver me out of the power of this enemy which had seized upon me, and at the very moment when I was ready to sink to despair and abandon myself to destruction—not to an imaginary ruin, but to the power of some actual being from the unseen world, who had such an astonishing influence over me as to bind my being—just at this moment of great alarm, I saw a pillar of light exactly over my head, above the brightness of the sun, which descended gradually until it fell upon me.

It no sooner appeared than I found myself delivered from the enemy which held me bound. When the light rested upon me I saw two personages, whose brightness and glory defy all description, standing above me in the air. One of them spake unto me, calling me by name, and said, pointing to the other— *"This is my Beloved Son, hear Him!"*

My object in going to inquire of the Lord was to know which of all the sects was right, that I might know which to join. No sooner, therefore, did I get possession of myself, so as to be able to speak, than I asked the Personages who stood above me in the light, which of all the sects was right—and which I should join.

I was answered that I must join none of them, for they were all wrong and the Personage who addressed me said that all their creeds were an abomination in His sight, that those professors were all corrupt, that "they draw near to me with their lips but their hearts are far from me, they teach for doctrines the commandments of men, having a form of godliness, but they deny the power thereof."

He again forbade me to join with any of them; and many other things did He say unto me, which I cannot write at this time. When I came to myself again, I found myself lying on my back, looking up into heaven.

Joseph Smith, Jr., and several colleagues organized the Church of Jesus Christ of Latter-day Saints in 1830.

(opposite) This cartoon features T. DeWitt Talmage's quote "The Chinese May Stay but the Mormons Must Go."

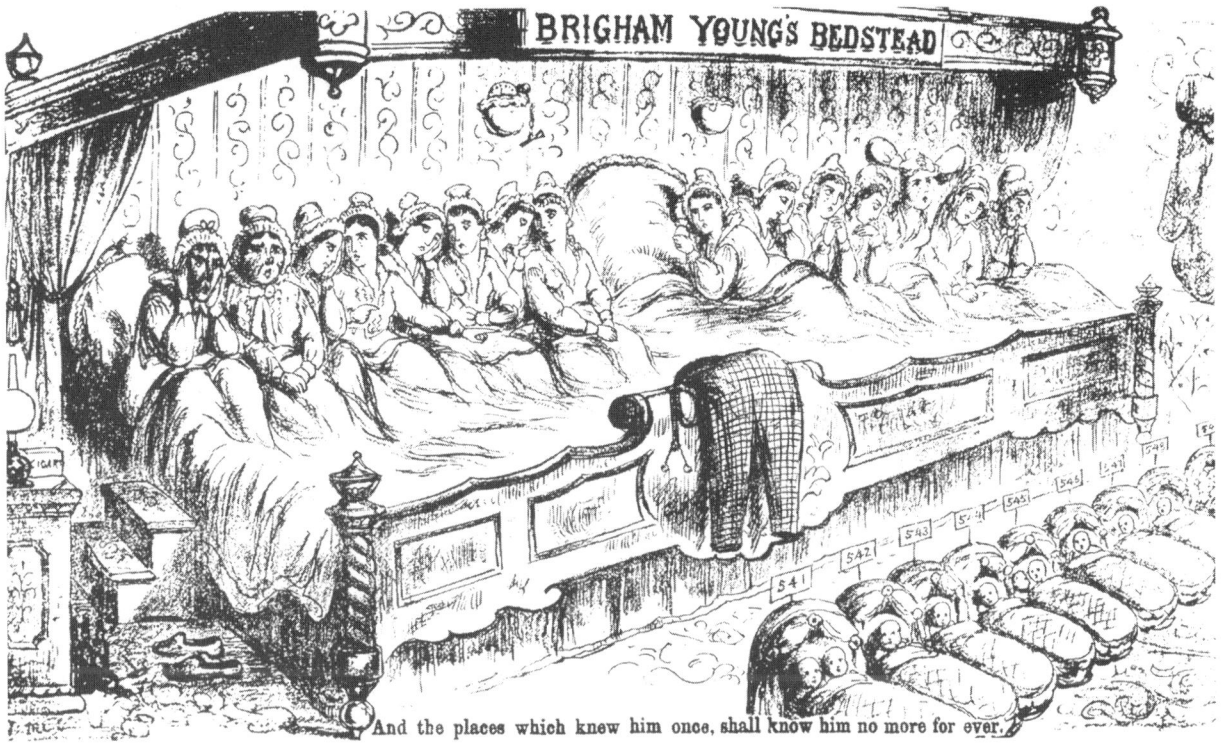

And the places which knew him once, shall know him no more for ever.

In spite of his pioneering accomplishments, easterners came to know of Brigham Young primarily as the husband of multiple wives.

The experiences of the Fox sisters, two of whom are pictured here, led to the founding of modern Spiritualism. Kate Fox Jencken is on the left, Ann Leah Underhill on the right.

(1836–1892) and her two sisters, Margaret (1833–1893) and Ann Leah (1814–1893), discovered that the rapping noises that they were hearing in their house seemed to respond rationally to their imitating the noises by clapping. They attempted to communicate and discovered that the noises originated with a person who claimed to have died in the house before the Fox family had moved in. Neighbors who heard about the rappings came to witness. The women's claim to be talking to a disincarnate entity was publicized, and even newspaperman Horace Greeley supported their veracity.

Soon, other people, such as Andrew Jackson Davis (1826–1910) of Poughkeepsie, New York, claimed that they could also communicate with spirit entities. Davis had been hypnotized in a mesmerism demonstration but soon discovered his ability to go into trance and have spirits speak through him. The practice of spirit communication became a national fad in the 1850s. Mediums, people believed to have the ability to sustain such communications, appeared on stage from Maine to California, and the movement was quickly brought to Canada and even England.

As the movement developed, it was viewed as a secular activity, but one with distinctly religious overtones. It purpose was simply to demonstrate the reality of life after death by communicating with what was believed to be the continuing spirit of the deceased. The movement found an audience among

Andrew Jackson Davis is credited with welding American Spiritualism into a coherent movement.

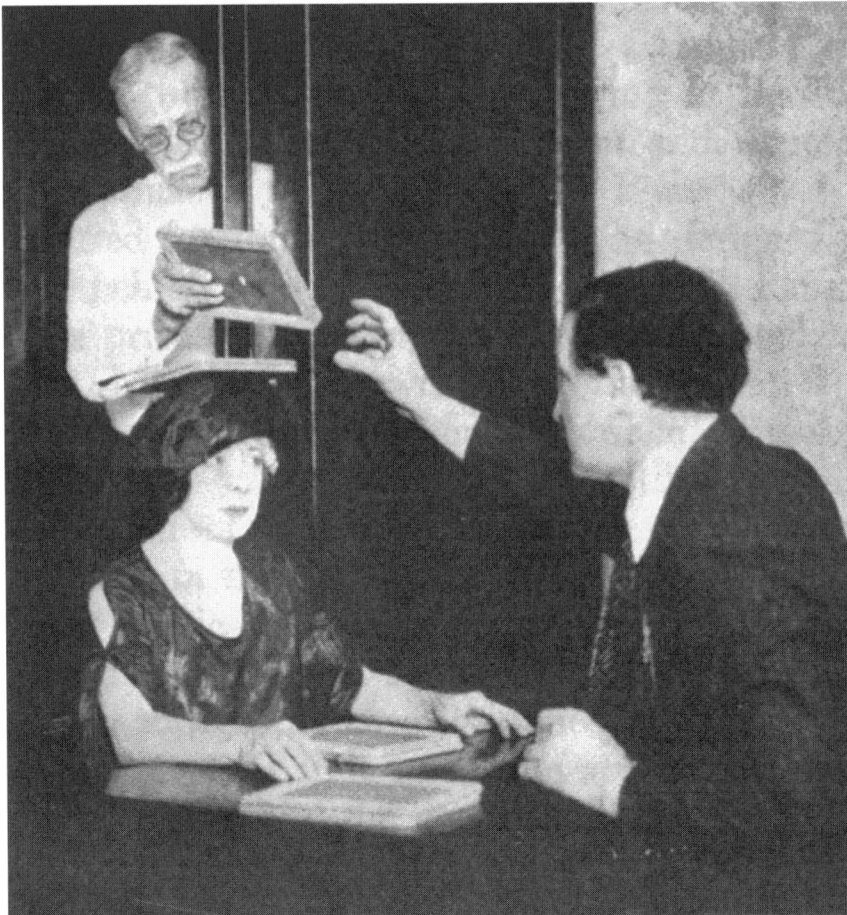

Harry Houdini demonstrating Spiritualist trickery.

Cora Richmond was a prominent Spiritualist medium of the nineteenth century.

The liberal-minded Hosea Ballou emerged as a major advocate of Universalism.

people in grief over the loss of a close friend, spouse, or family member. As critics offered purely naturalistic explanations for the phenomena, spiritualism began to develop a rationale for its existence. In a world in which science was increasingly becoming the authority, it claimed to demonstrate scientifically the truth of human survival of death in the face of a vocal skeptical community.

Spiritualism arose amid the conflict between the Christian churches and a range of movements dissenting from orthodox faith. The Deism of the eighteenth century found communal expression in the Deistical Society of New York (1794). Deism would in the nineteenth century give way to free thought, a popular form of atheism. Freethinkers would finally organize a national organization, the United Moral and Philosophical Society for the Diffusion of

William Ellery Channing facilitated the organization of Unitarians into a separate denomination.

Elias Hicks became the leader of Quakers who emphasized the Inner Light over the authority of Scripture in the generation after the American Revolution.

Useful Knowledge, in 1836. Spiritualism attempted to respond to the limited view of the world and human life offered by the atheists, by proving that what religion had talked about as heaven had some basis in fact. Of course, in the manner of their establishing their proof, and in the content of what the spirits actually said about the afterlife, the spiritualists soon alienated themselves from the mainline churches.

Latter-Day Saints and Spiritualists on one end and atheists on the other stretched the spectrum of American religions in ways that their more conservative Christian contemporaries abhorred and attempted to banish to the fringes of culture. Meanwhile, the dozen or more churches that were present at the founding of the nation were in the process of fragmenting into literally hundreds of different denominations, none with the power to assume religious hegemony. And none were yet ready to see these new movements as the heralds of an extraordinary religious pluralism that was coming, the product of that small phrase the Congress had inserted into the First Amendment to the Constitution.

CHAPTER 5

Urbanization and Pluralism

THE CIVIL WAR

The forces that had set the northern and southern halves of the United States on very different trajectories following the American Revolution culminated in the attempt to split the country and the war to prevent such a division. The division that had developed by the end of the 1850s between North and South penetrated every aspect of the society from economics to politics. However, in the public consciousness, all of the diverse and divisive issues focused upon the single issue of slavery and the moral offense it presented, even to most southerners.

Arguments over slavery had divided the larger Protestant groups and effectively paralyzed groups such as the Protestant Episcopal Church and the Roman Catholic Church that were able to stave off formal division. Every national church included the range of believers from abolitionists to staunch defenders of slavery as part of God's ordering of society. The demands of the abolitionists were blocked by the far larger number of antislavery advocates who opposed slavery but promoted a program of gradual reduction and ending of the plight of the Africans rather than a sudden abandonment of the South's "peculiar institution." No one came forward with a viable plan to end slavery in a way that could be accepted by slaveholders while providing a reasonable goal for the end of the problem. By 1860, the war that had been talked about for several decades finally could be postponed no more.

The war itself touched every person. More than half a million died in the hostilities, and every survivor could count a family member or loved one among the dead. Combined with the program of "reconstruction" imposed upon the South after its defeat, the war can be seen as the most dramatic change in the country's structure apart from that produced by the Revolution and the end of British rule. The South was left economically exhausted, and newly freed slaves had but minimal resources to support their effort to capitalize on the opportunities now before them. Along with the rest of the region, the southern churches had to struggle to recover from the ravages of the war and the competition from northern denominations that moved in to claim the spiritual spoils of the war.

St. George's Church, Philadelphia, was an early center for Methodism in America.

As the Protestant churches prospered, they developed numerous educational centers, such as Drew Theological Seminary in New Jersey.

AFRICANS CLAIM THEIR INHERITANCE

African Americans experienced the greatest change as a result of the war. They were now free to create their own lives in spite of numerous legal restrictions that had not been removed by the war. In many ways they remained second-class citizens, but leaders called them to exercise the new potentials that had been placed at their doorstep. First, they had to organize their own institutions. The primary need was education, and the churches would have to take the lead.

As the war ended, the strongest religious institutions serving the black community were the two African Methodist bodies. During the first half of the century, they had spread through black communities in the North and were poised to move into the South even before the war ended. The fate of more than 4 million African American souls hung in the balance. The African Methodist Episcopal Church (AME) followed the Union Army into the South. As large sections of South Carolina and Tennessee came under Union control in 1863 the first missionaries began work. The following year, its first southern conference was organized in North Carolina.

The majority of the former black members of the Methodist Episcopal Church South found their way into either the African Methodist Episcopal Church or the African Methodist Episcopal Zion Church (AMEZ), both old established denominations with experienced black leaders capable of acting in a predominantly white society. Free blacks from the southern cities were especially attracted to the AME and AMEZ where they found fellowship with northern blacks who like themselves had been able to avoid the stigma of slavery.

However, both former slaves and free blacks had additional opportunities. At its General Conference in 1864, the Methodist Episcopal Church (MEC) established a plan to move back into the South to reclaim territory lost at the time of the church's split in 1844. While not as successful as they had hoped, they were able to woo both white and black members who wanted to be reunited to what leaders declared to be the original Methodist Church in the country and identified with the victors in the war. Through the 1870s, the MEC was able to organize conferences across the South. Black churches were organized into separate conferences that allowed for some freedom of leadership development and programming, but they would remain segregated until late in the twentieth century.

A final option arose among those black members who had the strongest attachment to the Methodist Episcopal Church, South (MECS). As the MECS General Conference met in 1866, some 75,000 black members remained of the

WELCOME TO THE RANSOMED;

or, *Duties of the Colored Inhabitants of the District of Columbia*

By Daniel Payne

We are gathered to celebrate the emancipation, yea, rather, the *Redemption* of the enslaved people of the District of Columbia, the exact number of whom we have no means of ascertaining, because, since the benevolent intention of Congress became manifest, many have been removed by their owners beyond the reach of this beneficent act.

Our pleasing task then, is to welcome to the Churches, the homesteads, and circles of free colored Americans, those who remain to enjoy *the boon of holy Freedom.*

Brethren, sisters, friends, we say welcome to our Churches, welcome to our homesteads, welcome to our social circles.

Enter the great family of Holy Freedom; not to *lounge in sinful indolence*, not to *degrade yourselves by vice*, nor to *corrupt society by licentiousness*, neither to *offend the laws by crime*, but to the *enjoyment of a well regulated liberty*, the offspring of generous laws; of law as just as generous, as righteous as just—a liberty to be *perpetuated* by equitable law, and sanctioned by the divine; for law is never equitable, righteous, just, until it harmonizes with the will of Him, who is "*King of* kings, and *Lord* of lords," and who commanded Israel to *have but one law for the home-born* and the *stranger.*

We repeat ourselves, welcome then *ye ransomed ones*; welcome *not* to indolence, to vice, licentiousness, and crime, but to a well-regulated liberty, sanctioned by the Divine, maintained by the Human law.

Welcome to habits of industry and thrift—to duties of religion and piety —to obligations of law, order, government—of government divine, of government human: these two, though not one, are inseparable. The man who refuses to obey divine law, will never obey human laws. *The divine first*, the *human* next. The latter is the consequence of the former, and follows it as Night does the rising sun.

We invite you to our Churches, because we desire you to be religious; to be more than religious; we urge you *to be godly*. We entreat you to never be content until you are emancipated from sin, from sin without, and from sin within you. But this kind of freedom is attained only through the faith of Jesus, love for Jesus, obedience to Jesus. As certain as the American Congress has *ransomed* you, so certain, yea, more certainly has Jesus redeemed you from the guilt and power of sin by his own precious blood.

As you are now free in body, so now seek to be free in soul and spirit, from sin and Satan. The *noblest freeman is he whom Christ makes free.*

Bishop Benjamin W. Arnett of the African Methodist Episcopal Church.

200,000 members reported as the war began. They hoped to move in mass to an independent church. Feeling considerable responsibility for its black members, but also believing that an integrated church was not an option, over the next four years, MECS leaders facilitated the organization by blacks of what was then called the Colored Methodist Episcopal Church (now known as the Christian Methodist Episcopal Church).

With four relatively strong structures in place, the Methodists were in by far the best position to gather the harvest of potential members. As was the case among the whites, the majority of African Americans were not related to any religious institution. All of the major denominations initiated some work

10th Biennial Convention of Congrega[...]
Chattanooga Ten[...]

African Americans, such as these in the Congregational church, assumed a role in most major denominations after the Civil War.

among the freedmen, but the only other group ready to commit significant resources to the black community was the Baptist Church. As it had been able to spread through the white community after the Revolution through the instrument of untrained farmer preachers aided only by their knowledge of the Bible, their zeal, and their speaking ability, so in the same manner, the Baptist movement quickly took hold among blacks in the South. Preachers emerged both from the few Baptist churches already functioning in the South and from the African congregations and associations that had formed in the North. As the number of black congregations expanded through the 1870s, a generation-long struggle for control of the movement on the national level emerged and led to the formation of the major black Baptist denominations that still exist.

As the war came to a close, in 1864, the Western Colored Baptist Convention, which had formed a decade earlier to serve congregations west of the Mississippi River, reorganized as the Northwestern and Southern Baptist Convention. It presaged the establishment of state associations across the South, the

first of which, formed in Louisiana the following year. Fifteen years of growth among black Baptists would result in the formation of the Baptist Foreign Mission Convention as an initial national organization. But the immediate issue facing black Baptists at all levels was education. Systematic education of black children and youth had been neglected in the previous generation, and it was obvious to all that the ability of people to function in a free society was directly related to their access to knowledge. While state governments picked up much of the need for basic education, the denominations concentrated on the formation of colleges and seminaries.

The first Baptist school serving the black community began in 1865 with the effort of Massachusetts Baptist minister H. M. Tupper to establish a school for freedmen under the auspices of the American Baptist Home Mission Society. With some initial support from his friends in his home state, he moved to North Carolina, where he taught his first class, a theological course, in 1865. Then, through the efforts of some in the local black community, he was able to put up a building that became Raleigh Institute. Serious instruction began at both the high school and college level. Over the next decade, Tupper raised the money to purchase a tract of land upon which a real college could be built, and in 1875, Shaw University was incorporated. Similar stories would be played out across the South. The first African American theological school, Richmond Theological Seminary, was opened in 1867 in Richmond, Virginia.

The formation of colleges and seminaries signaled the emergence of an intelligentsia within the black church, although certainly men of eminent learning had been present in the church prior to the war. Among Baptists, the learned elite would assume positions as denominational and educational spokespersons. Their careers were nurtured by the American Baptists who raised large sums to undergird the development of the church among African Americans. Increasingly, however, many black Baptist leaders began to feel the need to separate from the predominantly white Baptist agencies and form their own independent structures. While American Baptists argued for the continuance of their prosperous working relationship, many blacks felt that it had led to an uncomfortable degree of white control and in the long run inhibited the development of the African American leadership.

The desire for independent black-led organizations resulted in the creation of the Baptist Foreign Mission Convention in 1880. It was followed by the American National Baptist Convention in 1886 and the National Baptist Educational Convention in 1893. Thus, black Baptists initially followed the pattern set by their white colleagues in setting up separate organizations to handle each task. Any particular congregation could then relate to all, one, or none of the conventions or continue to relate to the American Baptist structures. In 1895, these three national organizations merged into the National Baptist Convention, U.S.A., thus adopting an organizational pattern paralleling the Southern Baptist Convention. A majority of black Baptist congregations, but by no means all, shifted their allegiance to the new convention. The National Baptist Convention, U.S.A., would soon emerge as the largest black denomination in spite of experiencing a major schism in 1915 over the autonomy of its publishing enterprise, a schism which led to the formation of the rival National Baptist Convention of America. Most black Baptists would be affiliated through the twentieth century with one of the two National Baptist conventions or the American Baptists. Today, approximately a third of American Baptists are African American, and about a third of the churches in that denomination are predominantly African American.

The overwhelming majority of African American Christians were either Baptist or Methodist. However, the other large denominations also attempted to work in the African American community. The first black Episcopal con-

Wilberforce University, created by the AME Church, became a major institution in the recovery of African Americans from the years of slavery.

gregation, St. Philip's, had been opened in Philadelphia in 1795 under the leadership of former African Methodist Absalom Jones. Others also with black priests, opened in various northern cities. These congregations, however, did not lead to any large-scale effort devoted to evangelize Africans. Simultaneously, a few congregations, with white priests, arose in the South, usually built around a core of members who were slaves to an Episcopal master. The Episcopalians organized a Freedman's Commission after the war but marked its greatest success not in its attraction of black members but in its educational accomplishments. In like measure, the Presbyterians, Lutherans, Christian Churches, and Disciples of Christ created postwar missionary programs.

During the first generation after the Civil War, the rather meager efforts to bring Christianity to African Americans bore fruit as all of the denominational structures that had been created in the new nation were reproduced within the Baptist community. These provided the nexus for the organization of the black community and the platform from which a century-long struggle for civil rights would begin.

AMERICA'S PREMIER CHURCH

With the division of the larger Protestant groups, the Roman Catholic Church, which had struggled for its very right to exist in America in the previous century, suddenly became the largest religious body in the United States. John Carroll (1735–1815), a cousin of one of the signers of the Declaration of Independence, had become the first American bishop in 1790 and initiated what would become the vast system of Roman Catholic institutions of higher learning with the formation of St. Mary's Seminary the following year. He attracted to his side Elizabeth Seton (1774–1821), the founder of the American Sisters of Charity, the first American religious order. In 1808, he became the first American archbishop, with four bishops under him in Boston, New York, Philadelphia, and Bardstown, Kentucky.

Growth was slow through the first decades of the nineteenth century, but in the 1840s, just as Protestants were focused upon the slavery crisis, massive immigration from Europe diverted Roman Catholic attention as a new wave of German and Irish members swelled the church's ranks. With only a slight pause during the Civil War, immigration would continue unabated through World War I. Reacting to what they felt was a de facto Protestant establishment, the immigrants built their own parochial schools that provided education for children from elementary grades through college. The refusal of the government to provide support for Catholic education (as they had done in Europe) would be a continuing issue dividing Americans.

Typically, immigrants from a single country, all of whom spoke the same language, formed parishes and built their own churches. These churches initially were served by priests from the old country who also spoke the language and understood the peculiarities of the ethnic culture. In addition, members from different religious orders, most based in one country, moved to America. As parishes Americanized and as second and third generations adopted English as their primary language, the church's hierarchy was continually faced with the desires of parishes to retain their ethnic traditions and participate in ethnic communities that often strove, in effect, to reproduce the old country in the new.

In the meantime, the church's hierarchy set itself the task of creating a truly American church, of developing an adequate system of education (in the face of a Protestant-controlled public school system), and of providing for the training and deployment of clergy. Periodically through the nineteenth century, the church faced the pain of the transition to that Americanized church in the intense protests of members who wished to slow if not stop that process. Usually, that battle flared when a congregation rejected the assignment

As the first Roman Catholic bishop and then archbishop, John Carroll strongly supported religious tolerance and separation of church and state.

Elizabeth Seton, founder of the Sisters of Charity, was the first American canonized by the Roman Catholic Church.

of a priest to their parish from outside their ethnic group. As a whole, the church weathered the storms, and in only one case did a major schism result when Polish parishes in Pennsylvania organized to found the Polish National Catholic Church.

On one level, the Roman Catholic Church prospered through the nineteenth century. Although it was by far the largest church, it was outnumbered by the many Protestant groups who found a sense of unity in their common fear and dislike of the papal legions. Protestants were continually reminded of Roman Catholic theological errors and the actions taken against their ancestors by the Inquisition. Periodically, anti-Catholic sentiments led to outbreaks of violence against Roman Catholic churches and institutions. On several occasions, a wave of anti-Catholic sentiment invaded public life, the most notorious era being the 1850s, when the Know-Nothing party, with its platform of protecting America from foreigners and Catholics, emerged. In 1854, it showed surprising strength at the polls. English-speaking Americans resented their country's being invaded by foreigners who did not speak the language and seemed to show no interest in integrating into the English-speaking community. Protestants were upset with their bringing to America the very faith the Protestants' ancestors had attempted to distance themselves from.

The drive to build an American church thus became a delicate balancing act between the pull of the expectation of members whose ties to the old country were strong and the need to ground the church in the American experience. The issue remained open as emigration continued from predominantly Catholic countries through the century. In the years after the Civil War, another reality intruded upon the decision-making process of the American hierarchy, namely changes being instituted in the international leadership of the church in Rome.

The developing American church was prospering in a democratic country, but from a European perspective, it seemed a distant reality. Tumultuous changes were overtaking Europe in the wake of the French Revolution. Antimonarchical forces were growing, labor was organizing against business owners, and women were demanding new freedoms. In Italy, in particular, a drive had developed to throw off foreign rule and unify the Italian peninsula, unification finally occurring in 1861. Each change diminished the temporal

Pope Pius IX oversaw the First Vatican Council at which the question of papal infallibility was discussed and affirmed.

Cardinal James Gibbons was the leading spokesperson of American Catholicism at the end of the nineteenth century.

power of the Catholic Church, especially with the incorporation of the former Papal States into the new Italy and the steady reduction of papal lands to the miniscule Vatican State.

In the midst of these changes, forces demanding a new assertion of papal leadership within the church grew. They culminated in the pronouncements of the council that met at the Vatican in 1870 and 1871, at which the pope was declared infallible when he spoke *ex cathedra* on matters of faith and morals. Papal infallibility, which Roman Catholics understand as a rarely used and limited prerogative of the pope to define Catholic doctrine, was viewed by Protestants and others as further evidence of grandiose monarchical tendencies within the church. The additional fact that the pope actually ruled a foreign land, provided the opportunity for Protestant leaders to question the loyalties of Roman Catholics to the American government. This idea was given added substance by the naming in 1875 of John McClosky (1810–1885) as the first cardinal representing the American church.

As the nineteenth century came to a close, prominent American leaders such as Archbishops James Gibbons (1834–1921) and James Ireland (1838–1918) struggled to create a situation in which Roman Catholicism could take its place as one among the many religious bodies of the United States and again enter the public arena. However, the very success of the American church threatened many Catholics in Europe, where the idea of the Roman Catholic

CARDINAL GIBBONS'
DEFENSE OF THE KNIGHTS OF LABOR
February 20, 1887

6. Now let us consider for a moment the consequences which would inevitably follow from a contrary course, from a lack of sympathy for the working class, from a suspicion of their aims, from a hasty condemnation of their methods.

(a) First, there is the evident danger of the Church's losing in popular estimation her right to be considered the friend of the people. The logic of men's hearts goes swiftly to its conclusions, and this conclusion would be a pernicious one for the people and for the Church. To lose the heart of the people would be a misfortune for which the friendship of the few rich and powerful would be no compensation.

(b) There is a great danger of rendering hostile to the Church the political power of our country, which openly takes sides with the millions who are demanding justice and the improvement of their condition. The accusation of being, "*un-American*," that is to say, alien to our national spirit, is the most powerful weapon which the enemies of the Church know how to employ against her. It was this cry which aroused the Know-Nothing persecution thirty years ago, and the same would be quickly used again if the opportunity offered itself. To appreciate the gravity of this danger it is well to remark that not only are the rights of the working classes loudly proclaimed by each of our two great political parties, but it is very probably [not improbable— très probable] that, in our approaching national elections there will be a candidate for the office of President of the United States as the special representative of these complaints and demands of the masses. Now, to seek to crush by an ecclesiastical condemnation an organization which represents nearly [more than—presque] 500,000 votes, and which has already so respectable and so universally recognized a place in the political arena, would to speak frankly, be considered by the American people as not less ridiculous as it is rash. To alienate from ourselves the friendship of the people would be to run great risk of losing the respect which the Church has won in the estimation of the American nation, and of destroying the state of peace and prosperity which form so admirable a contrast with her condition in some so-called Catholic countries. Already in these months past, a murmur of popular anger and of threats against the Church has made itself heard, and it is necessary that we should move with much precaution.[12]

(c) A third danger, and the one which touches our hearts the most, is the risk of losing the love of the children of the Church, and of pushing them into an attitude of resistance against their Mother. The whole world presents no more beautiful spectacle than that of their filial devotion and obedience. But it is necessary to recognize that, in our age and in our country, obedience cannot be blind. We would greatly deceive ourselves if we expected it. Our Catholic working men sincerely believe that they are only seeking justice, and seeking it by legitimate means. A condemnation would be considered both false and unjust, and would not be accepted [and therefore, not binding—et ne serait pas acceptée]. We might indeed preach to them submission and confidence in the Church, but these good dispositions could hardly go so far. They love the Church, and they wish to save their souls, but they must also earn their living, and labor is now so organized that without belonging to the organization there is little chance to earn one's living.

Behold, then, the consequences to be feared. Thousands of the most devoted children of the Church would believe themselves repulsed by their Mother and would live without practicing their religion. The revenues of the Church, which with us come entirely from the free offerings of the people, would suffer immensely, and it would be the same with Peter's pence. The ranks of the secret societies would be filled with Catholics, who had been up to now faithful? The Holy See, which has constantly received from the Catholics of America proofs of almost unparalleled devotedness, would be considered not as a paternal authority, but as a harsh and unjust power. Here are assuredly effects, the occasion of which wisdom and prudence must avoid.

12. The English read, "Angry utterances have not been wanting of late, and it is well that we should act prudently."

Church's being anything but the dominant religious body was unthinkable. They identified the "Americanist" thinking of spokespersons like Ireland with the secular political liberalism that was seen as such an anti-Christian force by the Vatican.

The attempts to communicate the peculiar American situation to Vatican leaders in the 1890s failed, and in 1899, the pope issued an encyclical (pastoral letter) condemning Americanism. This encyclical, along with other supportive pronouncements, had the effect of elevating the most conservative forces in the church and driving it from public life. Through the first decades of the twentieth century, the church would turn inward and largely avoid the encounter with other Christians, public life, and those new intellectual currents that did not immediately affect its life. That situation would not change until the church was brought out of its shell by World War II.

THE MAINSTREAM

At the beginning of the nineteenth century, the churches that had been present in the colonial era found themselves faced with both the immense task and the opportunity of meeting the need of a country that within a generation moved from being a set of settlements along the Atlantic seaboard to a land stretching from the mouth of the Hudson River, to the mouth of the

Father Isaac Hecker was a leading advocate of the Roman Catholic Church's adaptation to American democratic life at the end of the nineteenth century.

The rise of Roman Catholicism in America did not occur without opposition, including periodic anti-Catholic riots in major American cities.

Mississippi River, to the mouth of the Columbia River. The Revolution opened land to the Mississippi, and the Louisiana Purchase doubled the American territory. Florida was added in 1819. Almost immediately, settlers began the push west, and the churches tried to move with them.

The Methodists were actually the best situated to respond to the frontier. The Congregationalists and Presbyterians were less successful, but there was room for all on the frontier, and slowly they established themselves. Many of their clergy were reluctant to invest their careers in the unknown territories. The new situation forced them to reevaluate their opinions of revivalism. Whatever their concern for the orderliness of church life, success obviously came to those who promoted the revivals and the camp meetings they spawned. Revivalism also led to a new appreciation of the Bible. In the absence of government authority and a state church, the Bible became the single authority to which all could appeal. And when ministers found themselves questioning the doctrines of one of the older churches, the Bible became their authority for leaving and starting a new independent ministry. Among the first ideas to be challenged by the frontier ministers was the idea of church organization. Most of the older churches had a strongly centralized authority structure based either in the episcopacy (Catholics, Episcopalians, Methodists) or in a synod/presbytery. In the free atmosphere operating on the frontier, ministers looking into the Bible found no justification for such hierarchical authority. When their own desires for pursuing their ministry conflicted with the leadership under whose rule they ministered, they found it convenient to reject such leadership and found new churches with a more democratic structure.

James O'Kelly (1757–1826), a Methodist minister in Virginia, rejected the Methodist policy of regularly moving their ministers to new fields and left to found the Republican Methodists, the first of a series of schisms the Methodists would face, the most substantive leading to the establishment of the Methodist Protestants Church in 1830. In Kentucky, Barton Stone (1772–1844) and five colleagues left the Presbyterian Church and subsequently issued the "Last Will and Testament of the Springfield Presbytery," in which they denied the validity of any church organization (above the congregation). Also leaving the Presbyterians on a somewhat similar basis was Alexander Campbell (1788–1866), whose followers became known as the "Disciples." Those congregations that accepted the basic free church ideal of O'Kelly, Stone, and Campbell would gradually come to fellowship with each other in a loosely organized movement that refused to see itself as a new denomination. They thought of themselves as just Christians, although names such as Churches of Christ, Disciples of Christ, and Christian Churches would gradually identify the major segments of the movement.

In the decades after the Civil War, the older churches and the more successful of the newer churches took on the appearance of a new established church. Every town had a selection of Protestant congregations from which to choose, and the larger communities experienced the entire spectrum from the ritualistic Episcopalians to the more informal Baptists and Disciples. On one level, they engaged in constant controversy and arguments over the superiority of one as opposed to the other, and debates between ministers of different churches were a popular form of public entertainment. On the other hand, ministers were ready to unite for a range of causes that demonstrated their control of the culture.

The rush across the country through the nineteenth century would allow some churches to emerge as successful national bodies while others would be left behind. As the frontier population grew and they settled in for the long haul, the need for education immediately came to the fore. More than 150 private colleges were established in the West prior to the Civil War, and the rate of founding new schools increased immediately after the war. These schools would not only provide indigenous leadership but would also be seedbeds for change and centers for abolitionism, women's rights, and a variety of social crusades. They would also be centers in which new challenges to theological orthodoxies would take root.

The last decades of nineteenth century could be characterized as an era of peculiarly Protestant dominance of American life. The churches had spread into every corner of American life. While the majority of people had still not been swept into membership, the wealthy families and the more cultured leaders identified with it. Leading ministers were regularly quoted in the papers and their Sunday sermons often reprinted in the Monday editions. Efforts begun in the decades prior to the Civil War (foreign missions, Sunday schools, social service programs) were developed into major enterprises. Charitable institutions, from orphanages to retirement homes, from hospitals to rescue missions, multiplied, especially in the cities. And as the cities grew, efforts were made to adapt revivalism to the cities.

Through the nineteenth century, as Americans learned to make their voices heard in the free society they had created, the country had been the scene of great crusades and crusaders. Church leadership had been essential to creating, sustaining and providing the moral underpinnings of abolitionism, the peace movement, temperance, and the rise of women. As the country secularized, crusades attempted to perpetuate Sabbath observance and had some success in the passing of laws preventing commercial and entertainment enterprises from operating on Sunday.

Frances Willard (seated, center) turned the Women's Christian Temperance Union into the largest women's rights organization in America at the end of the nineteenth century.

FRANCES WILLARD'S ARGUMENT FOR
THE ECCLESIASTICAL EMANCIPATION OF WOMEN

By a strange and grievous paradox, the Church of Christ, although first to recognize and nurture woman's spiritual powers, is one of the most difficult centers to reach with the sense of justice toward her, under the improved conditions of her present development and opportunity. The sense of authority is here so strong, and woman's capacities for reverence and humility are still so great, that, while we can not fail to deprecate, we need not wonder at the present situation. Here, as elsewhere, enlightened womanhood will come with the magic open sesame which shall erelong prevail even against these gates so sedulously barred: *Woman, like man, should be freely permitted to do whatever she can do well.*

Who that is reasonable doubts that if we had in every church, a voice in all its circles of power, it would be better for the church, making it more homelike and attractive, more endeared to the people, and hence more effective in its great mission of brotherly and sisterly love? By what righteous principle of law or logic are we excluded from church councils when we so largely make up the church's membership? Who that did not know it beforehand would believe that good men actually desire to keep us out? Antecedently I would have made my affidavit that nothing could have pleased them so much as to 'have us come in and share with them the power and honor, as we do the burdens and responsibilities, of the church home. Indeed, I can not help thinking that it might be said of us, "O fools, and slow of heart to believe all that the prophets have spoken!" We have not ourselves rightly understood the liberty wherewith Christ hath made woman free by introducing a religion that removes the world from a war footing to a peace basis, thus rendering science possible, with invention as its consequence, from all of which comes a civilization having as its choicest blossom the material comforts and contrivances of the modern home. We have not seen that old-time duties have been taken from our hands that we might enter upon higher ones, and that to make the whole world homelike is the province of one half the race. But as these truths take possession of our inmost hearts we shall go gently to our brothers, asking them to open to us every opportunity and to share with us every prerogative within the Church of Christ. In the United States, the generous spirit of whose manhood has nowhere been excelled, we have a vantage-ground in any effort that may be quietly and unitedly put forth for the opening of closed doors, ecclesiastical or otherwise. I have long thought that the spectacle of well-nigh a hundred thousand church edifices closed, except at brief intervals when meetings were in progress, was a travesty of the warm-hearted gospel of our Lord, and I rejoice to see that just as woman's influence grows stronger in the church, those doors stay open longer, that industrial schools, Bands of Hope, church kindergartens, reading-rooms, and the like, may open up their founts of healing, and put "a light in the window for thee, brother."

The time will come when these gates of Gospel Grace shall stand open night and day, while woman's heavenly ministries shall find their central home within God's house, the natural shrine of human brotherhood in action, as well as human brotherhood in theory.

Many of the causes found their convergence in arguably the most successful crusading organization, the Women's Christian Temperance Union (WCTU). Founded in 1874, the organization elected Frances Willard (1839–1898) to its presidency in 1879. She would see the evils of alcoholism as merely one among a series of issues affecting the women who made up her primary constituency and would, in announcing her "do-everything" program, turn the WCTU into the largest women's rights groups in the nation. Willard and the Union would champion clothing reform, education, labor reform, and most important, women's suffrage.

The growth of the cities also alerted church leaders to the problems faced by many Americans who were not prospering in the midst of the booming country. Increasingly, individuals who considered the plight of the poor were moved to found hospitals and food-distribution services. Rescue missions appeared, supplementing efforts to convert the poor with efforts to provide simple survival services from lodging for the homeless to hot meals. Along with the attempt to provide immediate assistance to the needy, others would begin to work on a more systemic approach, attempting to persuade the larger society of the need to reform itself into a more just social order.

While some reformers would concentrate on specific changes to assist particular groups of people, others would call for a major overhaul of the entire political order. The call to reform society in the image of the kingdom of God would become known as the "social gospel." In its most radical form, the social gospel would identify the equality and justice they sought with a relatively new political/economic perspective that was gaining in popularity, socialism.

Henry Ward Beecher was one of the best-known American preachers of the late nineteenth century.

CONTINUED IMMIGRATION

Through the nineteenth century, the English-speaking churches were carried forward by their evangelical efforts. Beginning the century with less than 15 percent of the population on their membership rolls, they experienced remarkable success. The population shot up from slightly more than 5 million in 1800 to more than 75 million in 1900. During that time, church membership went from less than a million to around 25 million, a remarkable achievement. The remarkable growth of American Protestantism in the nineteenth century had its price, the further splintering of the churches. From the 17 denominations at the time of the American Revolution, more than 100 had arisen. New churches often grew out of acrimonious debates that would take generations to heal; most offered new ways for Christians to structure their lives amid the varied demands of a changing world.

Most of America's population growth, however, did not occur in the English-speaking community; it resulted from massive emigration from continental Europe. Throughout the century, with few exceptions, the United States welcomed immigrants. As did earlier generations, the new immigrants represented those who had the fewest ties to their homelands and the fewest ties to the social structures, including religious structures, that they left behind. However, the number of irreligious was more than balanced by the many religious refugees, members of minority religions for whom discrimination and persecution had become a way of life in their homelands. Adding to the mix were the missionaries, the ministers and evangelists who took it upon themselves to care for the religious needs of the immigrant communities.

The largest wave of immigrants to the United States were German-speaking peoples of Lutheran, Reformed, and Roman Catholic background. Waves of German immigrants moved across America into the Midwest and on to California. They were followed by Scandinavians, almost all of Lutheran background, who concentrated in the upper Midwest from Michigan to Montana. Increasingly important as the century wore on were eastern Europeans of Orthodox background. They tended to settle in the Northeast, though many pushed westward to urban centers such as Detroit and Chicago.

Among the more interesting immigrant contingents to arrive in the United States were a group of Lutherans from Saxony. They were conservative Lutherans who rejected the rationalism that they felt had captured the church in their homeland. In 1839, they settled in Perry County, Missouri, just south of St. Louis. Over the next decades, they would prosper while retaining their conservative adherence to traditional Lutheran doctrine and practice. They

Carl F. W. Walther was the leading force in the founding of the Lutheran Church–Missouri Synod.

would eventually become the second largest Lutheran body in America, the Lutheran Church–Missouri Synod.

Lutheranism particularly benefited from immigration. As Germans and Scandinavians spread across middle America, they formed numerous Lutheran denominations, each representative of a different language group. Each also had a slightly different emphasis on Lutheran belief (the primary division being between those who valued the personal religious life and those who demanded adherence to the Lutheran confessions of faith). Many denominations formed because they were cut off geographically from other Lutherans who shared their language and perspective. At one time, there were more than 100 separate Lutheran bodies in the United States. As the communities they served

Philip Schaff, prominent Reformed theologian.

Americanized and communications improved, numerous mergers occurred through the twentieth century, and the overwhelming majority of Lutherans were brought into the two large Lutheran bodies, the Missouri Synod and the Evangelical Lutheran Church in America.

Joining the Lutherans in America were members of the Reformed Church, primarily of German and Dutch extraction. Both the German and Dutch churches had been present in the colonial era, and both continued to grow through the nineteenth century aided by the continued flow of immigrants, especially the Germans. However, both churches were inhibited by their opposition to revivalism and their slowness to Americanize. They continued their strong commitment to theological studies, and beginning with John William Nevins (1803–1886) and Philip Schaff (1819–1893), the anchors of the faculty at the seminary at Mercersburg, Pennsylvania, the German Reformed community produced a number of the outstanding theological leaders in American Christianity.

A new strain of German Protestantism entered the United States due to the action of King Frederick William II to unite the Lutheran and Reformed churches in his realm into a single body, the Church of the Prussian Union. Ministers from the church launched work in America in 1833 and by 1840 had created enough support to organize the German Evangelical Church Society

A. C. van Raalte was one of the founders of the Christian Reformed Church.

of the West, the seed of what would become the Evangelical Synod of North America.

The Dutch Reformed community was deeply affected by the split that occurred in Holland in 1834 when a group of ministers left the state church in protest of an attempt to bring the church directly under the control of the Dutch monarchy. They lived as a persecuted minority for a decade, but then, in 1847, they migrated in mass under their leaders, Hendrik DeCock, Henrik Scholte, and Albertus C. van Raalte. The group settled in western Michigan and joined their Dutch American colleagues in the Reformed Church in America. However, some found their American colleagues no more to their liking than those they had separated from in Holland and reorganized separately into what is today known as the Christian Reformed Church.

As the immigrant churches Americanized, they were quickly accepted into the mainstream Protestant community.

NOT THE MAINSTREAM

Not everyone felt comfortable with the new establishment provided by the larger Protestant churches. The popular emphasis on the authority of the Bible provided an opportunity for new leadership, subservient to no ecclesiastical authority, to arise completely outside those churches. The free religious sit-

(right) William Miller's predictions of the return of Christ in 1843 led to the founding of the modern Adventist movement.

(far right) Charles T. Russell, founder of the movement later known as the Jehovah's Witnesses.

(below) J. F. Rutherford, who succeeded Russell as head of the Jehovah's Witnesses.

uation provided new leaders with the opportunity to take their ideas directly to the public, regardless of the opinions of the learned preachers in the prominent pulpits. Through the century numerous new prophets arose, most gaining only a small following for a brief time. However, several found a significant audience and established an impressive addition to the emerging pluralism.

William Miller (1782–1849) startled people through the 1830s with his announcement, based upon his careful personal study of the Bible, that Jesus would return in 1843. His work was built upon the belief that the prophetic passages in the Bible, especially in the books of Daniel and Revelation, were to be read as if they laid out human history from the moment they were penned to the present. In particular, Miller believed that he had found the key to deciphering that history and understanding the chronology of predicted events. Christians from every denomination resonated with his abandonment of hope in this world and vision of a new world about to dawn. As the date drew closer, Adventist fellowships had emerged and thousands had committed themselves to the assurance that Jesus was about to physically deliver them.

The disappointment when Jesus did not return in 1843 (or the revised date of 1844), and Miller's own admission of error, did not destroy the movement; rather, it simply reorganized. Some groups of Millerites predicted new dates, and from each prediction, a new Adventist denomination arose. The most important of the date-setting groups arose in the 1870s around an independent teacher, Charles Taze Russell (1852–1916). Russell suggested that Jesus had returned invisibly in 1874 and that the end of the time of the Gentiles had begun. The beginning of World War I just forty years (a generation) later seemed to confirm his views, but he died in 1916 and the war ended without noticeable change in favor of God's people. New leadership arose in the person of J. F. Rutherford (1869–1942), who took Russell's Bible Students and welded them into a tightly knit evangelistic body that in 1931 took the name Jehovah's Witnesses.

Another group of Adventists had previously taken an approach similar to Russell's. Ellen G. White (1827–1915) assumed prophetic status and declared that Miller had been right about Christ's return but asserted that he had begun his return by entering the heavenly sanctuary (Hebrews 8) and would soon appear to cleanse the earthly one. White also became convinced that Sabbath worship had never been abrogated and led her followers to shift their worship gatherings from Sunday to Saturday. In 1865, her work was formally organized as the Seventh-day Adventist Church. It, like the Jehovah's Witnesses, instituted an impressive evangelization/missionary program that has spread to every corner of the United States and more than 200 countries of the world.

While the Adventists and Witnesses have looked for deliverance from this world, on the other end of the religious spectrum, teachers arose who looked

Ellen G. White and James White, co-founders of the Seventh-day Adventist Church movement.

Mary Baker Eddy
founded the
Christian Science
movement.

for salvation very much within this world. Mary Baker Eddy (1821–1910) was as unlikely a religious leader as one could imagine. A sickly widow in the years after the Civil War, she sought out a solution to her problems from various healers. Time spent with obscure mental healer Phineas Parkhurst Quimby became the catalyst for her own independent exploration of the Bible that led first to her own healing in 1866 and then to the formation of the Christian Science movement around her new approach to life.

Eddy believed that she had been healed after coming to the insight of the "Allness of God," a belief that found response in the atmosphere of the mystical metaphysics of Ralph Waldo Emerson. Eddy however, tied her insights to the Christian tradition and to the Bible. Unlike Miller, who saw the Bible as history, she saw it as allegory and developed a new tool, the *Key to the Scriptures*,

The Mother Church of Christian Science in Boston, Massachusetts.

Contemporaneously with Mary Baker Eddy, Boston minister Elwood Worcester launched a healing movement within the Episcopal Church.

attached to the movement's textbook, *Science and Health,* that facilitated her students' appropriation of the biblical message.

In their denial of illness in the face of the "Allness of God," Christian Scientists testified to the health that had come to them. Eddy went on to found the Church of Christ, Scientist, to perpetuate her views. Some who liked her teachings but rejected what they saw as the rigidity of the church left to found what became the New Thought movement. Emma Curtis Hopkins (1853–1925), for a short time the editor of the *Christian Science Journal,* became the teacher of these independents, who would go on to found the Divine Science movement, the Unity School of Christianity, and the Religious Science movement. To the emphasis on healing, they would add an emphasis on prosperity available to people from the abundance of God.

Pascal Beverly Randolph launched the modern era of Rosicrucianism in the United States.

While America was a fertile seedbed of religious innovation, Europe also continued to produce religious radicals, and new movements continued to appear across the Continent. However, Europe and America had very different levels of tolerance for minority religious communities, and a steady stream of members of persecuted churches and religions found their way to America. Most of these were Christian sectarian groups. The 1870s, for example, became an uncomfortable time for Mennonites, who had lived peacefully in Russia since the days of Catherine the Great, and several waves of German/Russian immigrants settled in the Midwest and plains states. The communally organized followers of Jacob Hutter (d. 1536) began their migration into South Dakota in 1874, and colonies eventually spread across the Dakotas and Montana and into the neighboring provinces in Canada. Over 300 such colonies had been founded by the end of the twentieth century.

Other noncommunal Mennonites moved into Kansas and Nebraska later that same decade and founded the Fellowship of Evangelical Bible Churches and the Mennonite Brethren Church. Members of a Ukrainian Evangelical movement, the Stundists, that had spread from Germany to the Transcaucasus, began to migrate in the 1880s. The Apostolic Christian Church began in

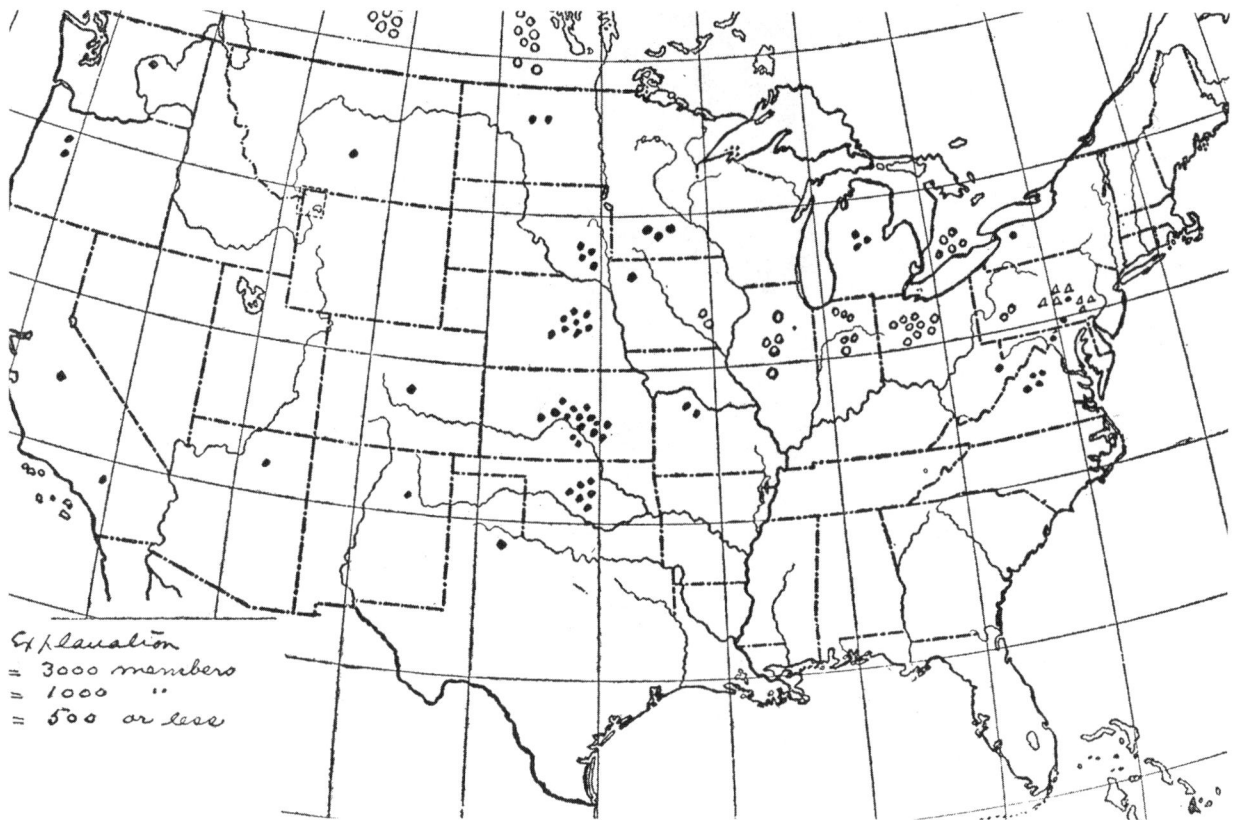

By the 1920s, the Mennonites had spread
across America from their original home in
Eastern Pennsylvania.

Rebecca Jackson, an African American
Quaker leader, was honored among the
Shakers for her mystical life.

*Men and women remained strictly
separated during Shaker worship.*

Switzerland under the preaching of Samuel Heinrich Froelich (1803–1857),
and its members began their migration in the 1850s.

Beginning with the arrival of Mother Ann Lee (1736–1787) and the
Shakers just prior to the Revolution, a variety of groups that practiced communal living relocated to America from Europe. Here the land was cheap and
groups could place their settlements in relatively isolated spots where their
experiments in utopian living could move forward with the least interference.
With help from the Quakers, the Society of the Separatists of Zoar moved from
Germany to Ohio in 1818. The Community of True Inspiration settled in
New York in the 1840s and moved on to Amana, Iowa, a decade later. About
the same time, the Icarians, French communalists, moved onto the land abandoned by the Mormons at Nauvoo, Illinois.

Shaker village.

As the nineteenth century came to a close, America had become the most diverse religious country ever known. Its pluralism recalled the heyday of the Roman empire and Rome's construction of the Pantheon to exhibit all of the deities worshiped in its expansive empire. However, the seemingly chaotic scene at the end of the century was but a foretaste of what was to come.

CHAPTER 6

Fundamentalism and Modernism

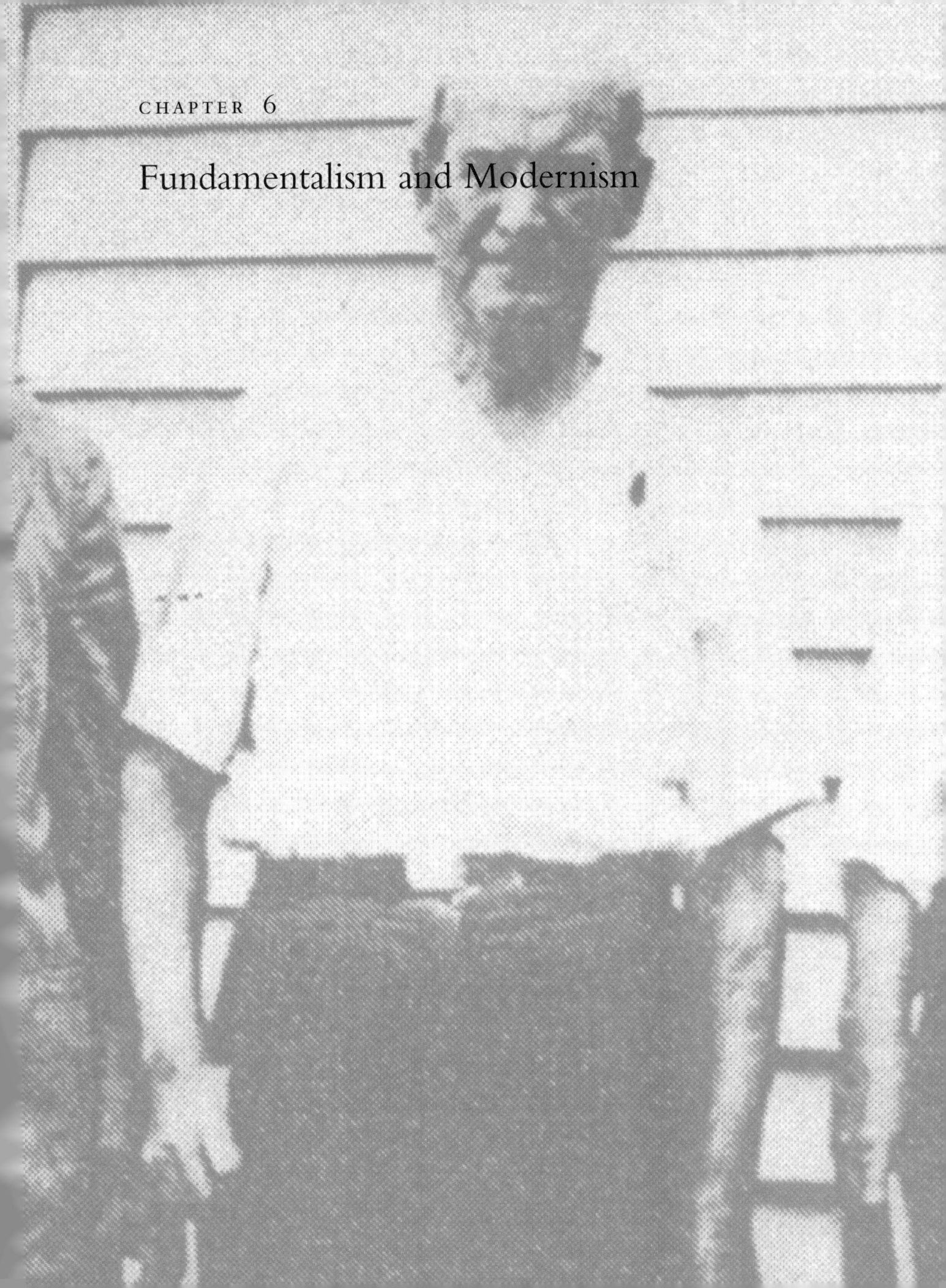

THE GREAT DIVIDE

During the late nineteenth century, Protestantism appeared to be in a major growth phase. Its power in the land was dominant. It was reaching out to the unchurched and the neglected with a variety of ministries and was supporting an expansive missionary program in other lands. Impressive, cathedral-like churches arose in the cities, and active parishes could be found in every community. However, amid all of the positive trends, a problem was developing that would in the twentieth century divide the Protestant community into two warring camps with very different visions of the Christian life. That division, still evident today, would change the face of American religion.

During the last decades of the nineteenth century, a host of transformations in how people lived and the manner in which they viewed the world began to converge. As important as any was the rise of the scientific perspective and the claims that science made as the authority in describing the natural world. Although scientists in previous centuries in the West had done yeoman service in their efforts to describe the world's phenomena, they had taken great pains to place their work in the conceptual framework provided by a literal reading of the Bible, especially the Book of Genesis. According to that literal reading, God created the world some 6,000 years ago. At one point he destroyed his creation with a worldwide flood and started over again. He intervened in his creation at various times and worked miracles.

The first challenges to this world-view came from geology and biology. Scientists began, for example, to observe the natural processes in the world, such as the mountain building that was occurring in volcanic regions. They concluded that the rate at which such mountain building occurred suggested a much longer time frame, tens of thousands of years, or even hundreds of thousands of years. More famous was the challenge made by Charles Darwin concerning the origin of species through a long process of evolution. He and his colleagues suggested not only that life had been present on earth for a much longer time frame than allowed by the Genesis account, but that one species emerged out of another. The Bible suggests that God created each species individually.

Ways to reconcile the observations of scientists with the biblical text might have been quietly worked out had not Darwin taken the next step and

Seminary president John A. Broadus emerged as a leading voice in the Southern Baptist Convention in the decades after the Civil War.

suggested that not only had the animal species evolved, but humankind had participated in that process. Humans may be, according to Darwin, the height of the evolutionary process, but they are nevertheless products of it. The new science struck at the very heart of the Protestant theological consensus as it existed in the nineteenth century. It challenged the veracity and hence the authority of the Bible, and in attacking the Bible, undercut the whole scheme of salvation.

The spirit of the new science also invaded biblical studies, especially in Germany, where scholars working on the first five books of the Jewish Bible (the Old Testament), traditionally ascribed to Moses, pioneered new techniques for examining the texts. These textual critics concluded that Genesis and the several following books were not the work of a single author (either Moses or anyone else), but the compilation of several documents that had been woven together into the present text by several editors. Such a view explained, among other things, the presence of parallel accounts of the same events (creation, the flood, the giving of the law, etc.) and the contradictions between the separate accounts. The new view of the text also led to the rewriting of the history of the rise of the Jewish nation.

Many scholars found the new view of the Bible very compelling and also understood the theological implications of what was termed the higher criticism. It challenged the integrity of the text and suggested that it was product of human history more than (or at least as much as) divine inspiration. Rather than reflecting God's progressive revelation to humanity, the Bible seemed the product of the conflict-filled history of the Israelites and their attempts to understand their history in light of the later consolidation of the Hebrew tribes into a single people.

If the intellectual attack upon the faith was not enough, the homogeneity of American society was under attack. Although the majority of Americans were of northern and western European extraction, an increasing number of emigrants from southern and eastern Europe began to arrive in the country as the century wore on. Massive migration from Poland and Russia began in the 1880s. Immigrants filled the cities to capacity and beyond. In the Far West, Chinese and then Japanese arrived in large numbers. The movement of people not only introduced new forms of Christianity, most prominently the ethnic strains of Eastern Orthodoxy, but also led to the establishment of the first communities of Buddhism, Hinduism, and Islam.

The presence of immigrants merely underscored the changes America was undergoing as it urbanized and industrialized. In the 1870s, Americans became aware of the evils that had developed in the workplace: the horrid work environment in many factories, the exploitation of labor (including the use of child labor), and substandard housing in the tenements. These were the products of an unbridled economic order in which wealthy factory owners were allowed free rein in their drive for a profit.

The discovery of the urban morass came just as the new discipline of sociology emerged. Sociology offered a view of social institutions and described their effect on individuals. Sociology also suggested the possibility of changing social structures to improve the condition of those living in them. Led by such thinkers as Washington Gladden (1836–1918) and Richard T. Ely (1854–1943), liberal Protestants attempted to integrate insights from sociology with Christian moral concerns. Increasingly, modernist theologians called for the restructuring of society, with the ultimate goal of creating a more egalitarian and just social order. What became known as the Social Gospel called Christians to the building of the kingdom of God. While more conservative voices called for reforms of the capitalist system, the more radical spokespersons tended to equate the kingdom with the visions of a new society proposed by socialism.

As these forces assaulted the social order and the churches so integral to it, church leaders arose who attempted to speak positively to and about the new realities. Already in the early and mid-nineteenth century, dissent had appeared primarily among the Congregationalists. Ministers and intellectuals had chal-

HOW MUCH IS LEFT OF THE OLD DOCTRINES
Washington Gladden

The main question before us implies that changes have been taking place in the old doctrines; that portions of them are obsolete or obsolescent; that in form and content they are different now from what once they were. This implication will at once be challenged. Doctrines that are true, it will be said, cannot be mutable; they must be as true for one generation as for another. A creed that is constantly reshaped must be a compend of error. But shall we say that the vine which has now of branches and of clusters fivefold more than it had five years ago is not true vine; or that the gray-bearded sage who thirty years ago was a man in his stalwart prime, and thirty years before that a ruddy-faced youth, just passing out of adolescence, and twenty years before that a helpless infant in his mother's arms is not a true man ? Is not every living thing constantly changing, not only its form, but its substance? If Christian doctrine is a living thing, it must be undergoing changes.

Christian doctrine consists of the opinions and beliefs of men concerning God and his kingdom. As the generations pass, and men learn more about themselves and the world in which they live and the works of God in the world, their point of view changes, and their doctrines are modified by their growing knowledge.

"Nay, but," some wise man will say, "Christian doctrine is all drawn from the Bible, and the Bible does not change; the truth is all there; all we have to do is to interpret it rightly, and then we have the everlasting and unchangeable truth." That statement is not quite correct, for our doctrines, if they arc true and complete, are drawn from other sources as well as from the Bible. They are drawn also from our knowledge of ourselves, and of the world in which we live. But, even admitting all this, it is still true that the enlargement of our knowledge, and the change in our point of view, lead us to interpret the Bible differently. We do not take the same view of the Bible itself that once we took; it is quite impossible that we should. We have studied it more carefully, we have gone to the Bible itself to find out what kind of book it is, and the Bible has plainly told us that it is not the kind of book that we once thought it to be. It is a better book, a far more useful book, but it is a different book. And therefore, because our view of the book has changed, and our methods of interpreting it have changed, our doctrines, even in their Biblical elements, must have undergone considerable change.

lenged traditional Christian affirmations of the Trinity and of the reality of hell and eternal damnation. These views had led to the founding of the American Unitarian Association (dissenting on the Trinity) and the Universalist Church (dissenting on hell). Members of both movements saw themselves as Christians who merely differed upon a single idea. However, orthodox church leaders saw Unitarianism and Universalism as more than simply another sectarian variation. Each had dissented from what was considered an essential doctrine, and the single (but different) doctrinal change made by each reverberated through the whole of their theological system. Changing either the doctrine of the Trinity or of hell, they charged, suggested an entirely new understanding of the Christian faith. The acceptance of the doctrine of the Trinity would thereafter emerge as a common standard by which Christians would define the boundary of their multidenominational community.

THE TRIUMPH OF MODERNISM

Throughout the post–Civil War period, individual church leaders attempted to create a dialogue between the Christian tradition and the challenges to the tradition posed by new scientific knowledge. They created theologies that accommodated evolutionary theories, responded to new views of the Bible, and attempted to deal with the realities of the new urban complexes. As knowledge of the world's religions grew, they reassessed the place of Christianity within the larger global community. Those who engaged in this pioneering effort that would lead to the promulgation of a wide variety of new theological approaches came to be termed modernists for their attempt to respond to the modern world. They were opposed to the conservatives, who saw in the changes primarily a new context in which to reassert the traditional affirmations.

Through the decades between the Civil War and World War I, first, modernism was denounced, and then its spokespersons were directly challenged. In the 1890s, for example, Charles Augustus Briggs (1841–1913), a professor at Union Theological Seminary, a prominent Presbyterian school, attacked the defense of biblical authority being made by his colleagues at Princeton. Further, having read and absorbed the work of the German biblical critics, he suggested that the Bible contained mistakes and errors on matters peripheral to its primary thrust.

For his efforts, Briggs was tried for heresy and, following his being found guilty, was defrocked. The trial led Briggs into the Episcopal Church, and showing their support, his colleagues withdrew Union from its affiliation with the Presbyterian Church. His would be but one of the more prominent such challenges and trials of seminary professors and pastors indicating a division of opinion that was arising in the larger Protestant denominations. The great (right) Horace Bushnell, an early modernist, opposed Calvinist demands for conversion in favor of a view of gradual religious development.

(far right) Charles A. Briggs' attempt to introduce German-style biblical criticism into the curriculum led to his ousting from the ministry of the Presbyterian Church.

majority of members still clung to a traditional approach to their faith, and their leaders attempted to establish its basis with ever more secure foundations. However, the majority of intellectuals and many of the pastors of the more prominent northern urban congregations were adopting a more liberal perspective. Support for modernism was growing, and conservatives were beginning to see it as a massive tidal wave threatening the whole of the Protestant Christian community.

Through the early decades of the twentieth century, very quietly, the faculties of most of the seminaries related to the Northern Baptist Convention, the Congregationalist Church, the Episcopal Church, the Methodist Episcopal Church, and the Presbyterian Church shifted their sympathies toward the modernist perspective. For them, the contemporary intellectual climate demanded an appreciation of the new role of science, especially sociology and biology; an understanding of the Bible as the product of human history; a theology that emphasized Jesus as a moral exemplar more than a sacrificial Savior; and an emphasis upon social change as a means of bringing about the kingdom of God.

The modernist approach would lead to theologies that tended to accept biological evolution and suggest that further human evolution (or progress) into a more perfect world was possible. Such evolution can be seen in our maturing understanding of God over the centuries, a development clearly demonstrated in the Bible. Jesus was held up as an ideal whose teachings should be followed and behavior copied. Rather than exclusively seek the personal salvation of individuals, Christians should be about the re-creation of society, which as a by-product will lead people into a relationship with God.

Rounding out the modernist agenda was a reappraisal of the missionary enterprise. During the nineteenth century, churches had devoted a substantial part of their financial resources and personnel into the conversion of the world. Thousands of American missionaries were at work around the world when, in 1932, Harvard professor William E. Hocking (1873–1966), whose own Congregationalist Church had taken the lead in the nineteenth-century missionary enterprise, completed his watershed reappraisal of that effort. *Re-Thinking*

(above) Methodist Bishop John Heyl Vincent founded the popular Chautauqua Movement, the fountainhead of continuing education programs for adults.

(left) Liberal Baptist preacher Russell Herman Conwell of Philadelphia founded Temple College (now University).

Missions called for a maturing of missions from an exclusive concern for the conversion of peoples into efforts focusing on a program of humanitarian service. Hocking's opinions reflected a view emerging in the more successful missions, where a considerable amount of missionaries' time was now taken up with overseeing a large body of believers and training a new generation of indigenous leaders.

Through the 1920s, liberal majorities assumed control of most Protestant seminaries and many prominent pulpits, and during the 1930s, they took control of most of the denominations' legislative bodies and administrative agencies. By the 1940s, the larger denominations declared the modernist controversy over. The theological task became the reconstruction of the tradition in such a way that Christianity could be at home in a world in which the authority of science, a pluralistic religious community, and the historical process of writing the Bible were assumed. While losing their most conservative ministers and members, these denominations would emerge after World War II as a new American establishment that would find its embodiment in the National Council of Churches of Christ in the U.S.A.

The conservatives did not go away, however embattled they felt by both the challenges of modern life and the departures from what they considered essential aspects of Christian faith by the triumphant modernists. Throughout the period of controversy, they retained a broad base of popular support among pastors and church members and developed a range of responses to the ever-changing situation.

THE RESPONSE TO MODERNISM

Possibly the most unique structure developed by American Christianity was revivalism. In previous centuries, Christians who had experienced times of spiritual dryness could be found praying for a revival of spirituality, but always in a context of an older Christian community perceived to have become complacent and emotionally dry. Little could bring a revival other than praying and expectant waiting. However, in the peculiar context of the religiously free and largely secular American frontier, the meaning of revival began subtly to change focus from the stimulation of the fervor of Christians to the conversion of unbelievers and from expectant waiting to feverish activity.

Through the first half of nineteenth century, Methodists and Baptists, soon joined by Disciples and Cumberland Presbyterians, took the lead in organized attempts to convert sinners through meetings specifically designed to invite attendees to change their religious thoughts and feelings. Those who established such meetings hoped that they would be God's instrument to revive the Christian community but, more important, that they would convert a large

number of attendees, the majority of whom did not profess any faith. The first structures to arise to promote revivals were the camp meeting and the protracted meeting. Camp meetings were effective tools in the rural frontier, and people from many miles around would travel to the designated site where they would camp out for a week or longer. The camp meetings were times to visit with neighbors, to be entertained by the music and the oratory of the preachers, and for many, to initiate a religious life.

Protracted meetings were held in a local church when the pastor or most often a visiting evangelist announced daily meetings that would continue as long as there was a meaningful response. If the community responded, the meeting could last for weeks. While the camp meeting was almost totally limited to rural areas, the protracted meeting could be held in the towns and cities that were arising. The heart of such meetings were sermons that called those in attendance to a decision, the most effective being those that aroused the emotions and were heard in the context of an accepting congregation.

Revivalism supplied American churches with a powerful tool, and those churches that adopted it experienced spectacular growth through the nineteenth century. Revival-oriented churches that were experiencing rapid expansion on the frontier also noted that the urban areas were the most resistant to their evangelistic endeavors. Charles G. Finney, who is credited with developing the idea of the protracted meeting, is also credited with expanding

Australian evangelist/healer John Alexander Dowie
founded the Zion Christian community, north of Chicago.

revivalism to the cities in the 1850s. As he had developed the famous "new measures" as effective means to revivalism's ends, he led in the creation of new structures that served the urban dweller, among the most important being the midday prayer meetings and worship services, which could be organized around the businessman's lunch hour. Such meetings exploded on the cities through the decade and picked up again after the Civil War.

Revivalism emerged as a program among two miniscule Christian churches (Methodists and Baptists) and turned them into the largest churches in America. Camp meetings and protracted meetings were such successful instruments that even the most staid denominations, from Lutherans and Roman Catholics to Unitarians, found themselves flirting with their use. The more conservative ministers from the older established churches condemned the practice. They saw revivalism as sacrificing sound biblical interpretation and theology in favor of feelings and emotionalism. More important, most evangelists operated apart from the control of these religious authorities, and their activity, in effect, subverted the traditional religious order.

The critics were, of course, accurate in their assessment of the revival movements, but the public did not care. They had not previously responded to the religious authorities and possessed commitments neither to seminary-trained ministers nor to the traditions they represented. The evangelists had discovered what leaders of new religious movements have realized ever since, that in an open society, many avenues exist that bypass existing religious structures and grant immediate access to a waiting public.

Fanny Crosby, blind from birth, wrote hundreds of America's most beloved hymns.

Dwight L. Moody, the most prominent Christian evangelist in the last quarter of the nineteenth century.

New forms of revivalism would arise as the nation grew and changed (although the older forms hung on in the countryside). In the decades following the Civil War, the great urban tabernacles that seated thousands of people appeared, and professional evangelists who devoted themselves full time to holding protracted meetings in urban settings arose. During the 1880s and 1890s, evangelists such as Dwight L. Moody (1837–1899) and J. Wilbur Chapman (1859–1918) were but the most successful of many evangelists that toured the country. They were generally accompanied by a team who performed all the tasks associated with a successful revival meeting from advanced publicity to music to fund-raising. By the end of the century, the development of a successful career in evangelism had become big business.

Increasingly, the more successful evangelist teamed with an equally talented musician, and often the pair became as famous as either individually. Moody traveled with Ira Sankey (1840–1908), and Homer Rodeheaver per-

Moody's camp grounds in Northfield, Massachusetts, became one of the most popular sites for summer gatherings of evangelical Christians.

Ira S. Sankey, evangelist Dwight L. Moody's song leader.

formed the same function in the next generation for Billy Sunday. Chapman himself wrote a number of gospel songs and compiled several hymn books. During an evangelistic campaign, the musicians expanded the effect of their presence by working with local church musicians to improve their performances. In the late twentieth century, Billy Graham carried on the tradition by teaming with George Beverly Shea, whose solos were always singled out as a highlight of Graham's services.

OH- CHRISTIAN -

HAVE YOU ANY SCARS TO SHOW IN THIS CONFLICT?

WHEN A WAR IS OVER HEROES HAVE SCARS TO SHOW AND THEY ARE PROUD OF THEM!

~A THIRD SAYS-"BILLY" MY OLD BACKS HAD A POWERFUL CRICK IN IT EVER SINCE ANTIETAM!"

ONE ROLLS BACK HIS SLEEVE AND SHOWS A GUNSHOT WOUND,

~ANOTHER PULLS DOWN HIS COLLAR TO SHOW A SCAR ON HIS NECK

CHRIST HAS SCARS TO SHOW!— SCARS ON HIS BROW— AND ON HIS HANDS AND FEET! HE WILL PULL ASIDE HIS ROBE OF ROYALTY AND SHOW THE SCAR ON HIS SIDE!

WHAT SCARS HAVE YOU TO SHOW?

Billy Sunday was the most popular evangelist and voice of fundamentalism at the beginning of the twentieth century.

As the modernist perspective found its strength in the cities, the urban evangelists took the lead in opposing the churches' shift away from the task of converting the unsaved in favor of social activism. The effort to convert the masses of people who were crowding into American cities had to take precedence over programs to clear up the urban areas, however laudable. Possibly the

Billy and "Ma" Sunday.

most prominent evangelist of the era was Billy Sunday (1862–1935), a former baseball player who attacked the cities with his flamboyant style. And his success in the Midwest would be matched on the West Coast by the equally flamboyant female evangelist Aimee Semple McPherson (1890–1944), who made her headquarters at Angelus Temple in Los Angeles.

Catherine Booth, co-founder of the Salvation Army, was an advocate of women's leadership in the church.

William Booth, co-founder of the Salvation Army, responded to modernist social concerns with a conservative approach.

CONSERVATIVE THEOLOGY

The evangelistic thrust symbolized by revivalism provided the heart of American religious life through the nineteenth century. The evangelist called people to immediate conversion and a change of life. The call to conversion was based upon the authority of the Bible and invited people to a salvation experience with the God of the Bible and his Virgin-born son, Jesus. Following their experience of salvation, new converts were invited to a life of studying the Bible, mastering its contents, and following its precepts. The whole of Protestantism had been built on the appeal to the authority of Scripture alone made by Martin Luther against the authority of the pope in the sixteenth century.

Any attack upon the Bible, conservatives believed, such as that made by the German critics and their students, eroded the foundation of the average Protestant Christian's faith. And that attack came from various directions.

Lecturer Robert G. Ingersoll emerged as the most popular spokesperson for atheism in the nineteenth century.

Adopting a skeptical scientific view, critics suggested that the accounts of miracles in the Bible should be judged by our knowledge of what is and is not possible. Stories that include impossibilities, such as floating ax-heads and people walking on water, could not be taken literally. And the beloved stories of the Bible such as the Garden of Eden, the Tower of Babel, and the universal flood were little more than historically unconfirmed folktales. Further, they questioned the integrity of the text, especially the first five books of the Bible. The so-called books of Moses were not simple writings of a single inspired author, whether Moses or someone else, but an edited text, stitched together from previously existing texts.

The most skeptical freethinkers of the era, of course, took the arguments much further and suggested not only that the Bible was a flawed book, but that it actually taught immorality. Atheists suggested that the practices of God's people in the ancient wars, the immorality of prominent biblical characters, such as David, and even the teachings of Jesus implied in the cursing of the fig tree were not worthy of the allegiance of modern people. Popular orator Robert G. Ingersoll (1833–1899), author of the often-reprinted lecture "Some Mistakes of Moses," found a popular audience for his religious dissent in the

Robert G. Ingersoll addressing a crowd.

late nineteenth century. Ingersoll and his colleagues provided the basis of organized unbelief in the twentieth century.

Many theological teachers attempted to ignore the German biblical critics and the challenge to biblical authority posed by the likes of Ingersoll with simple assertions of Christian tradition. Given the continued expansion of the churches throughout the nineteenth century, many felt that traditional

Christianity was being confirmed in its success. However, a small group of theologians at Princeton Theological Seminary took upon themselves the task of defining and defending biblical authority. Professors A. A. Hodge (1823–1886) and Benjamin Warfield (1851–1921) rejected Darwin's findings and the work of the German critics and, in their 1881 paper "Inspiration," defined what they saw as the plenary verbal inspiration of the Bible that left the church with an inerrant (as to matters of science and history) and infallible (when speaking on spiritual and religious issues) text. They were not unaware of the problems with the biblical text raised by its critics, but they claimed that these were problems of interpretation that did not directly challenge the sufficiency of the Scripture. There were, for example, apparent internal contradictions in the text, but these were resolved when one studied the Bible. And in the end, there could be no real contradiction between true science and God's revelation in the Bible.

Many welcomed the Princeton position. The Presbyterians, in particular, adopted it as part of their official teachings in 1892. Throughout the twentieth century a number of conservative Christian bodies would include language on the plenary and verbal inspiration and/or the infallibility and inerrancy of the Bible in their doctrinal statements. The Princeton position would find its greatest acceptance among those churches also rooted in the Presbyterian Calvinist theology, primarily the Congregationalists and Baptists.

The Princeton theology was by no means universally accepted, and many conservative Christian leaders, especially in the Wesleyan tradition, explicitly rejected its attempt to codify the nature of inspiration with terms such as inerrancy and infallibility. However, it attained an importance far beyond the numbers who accepted it when, after World War I, the Presbyterian and Baptist Churches became the two bodies in which the modernist controversy became most intense.

FUNDAMENTALISM

While modernism was growing in strength, another new movement was spreading through American churches, the dispensational theology of Irish minister John Nelson Darby (1800–1882). Darby had left the Church of Ireland to become the founder of a new free church movement that came to be known as the Plymouth Brethren (an informal name derived from the group meeting at Plymouth, England). While the movement embodied several distinctive features, it was the unique approach to biblical interpretation advocated by Darby that caught on with a broad base of Protestant Christians.

Darby advocated that the Bible should be divided into a number of historical eras, which he termed dispensations. Each dispensation was defined by a change in the manner in which God chose to relate to his people. Such

The Modern Fundamentalist movement can be traced to the efforts of Irish preacher John Nelson Darby.

changes were marked by specific stories in the Bible, for example, the fall of Adam into sin, God's making a covenant with Abraham, the giving of the law to Moses, and preeminently, the resurrection of Christ. According to Darby, we currently live in the dispensation of grace inaugurated by Christ's resurrection, a condition that is due to last until he soon comes again.

While the dispensational approach was not developed specifically to answer the attack of biblical critics, American Christians stinging under that attack found in dispensationalism the solution to many of these criticisms. Darby's system assigned each book of the Bible to its proper dispensation, and many of the seeming contradictions of Scripture disappeared in the understanding that what was operative in one dispensation would no longer be acceptable in the next.

Dispensationalism was also generally wedded to a belief in the imminent Second Coming of Christ, who would, following his return, establish his reign of a thousand years on earth, the millennium. This belief is generally referred to as premillennialism. Those who accepted dispensationalism also tended to develop an expectancy of Christ's soon return. Believing in Christ's return, dispensationalists also looked for signs indicating that they were living in the last days. While reminding his followers that no one knew the date, Jesus also pointed to signs that would be associated with that return. Unfortunately, the signs, for example, wars and rumors of wars, have been so general that believers in almost every generation have been able to identify with them.

As early as 1869, an interdenominational group of ministers (primarily from Calvinist denominations) who held to both the inspiration of the Bible and the imminent Second Coming began to hold annual meetings to discuss the essentials of the faith. In 1883, these meetings were moved to Niagara-on-the-Lake, Ontario, and were henceforth known as the "Niagara Conference on Prophecy." In 1890, the Niagara Conference passed a fourteen-point statement of what it considered the essential, fundamental affirmations of Christianity. Both the inerrancy of the Bible and the imminent Second Coming were included.

The Niagara Statement would become the manifesto of what would emerge as a new interdenominational movement defending traditional fundamentals of Protestantism and opposed to the divergences proposed by the modernists. The Niagara position would be embodied in several schools, such as the Moody Bible Institute and the Bible Institute of Los Angeles, designed to train a new generation of leaders, as well as in many less formal Bible conferences that proliferated around the country. Over the next decades, those who championed the Niagara perspective would come to be known as fundamentalists.

The fundamentalist movement became more defined in the years immediately prior to World War I. First, C. I. Scofield (1843–1921) published his famous reference Bible, which integrated dispensationalism into its numerous annotations. Then, with money supplied by Lyman and Milton Steward, two wealthy California Presbyterians, the booklets *The Fundamentals*, containing essays by leading conservative pastors and scholars, were distributed freely to thousands of pastors.

Through the 1890s and into the new century, conservatives in the major denominations were increasingly scandalized by the books, lectures, and public statements of those who challenged what they saw as Christian essentials. Periodically, conservatives called for the dismissal of pastors, denominational officials, and college and seminary professors who had made incriminating admissions, but in spite of occasional conservative successes, modernism continued to grow. But after the hiatus of World War I, fundamentalist leaders gained a new sense of solidarity and moved to root modernists out of positions of authority in both the Presbyterian Church and the Northern Baptist Convention.

Both Baptists and Presbyterians were called to action by Harry Emerson Fosdick (1878–1969), a Baptist serving as pastor of the prominent Madison Avenue Presbyterian Church in New York City. In 1922, Fosdick preached the sermon, later reprinted and widely distributed, "Shall the Fundamentalists Win?" He challenged belief in the Virgin birth of Christ, the inerrancy of the Bible, and the imminent Second Coming while calling for greater tolerance

THE FUNDAMENTALS
Volume I, Chapter I

THE VIRGIN BIRTH OF CHRIST

By the Rev. Prof. James Orr, D.D.,
United Free Church College, Glasgow, Scotland

It is well known that the last ten or twenty years have been marked by a determined assault upon the truth of the Virgin birth of Christ. In the year 1892 a great controversy broke out in Germany, owing to the refusal of a pastor named Schrempf to use the Apostles' Creed in baptism because of disbelief in this and other articles. Schrempf was deposed, and an agitation commenced against the doctrine of the Virgin birth which has grown in volume ever since. Other tendencies, especially the rise of an extremely radical school of historical criticism, added force to the negative movement. The attack is not confined, indeed, to the article of the Virgin birth. It affects the whole supernatural estimate of Christ— His life, His claims, His sinlessness, His miracles, His resurrection from the dead. But the Virgin birth is assailed with special vehemence, because it is supposed that the evidence for this miracle is more easily got rid of than the evidence for public facts, such as the resurrection. The result is that in very many quarters the Virgin birth of Christ is openly treated as a fable. Belief in it is scouted as unworthy of the twentieth century intelligence. The methods of the oldest opponents of Christianity are revived, and it is likened to the Greek and Roman stories, coarse and vile, of heroes who had gods for their fathers. A special point is made of the silence of Paul, and of the other writings of the New Testament, on this alleged wonder.

THE UNHAPPIEST FEATURE.

It is not only, however, in the circles of unbelief that the Virgin birth is discredited; in the church itself the habit is spreading of casting doubt upon the fact, or at least of regarding it as no essential part of Christian faith. This is the unhappiest feature in this unhappy controversy. Till recently no one dreamed of denying that, in the sincere profession of Christianity, this article, which has stood from the beginning in the forefront of all the great creeds of Christendom, was included. Now it is different. The truth and value of the article of the Virgin birth are challenged. The article, it is affirmed, did not belong to the earliest Christian tradition, and the evidence for it is not strong. Therefore, let it drop.

. . .

THE CASE STATED.

It is the object of this paper to show that those who take the lines of denial on the Virgin birth just sketched do great injustice to the evidence and importance of the doctrine they reject. The evidence, if not of the same public kind as that for the resurrection, is far stronger than the objector allows, and the fact denied enters far more vitally into the essence of the Christian faith than he supposes. Placed in its right set-ring among the other truths, of the Christian religion, it is not only no stumbling-block to faith, but is felt to fit in with self-evidencing power into the connection of these other truths, and to furnish the very explanation that is needed of Christ's holy and supernatural Person. The ordinary Christian is a witness here. In reading the Gospels, he feels no incongruity in passing from the narratives of the Virgin birth to the wonderful story of Christ's life in the chapters that follow, then from these to the pictures of Christ's divine dignity given in John and Paul. The whole is of one piece: the Virgin birth is as natural at the beginning of the life of such an One—the divine Son—as the resurrection is at the end. And the more closely the matter is considered, the stronger does this impression grow. It is only when the scriptural conception of Christ is parted with that various difficulties and doubts come in.

between fundamentalists and modernists. Fosdick was met with an angry reaction that soon forced him out of his pastorate. He would later become pastor of the new Riverside Church in New York City, an independent congregation that continues as a bastion of liberal Protestantism.

The Fosdick controversy began what were regular battles at every gathering of the Presbyterians' General Assembly and the Baptists' Triennial Convention. In the midst of these skirmishes, the focus of the battle suddenly moved into the Deep South, to the small community of Dayton, Tennessee. One of the most famous politicians of the era, three-time presidential candidate William Jennings Bryan (1860–1925), agreed to lead the prosecution of a high school teacher accused of violating Tennessee's law against teaching the idea of evolution. The teacher was defended by freethinking attorney Clarence Darrow (1857–1938).

The so-called monkey trial turned into a debate over evolution and the Bible. At the end of the intense confrontation, both sides claimed victory,

William Jennings Bryan, politician and lawyer and defender of the Fundamentalist cause at the famous "Monkey Trial" in Dayton, Tennessee.

Lawyer Clarence Darrow defended Tennessee schoolteacher John Scopes at the famous "Monkey Trial."

although the teacher was found guilty. Bryan appeared to have been broken by Darrow's broadsides and died shortly thereafter. Others argued that Darrow's arguments had made fundamentalism an indefensible position, a view seemingly confirmed by later generations.

Charles E. Fuller was the leading fundamentalist radio minister during the middle of the twentieth century.

In the years after the trial, fundamentalists in both the Baptist and Presbyterian Churches realized that they had lost control of the vital denominational structures—the seminaries, the denominational leadership, and the mission boards (that commissioned home and foreign missionaries). Through the 1930s, they came to grips with their defeat and assayed their chances of ever making a comeback. Concluding that their losses were permanent, many separated from their denominations and formed new fundamentalist ones. The General Association of Regular Baptists, the Conservative Baptist Association, the Orthodox Presbyterian Church, and the Bible Presbyterian Church are the primary results of the conservative leave-taking.

The end of the modernist-fundamentalist war came just as another war loomed on the horizon. When World War II began, the churches turned their attention to the war effort. However, a bridge had been crossed, and the last half of the twentieth century would be a time for reorganizing the whole Christian community in light of the division that occurred.

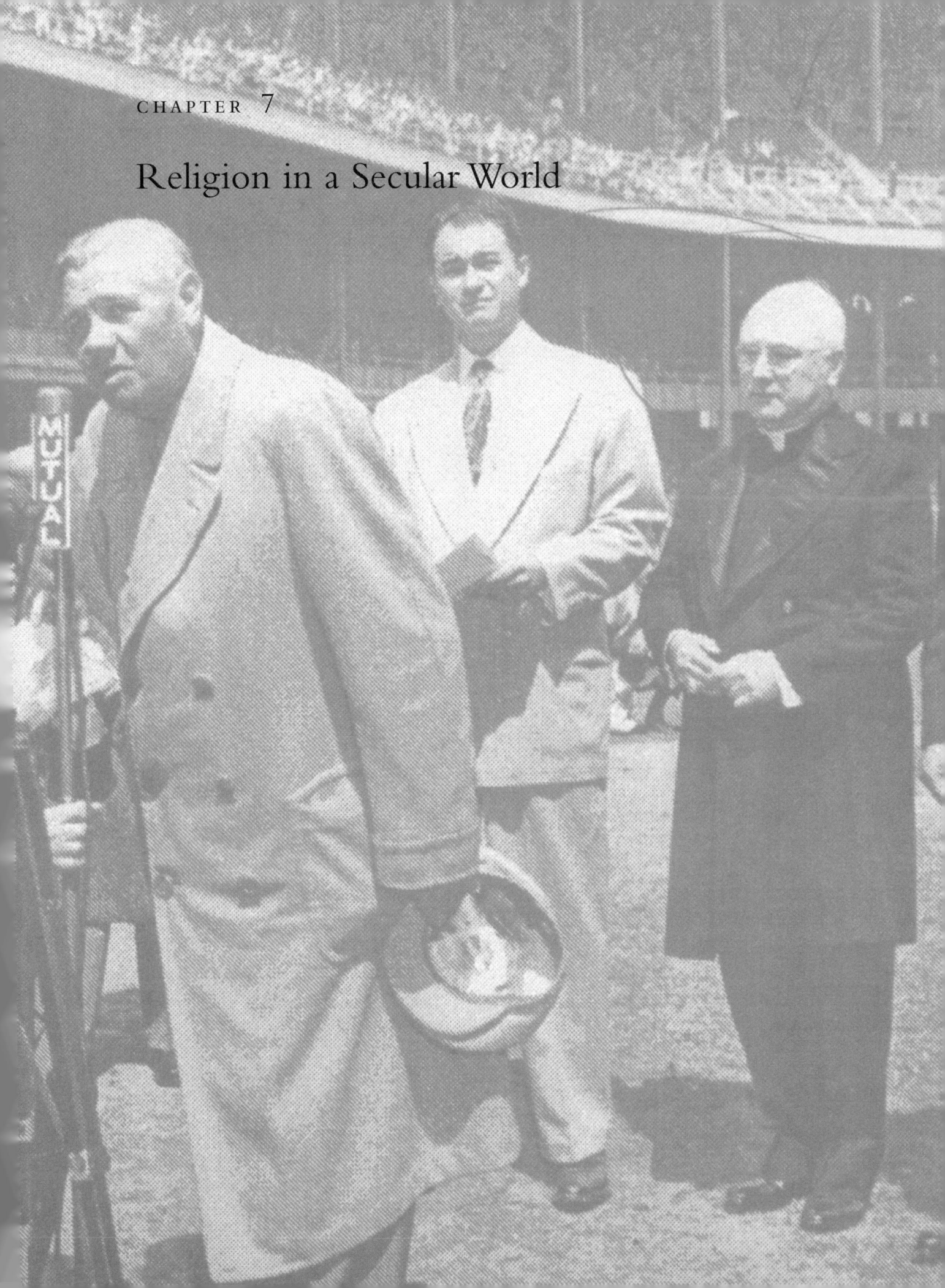

CHAPTER 7

Religion in a Secular World

Many observers have suggested that the great fact of contemporary life in the West is the growth of secularism and point to various trends in society as evidential. Most important, no single religious vision dominates either society as a whole or even individual countries. Rather, contemporaries are being shaped more by science; where religion continues to exist, it must reconstitute itself in a manner compatible with that science. At the same time, religion has relinquished its place in public forums, no longer supplying either the language or the context in which public discourse, be it politics or pop culture, proceeds. The price of separating church and state and of allowing so many different religions to exist peacefully side-by-side has been to push religious language, if not religion itself, to the periphery of the important processes of decision making.

At the same time, religion has not withered as many observers had predicted it would at the beginning of the twentieth century. Quiet to the contrary, one could hardly imagine a more vigorous religious community than that existing in America at the end of the twentieth century. Never in the history of America had the church claimed the allegiance of so many people (whether one considered percentages or membership figures), raised more money, or been more visibly present. In a land with no state church to speak for the people, the great majority of people have affiliated with one of the more than 2,000 different religious groups from which they could choose, continue to respect religious leaders, and freely acknowledge their faith. The coexistence of a pervasive secularism and a heightened religiosity have sent observers back to the drawing board in their attempts to redefine the nature of religion in the modern world and to discern its likely future. The half century of vigorous change in the decades following World War II provides the material for the reassessment. The religious ferment at the end of the century radically remade the religious landscape that was present at midcentury.

A SECULAR CONTEXT

While secularism has a life of its own propelled by the growing authority given to science in modern life, the twentieth century has been marked by the presence of activist groups characterized by unbelief, associations of believ-

*The National Cathedral
(Episcopal), Washington, D.C.*

ers who have asserted that they have no need for religion. A positive fulfilling life is possible without a belief in God (atheism), or religious sentiments (rationalism), or supernaturalism as a guiding principle for behavior (humanism). American atheists, rationalists, and humanists can trace their lineage to two Revolutionary War heroes, Ethan Allen (1738–1789), who shortly before his death released *Reason the Only Oracle of Man* (1785), and Thomas Paine (1737–1809), author of *The Age of Reason* (1794). Atheism and its cousin agnosticism flourished in the nineteenth century, although its leading exponents were often the victims of censorship, especially when their ideas were pushed into a questioning of sexual mores. Freethinkers took the lead in challenging bans on public discussions of sexuality, birth control, and the status of women.

While several associations and numerous periodicals emerged to serve the freethinking community, it would not be until the last half of the twentieth century that stable groups would arise that were able to appeal to middle America. Among the first atheist organizations to make an impact upon public life was the Freethinkers of America founded in 1915. In the 1920s, Joseph Lewis (1889–1968) assumed the presidency of the group and turned it into an organ for his own fight with religion embodied in his two most famous books, *The Bible Unmasked* (1926) and *Atheism* (1930). He also founded the Eugenic Publishing Company to disseminate books on sexology and recruited a number of physicians to write books that he issued as low-cost reading material. Lewis, himself a Jew, was among the first to write a popular book condemning the practice of circumcision, and he capped his long career with a deconstruc-

Revolutionary hero Thomas Paine stands at the fountainhead of modern rationalist/atheist thought.

tion of *The Ten Commandments* (1946). In the meantime, most of the up-and-coming voices of unbelief wrote for his magazine, the *Freethinker*.

Lewis's work, centered on New York City, set the stage for the arrival of a more broadly based atheist organization in the 1960s. At the beginning of the decade, a housewife in Baltimore, Maryland, filed a suit claiming that her son was a victim of religious discrimination at school because he had asked to be excused from participation in the daily exercises of Bible reading and the recitation of the Lord's Prayer, then a common practice in many public schools across the land. The case was decided in 1962, and the court ruled in her favor. Building on that decision, in 1963, she founded American Atheists, Inc., although due to some personal problems it would be the next decade before the organization became an effective voice for the cause. However, beginning in 1977, Madalyn Murray O'Hare (1919–1995?) emerged as an effective propagandist for atheism. She filed lawsuits seeking the removal of religion from various government contexts, frequently appeared on radio and television, occasionally debating Christian ministers, and built an effective national organization.

O'Hare had an abrasive personality that drove many people initially attracted to her ideas from her organization. Several other national atheist organizations, such as the Freedom from Religion Foundation and the Atheist Alliance, resulted from the reorganization of former members. In spite of her flaws, atheists are in debt to O'Hare for placing unbelief on the country's agenda and moving the debate over the existence of God and the government's tacit backing of Christian activities into the public consciousness. Since her disappearance under most mysterious circumstances in 1995, no other atheist has been able to claim her unique public role.

Growing up beside atheism, and sharing much of its perspective, humanism is distinguished by its emphasis upon building an ethical system without appeal to divine revelation and by its generally more favorable attitude toward "religion." Humanism traces its history not so much to the rejection of religion as to the radical religious perspective of Deism and the Free Religious Association, formed by the most liberal wing of Unitarians in the late nineteenth century. Among the early spokespersons of humanism were Unitarian ministers John H. Dietrich (1858–1957) and Curtis W. Reese (1887–1961), both midwesterners. At the end of the 1920s, the first humanist societies were founded in New York by Charles Francis Potter (1885–1962) and in California by Theodore Curtis Abell.

The cause of humanism was given a significant boost in 1933 with the issuance of the "Humanist Manifesto," a statement of the humanist perspective and an outline of humanist ethics that was signed by a number of leading public figures, such as philosopher John Dewey (1859–1952). The manifesto called for an ethic aimed at creating a complete realization of human personality. Religion was seen as a tool for realizing the highest values in life. As other humanist societies were founded, they came together in the American Humanist Association (AHA), founded in 1941.

Among humanists are those who see humanism as a religious philosophy, if a nontheistic one, and the AHA has what amounts to a ministerial training program leading to certification as a "celebrant" who can lead humanist organizations, officiate as humanist services, perform marriage and burial services, and counsel members. Others have rejected that idea and see humanism as a nontheistic philosophy but also assert that it is logically the opposite of religion. They have given their interpretation the name "secular humanism." At the end of the 1970s, philosopher Paul Kurtz (b.1925), one of the most active leaders of the AHA, left to found the Council for Secular Humanism and has subsequently emerged as a spokesperson for the more militantly antireligious wing of the humanist movement.

Kurtz had been a leading force in the writing and publication of and the gathering of signatories for the 1973 "Humanist Manifesto II," a document seen as reaffirming and updating the original "Humanist Manifesto." (In 1980, he followed with "A Secular Humanist Declaration."). He also used his position in the humanist movement to assist the formation of the Committee for the Scientific Investigation of the Claims of the Paranormal (CSICOP), an organization calling into question the burst of interest in psychic, occult, and related phenomena (from flying saucers to psychic hotlines). Kurtz believes that the growing popularity of belief in psychic reality is irrational and dangerous to democratic society, and CSICOP has crusaded against it.

A THEOLOGICAL RENAISSANCE

In the 1960s, organized unbelief received a most unexpected boost from a group of theologians, radical amid the postwar theological renaissance, who proclaimed the death of God. The death of God movement came and went within a single decade, but it called the public's attention to the changing times and the breakdown of the older world of secure theological affirmations. The death of God theologians were not atheists in the traditional sense, although many perceived them that way, but they held much in common with the community of unbelief in calling the larger religious world to the widespread loss of a traditional religious experience of God even by many church members. The seriousness with which the proclamation of the death of God was received, even by those who vehemently rejected it, alerted church members that change was in the air.

HUMANIST MANIFESTO I

The time has come for widespread recognition of the radical changes in religious beliefs throughout the modern world. The time is past for mere revision of traditional attitudes. Science and economic change have disrupted the old beliefs. Religions the world over are under the necessity of coming to terms with new conditions created by a vastly increased knowledge and experience. In every field of human activity, the vital movement is now in the direction of a candid and explicit humanism. In order that religious humanism may be better understood we, the undersigned, desire to make certain affirmations which we believe the facts of our contemporary life demonstrate.

There is great danger of a final, and we believe fatal, identification of the word religion with doctrines and methods which have lost their significance and which are powerless to solve the problem of human living in the Twentieth Century. Religions have always been means for realizing the highest values of life. Their end has been accomplished through the interpretation of the total environing situation (theology or world view), the sense of values resulting therefrom (goal or ideal), and the technique (cult), established for realizing the satisfactory life. A change in any of these factors results in alteration of the outward forms of religion. This fact explains the changefulness of religions through the centuries. But through all changes religion itself remains constant in its quest for abiding values, an inseparable feature of human life.

Today man's larger understanding of the universe, his scientific achievements, and deeper appreciation of brotherhood, have created a situation which requires a new statement of the means and purposes of religion. Such a vital, fearless, and frank religion capable of furnishing adequate social goals and personal satisfactions may appear to many people as a complete break with the past. While this age does owe a vast debt to the traditional religions, it is none the less obvious that any religion that can hope to be a synthesizing and dynamic force for today must be shaped for the needs of this age. To establish such a religion is a major necessity of the present. It is a responsibility which rests upon this generation. We therefore affirm the following:

FIRST: Religious humanists regard the universe as self-existing and not created.

SECOND: Humanism believes that man is a part of nature and that he has emerged as a result of a continuous process.

THIRD: Holding an organic view of life, humanists find that the traditional dualism of mind and body must be rejected.

FOURTH: Humanism recognizes that man's religious culture and civilization, as clearly depicted by anthropology and history, are the product of a gradual development due to his interaction with his natural environment and with his social heritage. The individual born into a particular culture is largely molded by that culture.

FIFTH: Humanism asserts that the nature of the universe depicted by modern science makes unacceptable any supernatural or cosmic guarantees of human values. Obviously humanism does not deny the possibility of realities as yet undiscovered, but it does insist that the way to determine the existence and value of any and all realities is by means of intelligent inquiry and by the assessment of their relations to human needs. Religion must formulate its hopes and plans in the light of the scientific spirit and method.

SIXTH: We are convinced that the time has passed for theism, deism, modernism, and the several varieties of "new thought."

SEVENTH: Religion consists of those actions, purposes, and experiences which are humanly significant. Nothing human is alien to the religious. It includes labor, art, science, philosophy, love, friendship, recreation—all that is in its degree expressive of intelligently satisfying human living. The distinction between the sacred and the secular can no longer be maintained.

EIGHTH: Religious Humanism considers the complete realization of human personality to be the end of man's life and seeks its development and fulfillment in the here and now. This is the explanation of the humanist's social passion.

NINTH: In the place of the old attitudes involved in worship and prayer the humanist finds his religious emotions expressed in a heightened sense of personal life and in a cooperative effort to promote social well-being.

TENTH: It follows that there will be no uniquely religious emotions and attitudes of the kind hitherto associated with belief in the supernatural.

ELEVENTH: Man will learn to face the crises of life in terms of his knowledge of their naturalness and probability. Reasonable and manly attitudes will be fostered by education and supported by custom. We assume that humanism will take the path of social and mental hygiene and discourage sentimental and unreal hopes and wishful thinking.

TWELFTH: Believing that religion must work increasingly for joy in living, religious humanists aim to foster the creative in man and to encourage achievements that add to the satisfactions of life.

THIRTEENTH: Religious humanism maintains that all associations and institutions exist for the fulfillment of human life. The intelligent evaluation, transformation, control, and direction of such associations and institutions with a view to the enhancement of human life is the purpose and program of humanism. Certainly religious institutions, their ritualistic forms, ecclesiastical methods, and communal activities must be reconstituted as rapidly as experience allows, in order to function effectively in the modern world.

FOURTEENTH: The humanists are firmly convinced that existing acquisitive and profit-motivated society has shown itself to be inadequate and that a radical change in methods, controls, and motives must be instituted. A socialized and cooperative economic order must be established to the end that the equitable distribution of the means of life be possible. The goal of humanism is a free and universal society in which people voluntarily and intelligently cooperate for the common good. Humanists demand a shared life in a shared world.

FIFTEENTH AND LAST: We assert that humanism will: (a) affirm life rather than deny it; (b) seek to elicit the possibilities of life, not flee from them; and (c) endeavor to establish the conditions of a satisfactory life for all, not merely for the few. By this positive morale and intention humanism will be guided, and from this perspective and alignment the techniques and efforts of humanism will flow.

So stand the theses of religious humanism. Though we consider the religious forms and ideas of our fathers no longer adequate, the quest for the good life is still the central task for mankind. Man is at last becoming aware that he alone is responsible for the realization of the world of his dreams, that he has within himself the power for its achievement. He must set intelligence and will to the task.

J. A. C. Fagginer Auer	William Floyd	Roy Wood Sellars
E. Burdette Backus	F. H. Hankins	Clinton Lee Scott
Harry Elmer Barnes	A. Eustace Haydon	Maynard Shipley
L. M. Birkhead	Llewellyn Jones	W. Frank Swift
Raymond B. Bragg	Robert Morss Lovett	V. T. Thayer
Edwin Arthur Burtt	Harold P. Marley	Eldred C. Vanderlaan
Ernest Caldecott	R. Lester Mondale	Joseph Walker
A. J. Carlson	Charles Francis Potter	Jacob J. Weinstein
John Dewey	John Herman Randall, Jr.	Frank S.C. Wicks
Albert C. Dieffenbach	Curtis W. Reese	David Rhys Williams
John H. Dietrich	Oliver L. Reiser	Edwin H. Williams
Bernard Fantus		

A statue of the Rev. Norman Vincent Peale now stands at the Marble Collegiate Church in New York City, where he preached for more than half a century.

Within the mainline churches, World War II proved the catalyst for change. The larger denominations entered the war years firmly in the hands of the modernists. They were firm believers that they were building the kingdom of God and that a bright future of progress into a more perfect society was occurring. The tragedies witnessed as a result of the Nazi Holocaust shook many out of their liberal ideals and reintroduced a new appreciation for the power of evil and depth of human sin. Much of the faith in the liberal agenda had already been destroyed in Europe by World War I, and on the Continent, theological reconstruction had already begun. The challenge of science to religion remained, but the challenge to faith presented by the enormity of Europe's devastation further destroyed the modernist theological world.

The combined reaction to the undeniable realities of modern life began in Europe, and following World War II, it was to Europe that Americans turned for some theological light. During the 1950s and 1960s, Germany in particular nurtured a community of theologians then coming into their maturity. Leading the field was Karl Barth (1886–1968), a Reformed theologian teaching at the University of Basel. His perspective, called neoorthodoxy, was built around the proclamation of a sovereign transcendent God, a new appreciation

(left) Edgar Sheffield
Brightman, early-
twentieth-century
Methodist theologian.

(left) German immigrant
Paul Tillich completed
his outstanding career
as a Christian
philosopher and
theologian in America.

(right) Reinhold Niebuhr
emerged in the middle of
the twentieth century as
America's leading liberal
Protestant theologian.

of the Bible (not as the word of God but as the instrument through which the word of God reached humans), and a theology freed from the changing findings of science. His work was joined by that of colleagues Emil Brunner (1889–1966), Paul Tillich (1886–1965), and biblical scholar Rudolf Bultmann (1884–1976), who called for a radical demythologizing of the Bible. By no means did these German theologians speak with a united voice, but each was seen as an outstanding thinker providing guidance for a theological community cast adrift. It did not take long for the American theological community to respond, and soon thinkers such as Union Theological Seminary ethicist Reinhold Niebuhr (1892–1971) emerged form the relative obscurity of their professorial study.

Radical Episcopal bishop James A. Pike (standing).

The memorable generation of theological voices in the postwar generation drew upon the century of critical theological and biblical work that had taken place in scholarly circles but had been largely uncommunicated to the great mass of church members. It became the task of a new generation of pastors to address to their parishioners the practical implications of the theological changes. A few churchmen took the lead in plainly stating what was occurring, none so articulate as Episcopal bishop James A. Pike (1913–1969), whose own grasp of the meaning of the new theology led to several books expressing his own doubts about some key traditional beliefs, such as the Trinity and the uniqueness of Christ. In the face of mounting criticism from his fellow bishops, in 1968 he resigned his position and moved to create a ministry to those like himself on the margin of church life, a ministry that never matured due to his untimely death the next year.

By the 1980s, the work of the postwar theologians had been absorbed, and a new liberal Protestant community emerged. Still somewhat settled on Main Street U.S.A., it no longer had the complacency of former generations. It had found a means of reaffirming the symbols of the heritage it represented but did so in a new context that recognized the ever-changing world, understood its own limitations and prospects, resided in a pluralistic environment, and reconciled to the constant need to re-create itself.

THE ECUMENICAL MOVEMENT

Concurrently with the theological renaissance, many church leaders responded to another problem, the hindrance to the church's mission caused by its fragmentation into numerous denominations. The problems of denominationalism had been raised by missionaries who saw the destructive reactions to the attempts to export centuries-old denominational squabbles to foreign lands. The early response to the problems of a divided Protestantism had been the formation of the Federal Council of Churches in 1908 by thirty-three of the most prominent Protestant bodies, the Southern Baptist Convention being the most notable nonmember. Through the 1930s, the Council would become the home of modernist thought, and critics would find ample ammunition for their ongoing war with liberalism in the socialist and pacifist pronouncements of prominent church leaders associated with the Council's program.

World War II exposed all of the weaknesses in the Federal Council structure, as well as the thought that undergirded it. At the same time, Protestant Christians were discovering new resources across denominational lines as they combined efforts to lead in the reconstruction of Europe following the war. While the hope of a world progressing into the kingdom of God had been lost, a new hope emerged, the hope of a reunited ecumenical church that could, it was believed, provide a unitive and more effective witness in the world.

The hope of a reunited Protestantism swept through Protestantism in the 1950s, its initial manifestation being the participation of many of the denominations of the Federal Council in the formation of the World Council of Churches in 1848. Two years later the Federal Council led in the complete reorganization of ecumenical life that included its replacement with a new organization, the National Council of Churches of Christ in the U.S.A. The ecumenical fervor led numerous member churches to enter into merger negotiations that would produce notable new ecclesiastical bodies such as the United Church of Christ (1957), the United Methodist Church (1968), the Presbyterian Church (U.S.A.) (1983), and the Evangelical Lutheran Church in America (1988).

By far the most far-reaching merger plan was put forth by the Consultation on Church Union (COCU) that called for the uniting of nine denominations including the Episcopal Church, the United Methodist Church, the three large African American Methodist bodies, the Presbyterian Church (U.S.A.), the Christian Church (Disciples of Christ), the International Council of Community Churches, and the United Church of Christ. Other churches have participated and sent official observers at various times since the inauguration of dialogue in the 1960s. While continuing into the new millen-

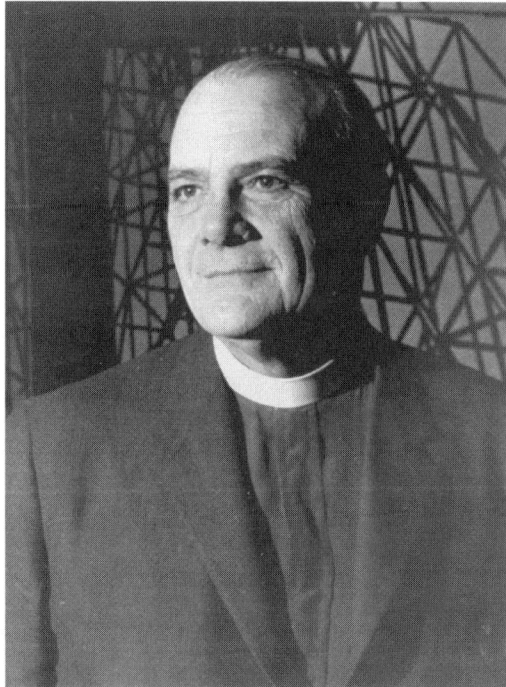

*Eugene Carson Blake,
Presbyterian minister and
ecumenical leader.*

nium, COCU has faced an uphill battle. While the ecumenical movement promoted a variety of successful church mergers, those have all been between closely related bodies with relatively few differences to resolve. COCU has proposed mergers across the major divisions in Protestantism but has been unable to overcome the more important denominational differences.

More important, it has more recently run into a new postecumenical world that has refocused its attention on other issues, as it has lost any faith in the promised benefits previously touted as coming through the amalgamation of denominations. Through the 1990s, ecumenical leaders have shown a noticeable lack of interest in promoting mergers and have remained content to work toward the building of positive relationships between church rather than a single united church body. Thus while COCU has continued, it now exists as a remnant of a movement that has itself passed from the scene.

THE SIXTIES

World War II called into question the liberal Protestant emphasis upon building the kingdom and social change leading toward a more just society. That program had been identified in many peoples' eyes with socialism and pacifism, both largely discredited philosophies by the 1950s. However, the commitments to social justice had been embedded in church documents,

Baptist minister Martin Luther King, Jr., led the civil rights movement of the 1960s.

most prominently the "Social Creed of the Churches," originally adopted by the Federal Council of Churches in 1908, and in statements by the larger Protestant denominations reflecting their particular social stance. The issue of social justice was taken off the back burner by the actions of a young Baptist minister in Montgomery, Alabama, in 1959. Martin Luther King, Jr., (1929–1968), responding to the refusal of an African American woman to give up her seat in the white section of a bus, mobilized the black community in a bus boycott that in turn sparked the black community in the creation of what became the most significant social movement since the days of abolitionism. King integrated his traditional Baptist theology with the nonviolent civil disobedience approach to social change exemplified in the career of Mahatma Gandhi. The formula worked.

Father Divine was a potent African American leader whose work heralded the changes of the 1960s.

The civil rights movement challenged the church at every level. King's own denomination, the National Baptist Convention in the U.S.A., refused to support his activism, and King's supporters were forced to pull out and organize separately as the Progressive National Baptist Convention. Black religious leaders across the South were called upon to choose to participate or continue to operate as they had previously, working for gradual change or placing their faith in the afterlife. White leaders in the South also had to choose, often forcing them to choose between their constituencies and their sense of moral rightness. Leaders in the North had to find their place in a movement led and directed by southern black leaders.

Over the 1960s, King's movement pushed through the Civil Rights Act and changed the racial makeup of the nation. The Civil War had ended slavery, but the hopes of freedom were largely blunted by the institution of segregation that found its way into the legal structure of the southern states in the last decades of the nineteenth century. The civil rights acts brought an end to those structures and, although they did not end racism, they altered relationships between the black and white communities in public space.

In the aftermath of the movement, churches across the United States have

Baptist minister Jesse Jackson rose to leadership in the civil rights movement following the death of Martin Luther King, Jr.

been forced to recognize the continuance of segregation in the existence of denominational bodies established in a segregated culture. On the one hand, numerous efforts have been made to end segregation, especially the disbanding of racially based structures within denominational bodies. At the same time, many black leaders found themselves empowered by the new liberties available as a result of legal changes and resisted the loss of power due to merging into desegregated church structures. Most church leaders, however, have supported

Black Muslim
spokesperson
Malcolm X was
assassinated soon
after his break
with the Nation
of Islam.

the pattern of efforts to find means of reconciling the black and white elements within their own community. During the 1980s, the Pentecostal community assumed a leadership role, recalling its own origins in the short-lived interracial revival in Los Angeles that gave it birth. Symbolic of their search to overcome racism was the disbanding of the Pentecostal Fellowship of North America and its replacement by the racially inclusive Pentecostal/Charismatic Church of North America.

The successes of the civil rights movement had repercussions far beyond the black community. It also empowered groups pushing for social change, the most important being women. On the heels of the civil rights movement, women emerged, and while they failed to past the Equal Rights Amendment to the Constitution, they have been able to pass numerous pieces of legislation that have embodied their major concerns. The churches also responded to their concerns. In these denominations, like the United Methodists, which already had provisions for women ministers, legislation was passed to recruit female clergy and to bring women into the church structure at every level from the bishopric and national agencies to the local church. Many denominations that had not previously allowed female clergy moved to admit women to ministerial status. The Episcopalians finally overcame their resistance after a highly publicized ordination service in 1974 in which four dissenting bishops ordained eleven women and forced their respective dioceses and the church as a whole to welcome them, which they did the following year. The Southern Baptist Convention and the Roman Catholic Church, the two largest denominations in America, while moving to empower lay women in many ways, remained resistant to attempts at introducing female clergy, a situation that shows no sign of changing in the near future.

By the 1980s, even the conservative Protestants learned of the effectiveness of organizing a national movement for support of their ideals. Their cause, the fight against abortion, blossomed as they aligned with Roman Catholics, a coalition made possible by the changes of Vatican II. Through the 1980s and into the 1990s, the antiabortion crusade mobilized a generation to defend the life of the unborn. It did not have the success of either the civil rights movement or the women's movement, but like them has been institutionalized to continue the battle into the next century.

Mahalia Jackson helped to shape the image of African Americans by introducing gospel music to white audiences.

The issue of homosexuality also emerged in the 1970s. Using the civil rights movements as a model, homosexuals found widespread support for their cause of ending discrimination against the members of their community. Such a presentation of their cause resonated with many church people who had worked on ending segregation and discrimination against females; however, the gay community ran into significant resistance over entrenched commitments by church leaders to the limitation of sexual relations to monogamous marriage. Liberal Protestants have found themselves pulled in separate directions on gay issues, and the larger churches ended the century conflicted over their response.

THE REBIRTH OF AMERICAN CATHOLICISM

American Catholicism largely disappeared from public life following the papal denunciation of "Americanism" in the 1890s. The church turned in upon itself and certainly, given the size of its membership, had plenty of work to do. Not the least of that work was the assistance to the large segment of first-generation Americans among its constituency. During the first half of the twentieth century, church leaders moved to create a Catholic subculture characterized by the promotion of parochial schools, a system of Catholic higher education focused in institutions such as Notre Dame and the Catholic University of America, a network of social service organizations, and a variety of programs of social action. While each of these structures made an impact on the larger culture, many Americans became conscious of the church's presence only on those rare occasions in which a Catholic ran for high office (as in the 1928 run for the presidency by Al Smith) and the regular pronouncements condemning books and movies by the Catholic League for Decency.

The end of the period of isolation for Roman Catholics in America began with World War II and the relationship developed with Protestants and others while working together on the common war effort. Then in the 1950s, scholars such as John Tracy Ellis and Thomas O'Dea launched an attack upon the Catholic abandonment of responsibility for American culture. Jesuits John Courtney Murray (1904–1967) and Gustave Weigel (1906–1954) took up the cause. These new forces found significant support in the 1960s with the pronouncements of the Second Vatican Council and the irenic spirit that made Pope John XXIII such a beloved leader far beyond the Roman Church.

The intellectual leadership of the scholars was supported on the more popular level by a spectrum of church leaders who found an audience far beyond the traditional Roman Catholic subculture. By far the most important of these was Fulton J. Sheen (1895–1979), who became a religious superstar with his several best-selling books and prime-time national television show. A first-rate scholar, Sheen also became a popular speaker on the *Catholic Hour* radio show in the 1930s. He jumped to television in 1951 for a successful six-year run, and after a hiatus, returned for several years in the mid 1960s.

The work of the scholars and popular spokespersons was made possible by a new forward-looking bishopric, most notable among them being Francis Joseph Spellman (1889–1967), named archbishop of New York in 1939 and cardinal in 1946. A friend of Pope Pius XII, he emerged from the war years as the most powerful Catholic bishop in the country. He used his power not only to bring the church out of its shell, but to begin to ask of the culture that it

Pope Leo XIII (1878–1903) struggled with the problems of Roman Catholicism, democracy, and the modern world.

Francis Cardinal Spellman (second from right) was the leading voice of Catholicism in the decades after World War II.

emerged in 1958 as Pope John XXIII. However, instead of sitting quietly in the Vatican City, he worked a revolution on the church by calling the first council of the bishops in over ninety years. Initially convening in 1962, the council would last through the remainder of his papacy. He would favor proposals that allowed the church to adapt to the modern age, and council leader responded with some radical changes in church life. Church members would feel the changes most with the dropping of the Latin mass in favor of local languages. For others, the most crucial statements concerned Catholic relationships with Protestants and the world's other religions.

American bishops and scholars played a leading role at the council, and the council's statements afterward sparked a revival in worship in the process of developing an English-language mass. Adding spice to the new situation, the council had also mandated the movement of the altar, the center of worship in any Roman Catholic church, in such a way that the priest faced the congre-

Imperial Wizard Hiram Wesley Evans and his Ku Klux Klan organization terrorized African Americans but also attacked Catholics.

With his brother Philip, social activist Daniel Berrigan represented one extreme of Catholic participation in the reshaping of Catholicism's American presence.

gation. An entirely new dynamic of parish life emerged. Although the church had to confront a dissident minority who demanded the retention of the Latin mass, in the end it gained far more than it lost when the most vocal of the dissidents (who also opposed other changes made by the council) broke away.

The council issued documents dealing with Protestants, their separated brethren, and with Jews, renouncing popular long-standing theological perspectives that placed special blame on the Jews for the death of Christ. Even prior to the council, John XXIII had founded the Secretariat for Christian Unity and invited official observers from eighteen denominations to the council. The council document placed the church squarely behind a new era of dialogue between Protestants and Catholics that affected every level of church life. At the international level, both the World Council of Churches and the leaders of the larger denominational families (beginning with Anglicans) opened formal dialogues with the Vatican. These highest level dialogues were reflected on the national and local level throughout the world. At the same time, the Vatican statements led to a new set of relationships between all Christians and the Jewish community, and mutual efforts emerged to educate Christians about the Holocaust, resolve issues over Israel, and recast traditional efforts at the conversion of Jews. Over the next decades, several of the larger Protestant churches publicly renounced any programs targeting Jews for conversion.

NEOEVANGELICALISM

Throughout the twentieth century, the Roman Catholic Church remained the largest in America, more than twice the size of its closest rivals, the Southern Baptist Church and the United Methodist Church. Thus, its return to an engagement of culture carried a certain element of triumphalism. In like measure, most of the liberal church bodies, united in the Federal (and later National) Council of Churches, were still enjoying a growth phase and approached the postwar world with a degree of optimism. Such could not be said of the older fundamentalist movement. It had lost severely during the 1930s, and no sooner had it recognized its defeat than fundamentalists began fighting among themselves.

The first battle concerned dispensationalism. The majority of fundamentalists were also dispensationalist, but that was certainly not the heritage of the Presbyterian Church and those conservative theologians at Princeton, such as J. Gresham Machen (1881–1937), who had carried the fundamentalist cause during its last phase. In 1932, Machen's vocal opposition to Hocking's *Re-Thinking Missions* became the catalyst of his break with the church, and with his supporters he established the Orthodox Presbyterian Church. He immediately ran into disagreement with a colleague, Carl McIntire (b.1906), who had

Phineas F. Bresee, founder of the Church of the Nazarene.

adopted a dispensational theology. Soon McIntire departed with his followers to found the Bible Presbyterian Church.

The second issue facing the fundamentalists concerned the relationship between those who left their denomination and those who remained. By no means did all fundamentalists move into the new denominational bodies. Many chose to remain and create pockets of conservative strength within the churches in which they had grown up. Those who did leave, however, tended to cite biblical passages about separation from heresy and unbelief as the rationale of their action, and many of these took the further step of condemning their former colleagues who chose not to separate from the "un-Christian" beliefs being advocated by the denominational leadership. Thus, three factions within the fundamentalist movement emerged: the separatists, the independents who had left the denominations but remained cordial to the conservatives, and the third group, the conservatives still within the denominations.

The separatists, the smallest of the three factions, launched a program of condemnation of both the liberal Protestant denominations and the conservatives who chose to remain within them. Carl McIntire emerged as the separatists' most visible leader, and in 1941, he led in the formation of the American Council of Christian Churches, which attempted to unite the remnant of true believers. McIntire also moved to locate fundamentalists in other lands and in 1948 launched the International Council of Christian Churches (ICCC).

Jerry Falwell, Independent Baptist and leading televangelist.

McIntire dominated both organizations for two decades but became the focus of a split in 1969, when he was removed from his leadership of the American Council. Pro-McIntire forces remained in control of the International Council. Anti-McIntire forces eventually created the World Council of Bible Believing Churches, while the International Council now works through the ICCC in America.

In the late 1930s, the nonseparatist fundamentalists and the conservative leaders still within the mainline churches engaged in a considerable amount of reevaluation of their position. They concluded that fundamentalism had been in error in its attempt to reject all of the changes that had occurred over the previous two generations. As a result, they were largely out of touch, and perseverance in their course could only continue to marginalize them. Out of these deliberation came the call for a new orientation that called for conservative Protestants, without dropping their allegiance to the Christian essentials and their zeal for world evangelism, to embrace contemporary scholarship and open a new era of engagement with the culture.

Those who embraced this message wanted to leave behind the image of the fighting fundamentalists who had cut themselves off from the new world of science and the larger Christian community, and they began to refer to themselves as evangelicals. While relatively small at their beginning, they felt that they had significant support within the Christian community and an important place in the future of the country. The initial conversations resulted in an organizational embodiment of the new evangelical movement in the National Association of Evangelicals. A new periodical, *Christianity Today*, soon emerged to serve the movement, and radio preacher Charles E. Fuller (1887–1969) gave the initial money to found a school, Fuller Theological Seminary in Pasadena, California, that quickly became the movement's intellectual center. Carl F. H. Henry (b.1919) and Edward John Carnell (1919–1967) took their place among the important theological voices of the next generation.

Evangelicalism's attempt to regain its position in American society was greatly aided by the emergence of a young, talented Baptist preacher. A former leader in the paradenominational Youth for Christ organization and then a college president, he suddenly became famous in 1949 when he traveled to Los Angeles to preach for two weeks at a revival meeting that lasted for two months. The following year he launched a radio program, *Hour of Decision*, and in 1952 gave up on his college job to become a full-time evangelist. It is unknown what would have happened to evangelicalism had William F. "Billy" Graham (b.1918) chosen a different trajectory. But there is little doubt that Graham won the masses to the movement. The integrity that came to the fore over his long ministry greatly enhanced evangelicalism's status in the land.

Evangelist Billy Graham counseled with many presidents, especially his fellow southern Baptist Jimmy Carter.

Graham will also be remembered for making the jump from radio to television. His first televised crusade was carried nationally from New York City during four months in 1957. Beginning with the organization of a conference on world evangelism in 1960 in Switzerland, he took the lead in calling together those with evangelical sentiments worldwide. And once on its feet, evangelicalism quickly made its presence felt. Liberal Protestantism had neglected evangelism through the mission field and had even redirected its energies on the mission field more toward social service. The results began to manifest in the 1960s, when church growth came to a halt and then began an alarming decline. In contrast, evangelicalism made evangelism both at home and abroad the major reason for its existence. It has continued to grow steadily.

Although it has yet to regain the strength and support it had prior to the 1930s, through the reconstituted evangelicalism, a traditional Protestantism has made an amazing comeback. It is now represented globally through the World Evangelical Fellowship that unites evangelicals in more than 100 countries.

THE CHARISMATIC MOVEMENT

Among the more unexpected movements to change the face of American Protestantism, in the 1970s both liberal and conservative churches found their set courses diverted by the emergence of pastors and groups of lay people advocating a new religious experience, speaking in tongues. Claiming authority from the New Testament description of Pentecost (Acts 2) and Paul's Epistle to the Corinthians (I Cor. 12), the new charismatics (from the Greek word for gift) suggested that the American church suffered from the lack of the presence of the spiritual gifts that so vivified the early church. The movement was rooted in the Full Gospel Businessmen's Fellowship, an organization formed in the 1960s that sponsored prayer luncheons and other gatherings for men who had found new life in charismatic spirituality. Once the charismatic life was transferred to the churches, it quickly spread through all of the large denominations, and national fellowships related to the larger denominational families (Presbyterians, Lutherans, Methodists, Baptists, Episcopalians, etc.) emerged.

The charismatic movement did not emerge in a vacuum but grew out of the older Pentecostal movement that had emerged at the turn of the century. The Pentecostal movement had in turn arisen from the holiness movement. While Presbyterians and Baptists were focusing upon the doctrinal changes occasioned by the rise of modernism, Methodists had turned to the problem of living the Christian life and the complacency that often entered into settled churches. This problem had been central to the rise of Methodism in England in the eighteenth century, and John Wesley had proposed a solution in the striving after perfection.

In the late nineteenth century, a revival of perfectionist thinking swept through Methodism (then split into several large denominations). Proponents argued that it was the duty of Christians to seek after sanctification (holiness), which was the immediate possibility of any believer by the grace of God through the Holy Spirit. Revival meetings by preachers of holiness proliferated in the 1870s and 1880s. However, the movement, so welcomed by the church's leadership at first, soon found itself under attack. The basic charge was that those professing holiness tended to look down on other believers as lesser members of the God's fellowship. Feeling alienated, in the 1880s, holiness believers initiated a series of movements out of Methodism, which led to the formation of a number of new churches such as the Church of God (Holiness), the Church of the Nazarene, and the Pilgrim Holiness Church. These churches would create a new family of Protestant denominations that continue to the present.

Holiness churches tended to emphasize behavior, and members frequently complained that it often drifted into legalism. Legalism led to a neglect of spirituality and direct experience of God, and even as the new churches were being created, leaders began to seek an experience of a deeper spiritual life. One such person was Charles F. Parham (1873–1929), an evangelist and the head of a small Bible school in Topeka, Kansas. Over the Christmas holidays of 1900, he set his students a problem. The Bible spoke frequently of a baptism

Charles Fox Parham, the founder of modern Pentecostalism.

of the Holy Spirit. What was this baptism and how would we recognize it? Returning shortly before New Year's, he listened to the reports of his students. They had concluded that when the blessing occurred, it was always accompanied by the experience of glossolalia, commonly referred to as speaking in tongues. The students having arrived at a consensus, Parham immediately led them into a time of prayer the object of which was that they receive the Spirit baptism. The first to receive it, on January 1, 1901, was Agnes Oznam (1870–1937). However, Parham and the others also experienced it and the related experience of tongues shortly thereafter.

Parham quickly moved to share the message with a larger audience, and it became the keynote of his evangelistic endeavors in Kansas, Oklahoma, and Texas for the next years. He eventually settled in Houston, Texas, and opened another Bible school. The most important event while in Houston was Parham's overriding of segregationist patterns of the time and allowing a black Methodist preacher, William J. Seymour (1870–1922), to sit in on the classes. In 1906, Seymour was called to pastor a small congregation in Los Angeles. He took Parham's ideas about the baptism of the Holy Spirit with him and there, among a small group of church members, the experience of the students in Topeka was repeated. From a center on Azusa Street in Los Angeles, Seymour began to preach the experience and launched one of the more notable movements of the century. Blacks, whites, and Hispanics came to Azusa Street to receive the baptism, and from the humble surroundings, within a decade, Pentecostalism had circled the globe and a new set of denominations, such as the Church of God (Cleveland, Tennessee), the Assemblies of God, and the Church of God in Christ, emerged.

Pentecostalism spread as a revival movement that first claimed holiness believers but soon reached out to Methodists, Baptists, and Quakers. Even as the movement grew, its adherents were hit with derisive labels such as "holy rollers," referring to the physical exercises that often accompanied the intense Pentecostal experience. The movement was dismissed as a primitive movement spreading among the ignorant. Nevertheless, the movement spread, established schools to train its leaders, and developed a sophisticated theology that integrated members' religious experience with traditional Protestant theological formats.

Having pushed Pentecostalism to the fringe, liberal Protestants and evangelicals were more than surprised when Pentecostalism suddenly spread within their churches. Baptists, who had developed an anti-Pentecostal polemic early in the century, were most offended. Liberal Protestants attempted to accommodate the new charismatics amid the diverse life that had emerged within their churches in other ways. However, at the congregational level, the

Aimee Semple McPherson,
Pentecostal evangelist and healer.

charismatics presented a problem that would not go away. As had been the case with holiness believers a century before, charismatic believers tended to look upon noncharismatics as having settled for a second-class Christian life. Some charismatics were able to remain in their previous fellowships by finding congregations dominated by charismatics. However, through the 1980s, a new set of charismatic denominations arose as believers found its easier to exist in an exclusively charismatic fellowship.

TELEVANGELISM

The diversification of the Christian community in the United States has been made possible in no small part by the availability of mass media that allow new religious leaders to bypass established authorities and appeal directly to the public. It is hard to conceive of evangelicalism's success apart from the radio. Among the first actions of the newly formed National Association of Evangelicals was the formation of National Religious Broadcasters. Through the 1940s, evangelicals began to dominate religious broadcasting and have continued to dominate the field to the present. At the same time, it is hard to picture the dramatic spread of the charismatic movement apart from television. In 1954, healing evangelist Oral Roberts (b.1918) launched a television ministry that continues to this day under his son Richard. He prepared the way for a young Baptist charismatic, Pat Robertson (b.1930), who in 1959 purchased a radio station in Virginia and two years later launched the Christian Broadcasting Network (CBN). CBN took off in the 1970s and was joined in the 1980s by Trinity Broadcasting Network, a second charismatic-based network, and in 1990 by a third, the Inspirational Network. All three networks were aided by the spread of cable television, which gave them entrance into an ever-increasing number of homes.

Televised religious programming matured quickly over its first generation. Roberts's original program featured his speaking against a plain background and scenes from his healing crusades. Rex Humbard entered the market with broadcasts of Sunday services, and Billy Graham broadcast revival services from various cities. CBN took off in part when it introduced a talk-show, *The 600 Club*, and gave time to a magnetic young couple, Jim and Tammy Faye Bakker. While Christian broadcasting has always been built around preaching, television allowed the professional staging of music performances and even the introduction of some choreography.

Evangelical and charismatic dominance of the airwaves occurred only after overcoming the attempt of the Federal Council of Churches to control religious broadcasting by having the national networks refuse to sell airtime to independent ministries and to allot free time to more established Protestant, Catholic, and Jewish groups. The National Council of Churches continued to

*Oral Roberts,
Pentecostal healer
and televangelist
pioneer.*

advocate a similar policy. Eventually, the policy failed, as television stations opted for the revenue that religious broadcasting generated. At the same time, many liberal Protestant leaders criticized religious broadcasting for shallowness and leading people away from church fellowships. Only in the 1990s did the marked success of religious broadcasting, even in the face of major scandals affecting several of its stars, prompt the mainline churches to mount a national response through the Faith and Values Channel, created by the National Interfaith Coalition. Though predominately Protestant, it also included Jewish, Muslim, and Mormon programming.

JUDAISM

Though present in America from the eighteenth century, the Jewish community came into its own during the last half of the twentieth century. The community had essentially developed in three stages. At the time of the American Revolution, the community was focused in a string of synagogues along the eastern seaboard. These synagogues were dominated by Sephardic Jews, those Jews who traced their lineage to medieval Spain and Portugal. Through the early nineteenth century, many Ashkenazi Jews (primarily from Germany and eastern Europe) moved to America. In Germany, a new form of Judaism, the Reform movement, had emerged. Reform Judaism sought to discard many anachronistic elements of traditional Judaism (including the use of Hebrew in worship) and emphasize the essential core of beliefs that had more universal significance. Outside observers could see many similarities between Reform Judaism and Unitarian Christianity.

In the United States, Reform Judaism found its center in Cincinnati, Ohio, where a large German American community had been created. The movement coalesced around Rabbi Isaac M. Wise (1819–1900), who had moved to the United States in 1846. His efforts resulted in the formation of the Union of American Hebrew Congregations in 1875 and the related Central Conference of American Rabbis in 1889.

Meanwhile, traditionalists within the American Jewish community organized in the face of what they saw as the Reformed challenge. While they had

Rabbi Isaac Wise, founder of Reform Judaism.

PITTSBURGH PLATFORM
[CENTRAL CONFERENCE OF AMERICAN RABBIS (1885) (REFORM JUDAISM)]

First—We recognize in every religion an attempt to grasp the Infinite, and in every mode, source, or book or revelation held sacral in any religious system, the consciousness of the indwelling of God in man. We hold that Judaism presents the highest conception of the God idea as taught in our holy Scriptures and developed and spiritualized by the Jewish teachers, in accordance with the moral and philosophical progress of their respective ages. We maintain that Judaism preserved and defended, midst continual struggles and trials and under enforced isolation, this God idea as the central religious truth for the human.

Second—We recognize in the Bible the record of the consecration of the Jewish people to its mission as priest of the one God, and value it as the most potent instrument of religious and moral instruction. We hold that the modern discoveries of scientific researches in the domains of nature and history are not antagonistic to the doctrines of Judaism, the Bible reflecting the primitive ideas of its own age, and at times clothing its conception of Divine Providence and justice, dealing with man in miraculous narratives.

Third—We recognize in the Mosaic legislation a system of training the Jewish people for its mission during its national life in Palestine, and to-day we accept as binding only the moral laws, and maintain only such ceremonies as elevate and sanctify our lives, but reject all such as are not adapted to the views and habits of modern civilization.

Fourth—We hold that all such Mosaic and rabbinical laws as regulate diet, priestly purity, and dress, originated in ages and under the influence of ideas altogether foreign to our present mental and spiritual state. They fail to impress the modern Jew with a spirit of priestly holiness: their observance in our days is apt rather to obstruct than to further modern spiritual elevation.

Fifth—We recognize, in the modern era of universal culture of heart and intellect, the approaching of the realization of Israel's great Messianic hope for the establishment of the kingdom of truth, justice, and peace among all men. We consider ourselves no longer a nation, but a religious community, and therefore expect neither a return to Palestine, nor a sacrificial worship under the sons of Aaron, nor the restoration of any of the laws concerning the Jewish state.

Sixth—We recognize in Judaism a progressive religion, ever striving to be in accord with the postulates of reason. We are convinced of the utmost necessity of preserving the historical identity with our great past. Christianity and Islam being daughter religious of Judaism, we appreciate their providential mission to aid in the spreading of monotheistic and moral truth. We acknowledge that the spirit of broad humanity of our age is our ally in the fulfillment of our mission, and therefore, we extend the hand of fellowship to all who operate with us in the establishment of the reign of truth and righteousness among men.

always made room for nonpracticing, secularized Jews, the idea of a Judaism that radically differed from that of the traditional life of the synagogue was a new phenomenon. The attempt to redefine traditional Orthodox Judaism against Reform was launched by Isaac Lesser. He created an Orthodox periodical, issued a new prayer book, and traveled extensively to counter Wise's efforts for Reform. It would not be until 1898 that the Union of Orthodox Jewish Congregations of America was formed.

In the meantime, a massive emigration from eastern Europe, primarily Poland and Russia, had begun in reaction to Russian pogroms against the Jewish community. They brought with them a traditional Judaism that added immensely to the strength of the previously existing Orthodox community. However, there also arose among these new immigrants a third perspective, those who advocated an allegiance to traditional Judaism but were ready to drop a strict adherence to all of the Orthodox strictures. This group gradually emerged as what had become known as Conservative Judaism. This distinctive path led to the formation of the United Synagogue of Judaism in 1913. In the 1930s, Conservative Judaism would become the birthing ground of a fourth Jewish community, the Reconstructionists.

Rabbi Alexander Kohut, one of the founders of the Conservative branch of Judaism.

Through the twentieth century, the Jewish community has been dominated by two intertwined issues, Zionism and anti-Semitism. In the 1890s, Viennese journalist Theodore Herzl had proposed the establishment of a Jewish state in Palestine as an answer to a variety of problems faced by the Jewish community that had suffered for centuries as a minority community in Christian Europe. His suggestion, while received somewhat coldly in segments of the Jewish world, found enough immediate support to make it a continued source for discussion and debate. Gradually, a majority accepted Herzl's suggestion and began to work for its realization. England began to back the idea in 1917.

Anti-Semitism was the major problem that Zionism was designed to solve. Jews had periodically been the subject of intense persecution at the hands of their Christian neighbors and lived with the negative stereotypes that flowed through both secular and religious literature in Europe and North America. Early in the twentieth century, Jewish leaders had formed the Anti-Defamation League, specifically designed to counter anti-Semitism in America.

Both the impetus toward Zionism and the efforts to rid the world of anti-Semitism took on a whole new meaning in the aftermath of World War II. The destruction of one-third of world Jewry by the Nazi Holocaust was a phenomenon that even those most attuned to the anti-Semitism of prewar Nazi propaganda could not predict and that many had trouble comprehending. The fact of the Holocaust completely restructured the Jewish community. Initially, it led to the migration of numerous Jews, primarily from Europe, to Palestine and the creation of the state of Israel in 1948. The fact of Israel's existence completed the first phase of Zionism, which reordered its priorities toward support for perpetuation of the country and the alignment of all of Judaism in diaspora around its continuation.

The Holocaust also led to the emergence of still another segment of the Jewish community in America—Hassidism. The Hassidic community represents a mystical strain of Orthodox Judaism generally traced to the career of Israel Ba'al Shem Tov (1700–1760). The teachings of Hassidism are centered on the Gnostic magical teachings of the kabbala, a view of the universe in which creation has emanated from God through a number of realms that connect heaven and earth. The Hassidic life provides means of traversing the spiritual realms back to God.

Hassidism had exploded across Europe during the nineteenth century and in many places rivaled the older Orthodox community in strength. The community in Hungary, Poland, Ukraine, and the western part of Russia was obliterated by the Nazis, and the few survivors fled to the United States and Israel. There had been several small Hassidic communities in the United States prior to World War II, but in the years immediately after the war, more than twenty-

Robert Gordis, leading Reform Jewish theologian.

five different Hassidic communities relocated to the United States. The largest of these was the Lubavitch community headquartered in Brooklyn.

Through the 1950s and 1960s, the American Jewish community came to grips with the full extent of what had befallen the world Jewish community. Concurrently, a handful of Christian scholars and church leaders also educated themselves concerning the Holocaust and initiated the reflection upon the Christian community's complicity in it. As the Jewish community organized efforts to ensure that the history of what had occurred would never be forgotten, Christians began the hard task of comprehending the meaning of the Holocaust for them. What guilt adhered to the churches for the centuries of Christian anti-Semitism and the years of silence as the Nazis rose to power and began to systematically kill the Jews in the lands under their control? That question formed the basis of a generation of Christian-Jewish dialogue amid admissions of guilt by Christian leaders and prayers for forgiveness.

The Holocaust created a new level of cordial if complex relationships between Christian and Jewish leaders. Discussions on the Holocaust, for example, led into discussions of two related issues, support for Israel and attempts by Christians to convert Jews. Evangelicals have been strongest in support for Israel, while liberal Protestants have been quick to renounce proselytization efforts within American Jewish communities. At the same time, evangelicals have nurtured Jewish missionary efforts, which found new life in the 1960s through the Jews for Jesus that emerged among the "street people" of the 1960s and the Messianic synagogue movement and its creation of Christian synagogues composed of people who are ethnically and culturally Jewish but who have become Christians. Liberal Protestants, on the other hand, have provided strong support for the Palestinians displaced by the creation of Israel in 1948.

A half-century after the Holocaust, something resembling normalcy has returned to the Jewish community, although it will be decades if not centuries before the trauma of the Holocaust is healed. The instability of Israel's position as a Middle Eastern nation is a constant reminder of the fragile nature of Jewish existence. At the same time, the Christian community has been made visibly aware of the dangers of religious prejudice and not only has taken steps to rid itself of the last remnants of anti-Semitism, but has increased efforts to ferret out and erase other prejudicial elements in its life.

CHAPTER 8

Contemporary Faiths

Through most of the country's history, the story of American religion was the story of the development of Christianity. As Europeans settled the land that became the United States at the end of the eighteenth century, they tended to push Native Americans aside and then launched an aggressive missionary effort that replaced native religions among the great majority of the Native American peoples. As a whole, these native religions were seen as primitive and of little value, and rarely did any meaningful interaction apart from the mission efforts occur. Only in the late twentieth century, with a reevaluation of native religion, did that situation change.

Christianity arrived in America, in the wake of the divisiveness of the Reformation, not as one religious body, but as a set of different denominations competing for the attention of the public and the approbation of the authorities. The battles between denominations in the new territory led to the experiment in religious freedom that has so characterized American history. The Constitution, especially the Bill of Rights, had the effect of establishing denominationalism as the way of religious life in America. No groups were given the special relationship that state churches in Europe enjoyed, especially financial support, and individuals were free to support one group or the other or no group, as they saw fit. The larger groups were able to establish national fellowships. Smaller dissident groups could organize as resources allowed and could become large groups if they had an effective message and program. In fact, the Methodists, Baptists, and Roman Catholics, all relatively minuscule at the time of the American Revolution, would rise in the nineteenth century to become the largest religious denominations in America. In the late twentieth century, the Church of Jesus Christ of Latter-day Saints, founded in the 1830s, would surpass most of the religious communities present in the colonial era.

Denominationalism is the basic structure that religion adopts within a free society. Denominations are societies of like-minded and like-hearted individuals who associate for worship, the maintenance of moral standards, fellowship, and the facilitation of good works. They are defined by their adoption of a theological stance or set of beliefs, a system of organization, a style of worship, and some rules of behavior. Local centers of the denomination then provide the ongoing community that nurtures faith for the lifetime of the adherents. Denominations have taken names from their founder (Lutherans), their theology (Reformed) their organizations (Presbyterians), or a particular practice (Methodists, Baptists). More recently, new denominations have searched the Bible for names and adopted terms such as the Vineyard, Church of the First Born, and Assemblies of God.

Denominations and their continuing drive to perpetuate themselves are the basic fact of American religious life. Their impact is no more clearly demonstrated than in the repeated calls to move beyond denominationalism, calls that began soon after the founding of the country. Possibly the first was the Church of God movement led by John Winebrunner, which decried the growing splintering of Christianity and offered solutions to move beyond the denominational divisions. Having lost the option of a united religious community imposed by the authority of the state, early leaders of the Church of God and then the Christian Church (that grew out of the work of Barton Stone and Alexander Campbell) called for a dropping of sectarian distinctives and a return to the simple truths and practices of primitive Christianity. Each of these efforts, however appealing, failed to reach its ideal and soon resulted in the formation of a new denomination. This process would be repeated many times in subsequent decades. Also, since Winebrunner's original designation of those in fellowship with him as the "Church of God," more than a hundred separate new denominations have followed his lead. The different Churches of God are now distinguished by various additional descriptors.

In the 1830s, Joseph Smith, Jr., would call for an end to denominational division through a newly established point of unity, the apostolic authority passed to the Church of Jesus Christ of Latter-day Saints. Only a small number were drawn to the new church, and even as it formed, it became the source of additional new denominations. Of the many splinter groups that formed, more than fifty remain, most having adopted a variation on the name Church of Jesus Christ or Church of Christ.

In the late nineteenth century, missionaries returning from foreign fields reported on the harm done to missionary efforts by the exportation of denominational battles where they had little relevance. The result was the ecumenical movement and its attempt initially to create a friendly, respectful atmosphere between Protestant denominations and eventually, by negotiation, find a means of reuniting Protestantism. Through the first half of the twentieth century, that movement led to the formation of various interchurch councils and the merger of many otherwise closely related denominations.

The ecumenical movement peaked in the decades immediately after World War II as churches united resources to rebuild Europe and responded to

Vatican II and the resultant changes in Protestant–Roman Catholic relationships. In this era of good feelings, many concluded that the few doctrinal issues that had originally separated the denominations were obsolete and could be overcome by dialogue. Movement leaders pronounced the age of denominations dead and looked for the formation of a large, united, liberal Protestant church like those already created in several countries such as India, Korea, and even Canada. However, dialogue merely brought to the fore the insight that sectarian differences were symbolic of serious doctrinal divergences and represented very different ways of approaching the entirety of the Christian life. Those engaged in merger negotiations came away with a healthy respect for the continuing power of theological ideas in the modern world and left behind their naiveté in thinking that overcoming denominationalism would be easy or desirable.

At the same time, some older pandenominational divisions in American Christianity became more solidified as they were incorporated in new "ecumenical" structures. The fundamentalist-modernist controversy had created the most significant chasm in American religious life. Separatist fundamentalists organized the American Council of Christian Churches and later a multinational affiliate, the International Council for Christian Churches. The neo-evangelicals, who would make a significant comeback in the last half of the twentieth century, found their focus in the National Association of Evangelicals and its international affiliate, the World Evangelical Fellowship. Liberal Protestants reorganized into the National Council of Churches and became part of the largest global association of church bodies, the World Council of Churches, which experienced significant growth when the Eastern Orthodox Churches also affiliated. Meanwhile, those denominations associated by their sharing of the same sectarian heritage also strengthened their ties by forming new ecumenical groups servicing a single denomination tradition—Baptist World Alliance, World Methodist Council, World Alliance of Reformed Churches, etc.

The late twentieth century did not lack renewed call for the formation of nondenominational churches. Like those in the Church of God movement in the nineteenth century, nondenominationalists wanted to overcome both the labels and divisions of the older denominations and the hierarchical governing structures that tended to limit the spread of rejuvenating movements, such as the charismatic movement. The charismatic movement introduced most of the liberal Protestant denominations to the experience of the charismatic gifts of the Spirit. In charismatic gatherings Lutherans, Baptists, Methodists, and Presbyterians worshiped with Episcopalians and Roman Catholics. Older denominational differences seemed to pale beside the unity of the spiritual experience. Leaders saw in the movement the beginning of the era of post-denominationalism; however, only a small percentage of church members were touched by the charismatic movement. Eventually, new charismatic churches arose, and while they united members across older denominational barriers, as they formed new associations, they discovered a whole new set of issues that divided them. The movement was soon restructured into an additional set of new denominations.

In 1800, America was home to some 15 Christian denominations, and the single most stable trend in American religion through both the nineteenth and twentieth centuries has been the steady increase in the number of new denominations. By the end of the twentieth century, there were more than 1,000 distinct denominations. During these same two centuries, the country's population grew (from 10 million to 75 million to approximately 280 million) and has become increasingly urbanized. No evidence suggests that this two-century-long trend will cease in the near future.

During the nineteenth century, church membership rose from some 10 to 15 percent to more than 30 percent. By around 1940, half of the population

John Henry Barrows, organizer of the World Parliament of Religions in 1893.

Abd-el-Rahman's Transcendent Science was typical of many new faiths that came to America in the early twentieth century.

had become church members, and that percentage continued to grow for several more decades. It finally leveled off in the 1960s with a peak of around 70 percent. During the nineteenth century, with the exception of a relatively small Jewish community, Christianity operated virtually unopposed as the dominant religion of America. Churches of every size and variety were established across the United States. By the end of the century, leaders of the larger denominations began to think of themselves as having created (however unofficially) a new American religious establishment. As the country celebrated the centenary of the events that led to its founding, Christianity reigned supreme.

However, even as church leaders asserted their new role in America, the new Protestant Christian nation, the challenges to that new establishment were making their appearance. The primary challenge came from the massive immigration that would, beginning in the 1880s, lead to the radically pluralistic environment of the contemporary United States.

CHINESE LEAD THE WAY

Among the largely forgotten effects of the discovery of gold in California in 1849 was the creation of the Chinese community in American life. Following the spread of news of the strike, thousands of Chinese set out for San Francisco, and their junks sat beside the schooners abandoned in the bay by gold miners. While many of the Chinese were Christians, products of the missionary efforts, others were Buddhists, and soon the first Buddhists temples, called joss (or "God") houses, appeared on the edge of the mining towns. Few Chinese '49ers found wealth in either the gold or subsequent silver mines. However, they did find a place in California and enough opportunity that a steady flow of immigrants followed them. In 1868 the United States signed a treaty with China giving the Chinese the right to unlimited immigration. More than 100,000 stepped through the open door.

By the end of the 1870s, the growth of harsh anti-Chinese sentiments among Americans of European heritage launched a push to block further immigration. The 1882 Chinese Exclusion Act not only blocked Chinese entry, but encouraged the return to China of those who had previously come. Many returned home, and others moved to British Columbia. Few took notice that Buddhism had gained a beachhead in the Far West. While politicians worried about Chinese in California, Japanese were migrating to Hawaii to fill labor needs on the large plantations. Buddhist leaders were slow to respond, but in 1889, the first Buddhist temple was opened in Hilo, Hawaii, and Buddhism would become fully established as a spectrum of priests from the different Buddhist organizations arrived over the next decade.

Contemporaneously with the arrival of Buddhists in California, American

The Dalai Lama,
the leader of Tibetan
Buddhists worldwide.

intellectuals were receiving massive feedback from the European colonies around the world where Christians had established missions. The encounter with the indigenous religious leadership from Asia and the Middle East and the growing body of information that was being accumulated about the world's religions were forcing Western Christian scholars to rethink the relationship between Christianity and other religious communities. Where had these religions originated, and how did they fit into God's plan for humanity? While conservative Christians continued to view non-Christians exclusively as targets for evangelistic efforts, liberal Protestants found the existence of the world's religions as, like Darwinism, an additional challenge to the uniqueness and supremacy of Christian faith.

Pioneer comparative religionists such as Unitarian James Freeman Clark suggested that religions had evolved from primitive animistic tribal religions into polytheistic religions such as Hinduism into monotheistic religions such as Judaism. The superior religion, they said, was Christianity, which capped religious evolution, as a universal faith for all humanity. Liberal Protestantism was the superior form of Christianity as it had evolved out of and further purified Roman Catholicism.

While no one today would attempt to defend Clarke's approach, his perspective was widely held in the 1890s and gave birth to one of the more important gatherings in American religious history, the Parliament of the World's Religions held in Chicago in the summer of 1893. Organized by the Chicago-based League of Liberal Churchmen, the parliament was designed as a showcase of world religious thought and practice and, so the founders thought, as a demonstration of the superiority of Christianity in general and liberal Protestantism in particular.

Parliament chairman J. H. Barrows, a Presbyterian minister, received widespread cooperation. Most of the larger denominations and many of the smaller groups sent a delegation and representative speakers. From around the world, each of the other major religions sent one or two speakers. Though definitely in the minority on the program, they would have a major impact. A new building, now the Art Institute of Chicago, was constructed to house the vast gatherings. Conservative Christians boycotted the parliament and staged counter-meetings throughout Chicago.

Barrows and his colleagues assumed that the superiority of Christianity would be evident to all who attended the conference. Such was not to be. Instead, for the first time, many of Chicago's elite heard articulate spokespersons from the world's religions and were introduced to the sophistication of the Buddhist, Hindu, and Muslim faiths. The stars of the event turned out to be the Indian teacher Swami Vivekananda (1863–1902) and the new leader of

SPEECH OF REV. AUGUSTA J. CHAPIN, D.D.

[After speaking of the unique dignity of this assembly, amid the many congresses on many special themes, and of the claims of this to a universal human interest, Miss Chapin proceeded with great felicity to speak of its singular opportuneness, especially in regard to women's share in it.]

The world's first Parliament of Religions could not have been called sooner and have gathered the religionists of all these lands together. We had to wait for the hour to strike, until the steamship, the railway and the telegraph had brought men together, leveled their walls of separation and made them acquainted with each other—until scholars had broken the way through the pathless wilderness of ignorance, superstition and falsehood, and compelled them to respect each others' honesty, devotion and intelligence. A hundred years ago the world was not ready for this Parliament. Fifty years ago it could not have been convened, and had it been called but a single generation ago one-half of the religious world could not have been directly represented.

Woman could not have had a part in it in her own right for two reasons: one that her presence would not have been thought of or tolerated, and the other was that she herself was still too weak, too timid and too unschooled to avail herself of such an opportunity had it been offered. . . . Now the doors are thrown open in our own and many other lands. Women are becoming masters of the languages in which the great sacred literatures of the world are written. They are winning the highest honors that the great universities have to bestow, and already in the field of Religion hundreds have been ordained and thousands are freely speaking and teaching this new gospel of freedom and gentleness that has come to bless mankind.

. . . I can only add my heartfelt word of greeting to those you have already heard. I welcome you, brothers, of every name and land, who have wrought so long and so well in accordance with the wisdom high heaven has given to you; and I welcome you, sisters, who have come with beating hearts and earnest purpose to this great feast, to participate not only in this Parliament, but in the great Congresses associated with it. Isabella, the Catholic, had not only the perception of a new world but of an enlightened and emancipated womanhood, which should strengthen religion and bless mankind. I welcome you to the fulfilment of her prophetic vision.

*Abdu'l-Baha led
the Baha'i Faith at
the time of its spread
to the United States.*

*Swami Vivekananda,
founder of the Vedanta Society.*

P. C. Mozoomdar was the first spiritual teacher from India to visit the United States.

Dharmapala represented Sri Lankan Buddhists at the World parliament.

the Theosophical Society, Annie Besant (1847–1933). Each time they spoke, meeting halls had to be rearranged to accommodate the crowds.

As a result of the parliament, American attendees impressed with what they had heard effectively launched Islam, Hinduism, and Buddhism in the United States. Immediately after the parliament, for example, Alexander Russell Webb (1846–1916), an American convert to Islam, opened a mosque in New York City. Swami Vivekananda stayed in America for two years touring, and before returning home, he founded the Vedanta Society and arranged for several young swamis to come to the United States as permanent residents.

Buddhism had, of course, already been established in California, but prior to the parliament was confined to Asian ethnic communities. As a result of his coming to America, the Ceylonese leader Anagarika Dharmapala (1864–1933) organized a chapter of the Maha Bodhi Society and formally received the first Western converts to Buddhism. More important for the American Buddhist community, the Japanese Zen teacher Soyen Shaku (1859–1919) returned to Japan to support the view of his teacher Imakita Kosen that Western culture should be taken seriously and to argue for the sending of Buddhist missionaries to the West.

During the generation following the parliament, millions of immigrants from around the world would flock to the United States, bringing their religion and their religious leaders with them. Heretofore, the majority of immigrants had been from the British Isles and western Europe. In the 1890s, a massive number of immigrants from southern and eastern Europe arrived and were joined by Middle Easterners and Asians (primarily from Japan, the Philippines, and India).

In the wake of Vivekananda's success at establishing the Vedanta Society and its Indian affiliate in the 1890s, other Indian teachers initiated work in the United States. Their work was truly groundbreaking, and while able to build stable centers, they were not able to attract the following that would come only late in the century. Of the several gurus (teachers), Swami Paramahansa Yogananda (1893–1952) had by far the greatest impact. Arriving for a meeting set up through the American Unitarian Association in 1922, Yogananda stayed to found the Self-Realization Fellowship (SRF) and to teach a form of Hinduism based on the practice of kriya yoga (a secret technique taught only to members). He started a magazine, wrote a number of books, including the best-selling *Autobiography of a Yogi* (1946), and spread his movement through a correspondence course. The SRF was the first Hindu group to build a national following.

Buddhism reached beyond the Japanese community primarily through Zen. During the first decades of the new century, other students of Imakita

This Buddhist center in Washington, D.C., is representative of the wave of immigration into the country following the Vietnam War.

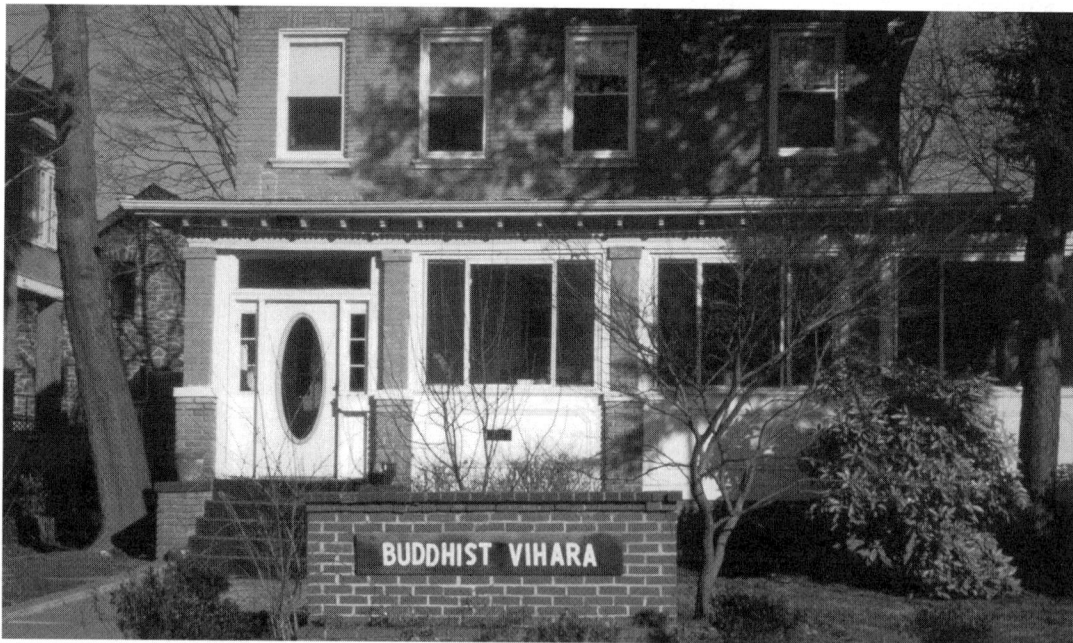

The Buddhist Vihara in Washington, D.C., is the oldest Theravada Buddhist organization in America.

Kosen and a few independent Zen masters with an openness to the West would find their way to America and begin to teach westerners. However, possibly the most important event laying the foundation for American Buddhism was the relationship that developed between Daisetz Teitaro Suzuki (1870–1966) and publisher Paul Carus. For twelve years (1897–1909), they worked on the translation into English and publication of important Buddhist texts. Then as a professor at Otani University, Suzuki wrote numerous books and articles in English. Beginning with the post–World War II wave of interest in Buddhism, Suzuki's books were among the first books on Buddhism encountered by Americans who became interested in it as a personal faith.

Swami Yogananda.

Swami Paramananda was one of the cadre of Vedantist teachers who relocated to America from his native India.

Rt. Rev. Reuchi Shibata introduced Shintoism into America.

ORTHODOXY

A high percentage of the immigrants from southern and eastern Europe were Eastern Orthodox Christians. Orthodoxy had been introduced in what became the United States as the Russians began a mission in Alaska and then extended it south along the Pacific coast to San Francisco. Greeks began to arrive in Florida as early as 1767, but the first church did not open until 1864 in New Orleans. It is a common principle that the first Orthodox church to reach a new land has primacy, and initially the Russians facilitated the establishment of a wide range of ethnic parishes. However, through the late nineteenth and early twentieth century, most of the distinctive national groups (from Ukrainian to Syrian) had established their own dioceses, each attached to a single national or linguistic group.

Over the twentieth century, all of these language groups would Americanize, but each retained a variety of ethnic distinctives. In addition, the international center of many of the churches would come under the control of either the Soviet Union following the 1917 revolution or a Marxist government following World War II. The rise of atheist totalitarian governments in Russia, Belarus, the Ukraine, Albania, Bulgaria, Romania, and Yugoslavia tested the loyalties of American believers to the ancient patriarchates. Most American dioceses experienced bitter splits that were only beginning to be healed in the years since the fall of communism.

Greek Orthodox Church, Washington, D.C.

During the last half of the century, those churches that remained loyal to the ancient patriarchs moved to create a national Orthodox church, one that was truly American and inclusive of the many ethnic groups. Ultimately it ran afoul of competition between the Russian church (the oldest) and the Greek church (the largest), and the Russian church simply asserted its primacy and adopted a new name, the Orthodox Church in America. The Orthodox also have entered into the ecumenical world, and most of the larger denominations are members of the National Council of Churches and through their patriarch, of the World Council of Churches.

TRYING TO STOP PLURALISM

The migration through the 1890s up to World War I significantly changed the spiritual complexion of America, especially the large cities. Older residents noticed the change, as the majority of new arrivals did not speak English, many dressed strangely, and they did not practice the dominant Protestant faith. If they were not Roman Catholic, they were Eastern Orthodox, and depending upon where one lived, might be Muslims, Hindus, or Buddhists.

Forces favoring a linguistic and racial unity in society began to build through the early twentieth century and demanded an end to immigration from any area other than northern and western Europe. Various measures were passed limiting immigration, and then in 1924, a comprehensive new bill passed that reduced immigration from most of the world to miniscule proportions. It also limited American citizenship to what was vaguely defined as white people. As a result of this legislation, Asian immigration was effectively stopped, and many Asians who had gained citizenship lost it.

The new immigration law effectively blocked the progress of a variety of groups, especially Hinduism and Buddhism. However, other very unorthodox groups discovered the early twentieth century to be a time of vital growth. In particular, the Church of Christ, Scientist, and the New Thought movement continued to expand across America. During its first generation Christian Science experienced two organizational crises—the first in 1889, when Mary Baker Eddy actually dissolved the church for three years, and the second in 1910, following her death when the issue of the leadership of the church by the board of directors was challenged. However, the church itself prospered until medical science began to come into its own. Only after World War II did the church's growth stop and membership begin to decline.

The New Thought movement, which differed from Eddy's on several points, including her complete break with physicians, also prospered and spread internationally. In 1914, the founding of the International New Thought Alliance, which became home to both the large metaphysical denominations

At the end of the nineteenth century, Horatio Dresser emerged as a major theoretician of the New Thought metaphysical movement.

and numerous independent New Thought congregations, signaled the movement's coming of age. New Thought had already assumed a role as the organizational expression of popular American spirituality. Since the 1890s, New Thought authors have written a series best-selling spiritual books, beginning with *In Tune with the Infinite* (1897) by Ralph Waldo Trine (1866–1958). In the 1950s, a minister of the Reformed Church introduced New Thought to an even larger audience with his phenomenal bestseller *The Power of Positive Thinking* and an inspirational monthly, *Guideposts*. Norman Vincent Peale (1898–1993), pastor of the oldest congregation in America, the Collegiate Church in New York City, wooed America for a generation, and his work has been continued by televangelist Robert Schuller (b.1926) under the slogan "possibility" (positive) thinking.

The same year that Christian Science was launched, three students of the esoteric tradition, Helena P. Blavatsky (1831–1891), Henry Steele Olcott (1832–1907), and William Q. Judge (1851–1896) created the Theosophical Society. The three were familiar with spiritualism and its attempt to demonstrate the reality of life after death but also wished to appropriate the rich resources of the older Western Gnostic esoteric spirituality that had for almost two millennia been the major alternative to Christianity. Throughout the years of Christian dominance of Western culture, there repeatedly arose dissenting

Madame Blavatsky, cofounder
of the Theosophical Society.

Annie Besant, an outstanding orator,
succeeded Madame Blavatsky as head
of the Theosophical Society.

groups that proposed a spiritual vision that envisioned an unknowable transcendent deity (rather than a personal deity to which one could relate) who produced the world through a series of emanations (rather than a single act of creation). Rather than creatures of God, this tradition suggested, humans were in fact particles of God trapped in the lesser reality called matter. Salvation consisted of leaving the world of matter behind and escaping through the levels of spiritual reality created by successive emanations back to God's realm. Assisting humans in their efforts to escape were various master teachers who existed on the spiritual levels and evolved beings in this life who were in contact with these masters.

Through the eighteenth and nineteenth centuries, esotericism had found expression in movements such as Rosicrucianism and Speculative Freemasonry. The Theosophical Society, however, aligned the tradition with new perspectives about science and evolution, and it struck a responsive chord in many. Thousands of people around the world flocked to its banner, and the society grew in spite of scandals that surrounded Blavatsky and several other leading Theosophists during its early years. Then during the 1920s, the society promoted a young Indian teacher, Jiddu Krishnamurti (1895–1986), as the embodiment of the coming World Savior, who would lead humanity into its next phase of spiritual evolvement. In 1929, after traveling around the world for several years on this campaign, Krishnamurti suddenly resigned his messianic role. The blow, coming just as the world plunged into an economic depression, severely undercut the society, and it has spent the intervening years trying to recover.

If one measured success in terms of membership, the Theosophical Society would not rank very high. However, its influence in attracting people to the Gnostic vision had been immense. In the United States alone, over 100 esoteric organizations can be traced directly to the society. It was also among these esoteric groups that a new movement was born that remade its image in the

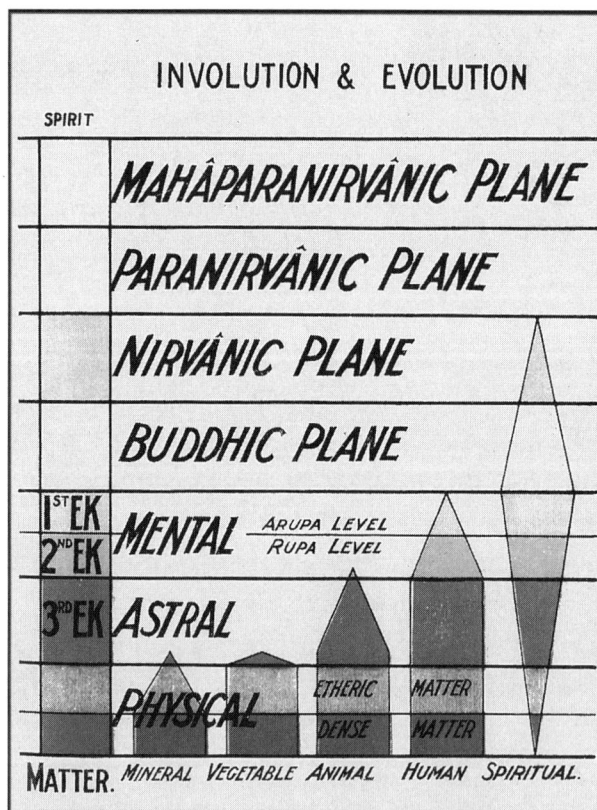

Theosophists picture the spiritual world as divided into many levels above the physical existence.

*JZ Knight, here channeling the
Enlightened entity named Ramtha,
was the most successful channeler
of the 1980s.*

1970s. The New Age movement accepted all of the elements of the esoteric tradition, from contact with highly evolved masters to the use of various occult practices like astrology and meditation. Where Theosophy had brought thousands into occult teachings, the New Age movement attracted millions to the transformative vision of a golden age of wisdom and peace.

Throughout the first half of the twentieth century, communities representative of the entire spectrum of the world's religious belief settled in America. There were Hindus, Muslims, Buddhists, and Hassidic Jews. There were Mormons, spiritualists, Theosophists, and Christian Scientists. If that were not enough, independent teachers emerged with various forms of metaphysical and spiritual teachings, such as the flamboyant African American Father Divine, who emerged in Harlem during the Depression with a message of the Allness of God and demonstrating God's abundance in the midst of human poverty.

TESTING DIVERSITY

The presence of so much religious diversity was destined to cause friction in those spaces where new religious communities appeared to be invading territory that older groups had considered their own. Decade by decade, cases landed in the law courts that served to expand the implication of the phrase in the Constitution concerning the free exercise of religion. Several cases arose as Congress moved to stamp out Mormon polygamy. In *Reynolds v. U.S.*, for example, a Mormon challenged antipolygamy legislation based on the principle that it was a religious practice. The court ruled that his belief could not override a more pervasive American commitment. The case set limits to allowable religious behavior that broke the law.

During the 1940s and 1950s, the Jehovah's Witnesses took a number of cases to the high court dealing with the church's very active proselytizing on the street and in door-to-door solicitations. In winning the overwhelming majority of these cases, they helped to establish an understanding that the right to tell someone else about one's religion is an integral part of religious free-

The deaths of members of the Peoples Temple, led by the Rev. Jim Jones, became a seminal event in the spreading pluralism of the late twentieth century.

Aldous Huxley was among the first to promote the religious use of psychedelic drugs.

dom. One of the more interesting cases that came before the court during World War II concerned the "I AM Religious Movement," a group in the Theosophical tradition that believed that its leaders were messengers of the ascended masters. At the end of the 1930s, several of the members of the group left and convinced the government to bring changes of fraud against the leadership. The case rested in large part on arguments that the teachings of the group were so unbelievable that even the leaders could not hold a sincere belief about what they were saying. They were simply operating a religious confidence scheme. At the Supreme Court, the case prompted a ruling written by Justice William O. Douglas that has became integral to the interpretation of American law: religious freedom means that one cannot put a person's religion on trial. The body of case law written in the 1940s and 1950s would become especially important with the radical increase in religious pluralism through the rest of the century.

UNITED STATES v. BALLARD (1944)
OPINION BY WILLIAM O. DOUGLAS

...We do not agree that the truth or verity of respondents' religious doctrines or beliefs should have been submitted to the jury. Whatever this particular indictment might require, the First Amendment precludes such a course, as the United States seems to concede. "The law knows no heresy, and is committed to the support of no dogma, the establishment of no sect." *Watson v. Jones*, 13 Wall. 679, 728. The First Amendment has a dual aspect. It not only "forestalls compulsion by law of the acceptance of any creed or the practice of any form of worship" but also "safeguards the free exercise of the chosen form of religion." *Cantwell v. Connecticut*, 310 U.S. 296, 303. "Thus the Amendment embraces two concepts,—freedom to believe and freedom to act. The first is absolute but, in the nature of things, the second cannot be." *Id.*, pp. 303–304. Freedom of thought, which includes freedom of religious belief, is basic in a society of free men. *Board of Education v. Barnette*, 319 U.S. 624. It embraces the right to maintain theories of life and of death and of the hereafter which are rank heresy to followers of the orthodox faiths. Heresy trials are foreign to our Constitution. Men may believe what they cannot prove. They may not be put to the proof of their religious doctrines or beliefs. Religious experiences which are as real as life to some may be incomprehensible to others. Yet the fact that they may be beyond the ken of mortals does not mean that they can be made suspect before the law. Many take their gospel from the New Testament. But it would hardly be supposed that they could be tried before a jury charged with the duty of determining whether those teachings contained false representations. The miracles of the New Testament, the Divinity of Christ, life after death, the power of prayer are deep in the religious convictions of many. If one could be sent to jail because a jury in a hostile environment found those teachings false, little indeed would be left of religious freedom. The Fathers of the Constitution were not unaware of the varied and extreme views of religious sects, of the violence of disagreement among them, and of the lack of any one religious creed on which all men would agree. They fashioned a charter of government which envisaged the widest possible toleration of conflicting views. Man's relation to his God was made no concern of the state, he was granted the right to worship as he pleased and to answer to no man for the verity of his religious views. The religious views espoused by respondents might seem incredible, if not preposterous, to most people. But if those doctrines are subject to trial before a jury charged with finding their truth or falsity, then the same can be done with the religious beliefs of any sect. When the triers of fact undertake that task, they enter a forbidden domain. The First Amendment does not select any one group or any one type of religion for preferred treatment. It puts them all in that position. *Murdock v. Pennsylvania*, 319 U.S. 105. . . . So we conclude that the District Court ruled properly when it withheld from the jury all *questions* concerning the truth or falsity of the religious beliefs or doctrines of respondents.

Justice William O. Douglas wrote the significant
opinion in United States v. Ballard *that has become*
a hallmark of religious freedom in the United States.

1965, A NEW BEGINNING

The great variety of religion present in the United States throughout the first half of the century touched only a miniscule element of the population. Of the non-Christian religions, only the Jewish community was represented in all parts of the nation. All that would change in 1965 with the rewriting of the immigration laws. The 1924 law excluding Asians was set aside, and new quotas from most Asian countries were set in place. Muslims, Hindus, and Buddhists began to sweep into the country by the tens of thousands annually and establish their places of worship in every major urban center. At the same time, unattached missionaries began to arrive and proselytize among the younger generation.

It just so happened that the arrival of the new wave of Asian spiritual teachers coincided with the coming of age of the baby-boom generation. Most remembered as the hippie generation, the baby boomers placed more pressure on the society than it could accommodate. Too many people were reaching adulthood than could be absorbed into the job market. Large numbers of them took to the street and the countryside. They had few commitments and had been introduced to a new world of mind-altering substances and psychedelic drugs, especially LSD.

While most baby boomers would sooner or later return to the mainstream, some were attracted to the new wave of teachers offering life in an alternate religious perspective. Among the first was A. C. Bhaktivedanta Swami Prabhupada, founder of the International Society of Krishna Consciousness, who taught a form of devotional Hinduism (bhakti yoga). The dancing and chanting of "Hare Krishna" by his shaven-headed devotees became the image of the baby boomers' religious experiments.

At the same time that the Asian teachers arrived, a competing new generation of evangelical Christians also moved onto the streets. A massive movement swept through the street people, whose converts began to call themselves "Jesus People," and rediscovered the communal living practice of the early church. As the Jesus People movement held many young adults as they made the transition back into middle America, the movement also produced its new radical spin-offs, none more noteworthy than the Children of God. The literal biblical faith preached by founder David Berg led him to put a twist to the millennialism so much a part of evangelical faith. He came to believe that he was the messenger of the endtime and destined to found a worldwide missionary organization, and through the early 1970s, the members of the Children of God scattered into more than fifty countries.

The Children of God, one of the new religions of the 1970s, whose publication is shown below, assumed a high profile as a result of their public demonstrations.

David Berg, founder of the Children of God, now known as The Family.

Before the Children of God departed, however, they had nurtured the beginning of a reactionary movement by parents of the young people who were joining the alternative religions that had suddenly emerged into the spotlight. These parents denounced the new groups that made high demands upon members and diverted them from finishing their college education. They were cults, and someone should do something about them. Through the mid 1970s, parent support groups appeared across the country, many not content to sit by and wait. They welcomed the suggestion of one Theodore Patrick that they try a process he had developed called deprogramming. For a fee, Patrick would snatch a young person at his or her parents request and attempt to pressure the person out of the new faith.

Of the new generation of religious leaders, none so angered parents as Korean minister Sun Myung Moon (b.1920), founder of the Holy Spirit Association for the Unification of Christianity (the Unification Church) out of continuing revelations he had received beginning in 1936. Americans had a hard time with his messianic claims to be fulfilling the work left uncompleted by Jesus, his arranging international and interracial marriages for his followers, and fund-raising activities of young believers on the street. By the mid 1970s, the Unification Church had become the major target of the anticult movement, and the church's members were experiencing the largest number of deprogrammings.

Having more success in gaining adherents than either ISKCON, The Family, or the Unification Church, the Church of Scientology had been founded in 1954 by students of L. Ron Hubbard (1911–1986). In creating Scientology, Hubbard drew on themes from the same esoteric roots as Theosophy but was unique in developing a spiritual technology to facilitate the human quest for religious Truth. He posited the existence of a soul-like entity, the Thetan, the true self, which had existed for millennia but was now trapped in ignorance and physicality. Scientology offered a number of techniques, including a form of counseling called auditing, that would allow the Thetan to discover its true nature and become free of encumbrances that kept it from operating at its fullest potential.

Scientology not only experienced more success than the other new religious movements that rose to prominence in the 1960s, but also faced a higher level of controversy, some attracted by its use of an instrument called the E-meter, an integral element in its counseling procedures and some by its adoption of a schedule of set donations for the receiving of church services. The latter structuring of its life led to scrutiny by the Internal Revenue Service, which only after a lengthy and thorough investigation finally agreed that the church and its various corporations could maintain their tax-exempt

Sun Myung Moon, founder
of the Unification Church,
and Mrs. Moon.

L. Ron Hubbard, the founder
of Dianetics and Scientology.

Scientologists engage in religious counseling called auditing.

status as a religious organization in 1993. That ruling resolved most of the church's problems in the United States, though it remains embattled in several European lands.

The problem of the new religions might have been worked out had it not been for an event in the jungles of South America in November 1978. Through the 1970s, a pastor in the Christian Church (Disciples of Christ) had built a large congregation called the People's Temple. The pastor, Jim Jones, was white, while most of his members were black. He preached a form of Marxist liberation theology and carried on an active social ministry. At the same time, he and the movement became more and more alienated from their life in San

Francisco, and in 1977, more than 900 of them moved to rural Guyana, where they had previously started an agricultural colony, Jonestown. Then on November 18, 1978, for reasons still not fully understood, members of the group killed a visiting U.S. congressman and his entourage and then turned on themselves. The minority that did not commit suicide were murdered.

In that moment, the People's Temple was transformed from radical church to "cult," and the term "cult" took on a new sinister connotation. In the wake of Jonestown, the very decentralized anticult movement moved to create viable organizations that could respond to what it saw as the cult problem in America. The Cult Awareness Network was the more important of these new organizations. An activist group, it promoted deprogramming and the theory that new religions practiced a form of brainwashing on their members. Brainwashing became the subject of a series of court cases during the 1980s until the idea was dealt a blow in federal court in 1990 and subsequently the Cult Awareness Network was found liable in a lawsuit brought by one Jason Scott, a Pentecostal church member who had been unsuccessfully deprogrammed. The judgment against the Cult Awareness Network forced it into bankruptcy and ended the practice of deprogramming.

THE NEW PLURALISM

Meanwhile, as attention was focused upon the cult controversy, hundreds of new religious communities, representative of every religious tradition of any size in the world, were quietly established across America. Possibly most important for America's future were the Muslim groups. Muslims, primarily from the Middle East, had settled in the Midwest early in the twentieth century and opened mosques in such places as Detroit, Michigan; Toledo, Ohio; and Chicago, Illinois. They remained a relatively small community until the 1970s, when immigration to the United States radically increased from Muslim countries (which include a strip that begins in North Africa and proceeds across the Middle East to Pakistan, Bangladesh, and Indonesia). During the last two decades of the century, more than a million Muslims arrived and, in the face of continuing Middle East tensions, quickly organized as a new political force threatening the position so carefully developed by the Jewish community.

However, like other religious communities, the Muslims have also presented themselves as a highly diverse community. They not only are divided into the two major orthodox camps of Sunnis and Shi'as, but include numerous Sufi (mystical organizations) and a variety of Islamic-inspired groups not recognized by the orthodox Muslims. Most prominent of these are the so-called Black Muslims, heirs of a century-long search to find a nondiscriminatory place for African Americans in American life. The antidiscriminatory

Elijah Muhammad, founder of the
Nation of Islam

Louis Farrakhan revived the Nation
of Islam, the main of which had been
integrated into the orthodox Muslim
community in America.

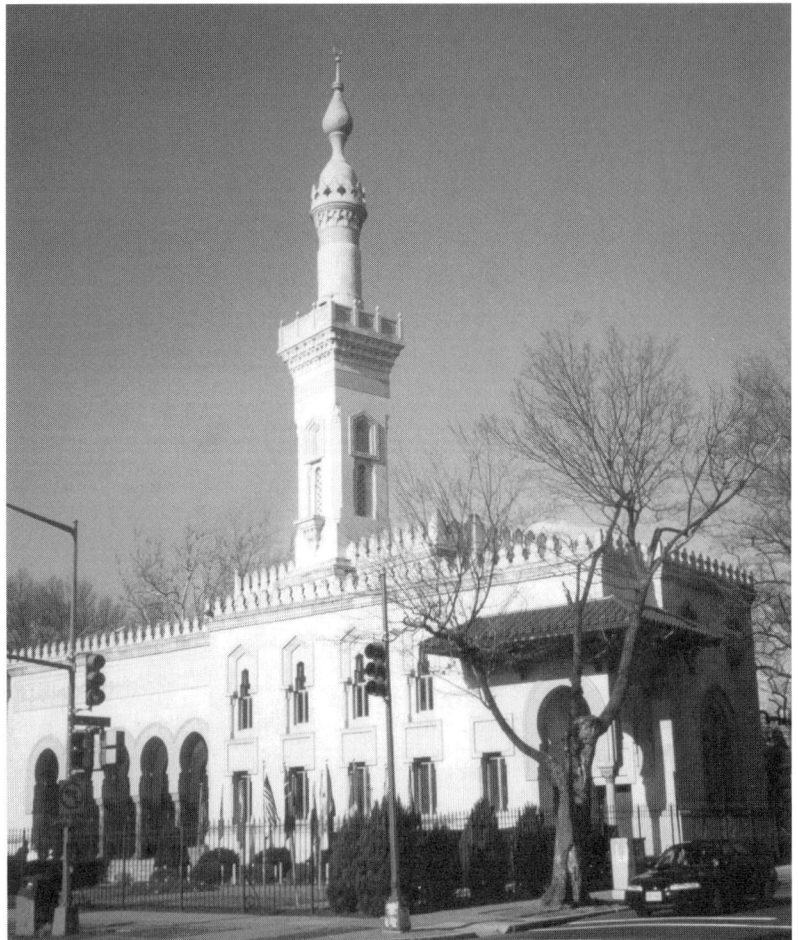

The growing Muslim community in
America has a symbolic focus in the
Islamic Center in Washington, D.C.

stance of Islam was welcomed by many African Americans, but some, most notably Elijah Muhammad (1897–1975), turned it into an expression of the aspirations of the black community in such a way that Islam was captured by the very racism it opposed. The measurable good it accomplished for its members and the black community was often compromised by its antiwhite (and at times anti-Semitic) rhetoric.

During the last thirty-five years of the twentieth century, America took a quantum leap in religious pluralism. It became home to all of the major traditions of the world's religions and many of the minor ones. By the end of the century, some 2,000 different religious communities existed in the United States (compared to 350 in 1900). More than half of these had been formed since 1965. Some 65 percent of the American public were church members but were split among the more than 1,000 Christian denominations. Another 20 percent could be found in the remaining 1,000 groups. In addition, there were many people who thought of themselves as believers in a spiritual reality but were unattached to any particular religious community.

INTO THE TWENTY-FIRST CENTURY

America has emerged at the beginning of the new millennium as the most religious nation ever known. Completely apart from any government coercion, the great majority of its citizens have chosen to affiliate with a religious community. Devoid of government financial support, religious communities have to survive and justify their existence to people who voluntarily give of their income to support them.

Religion in America exists in every variety. Not only is there an amazing array of beliefs among the different communities, but there are differing levels of commitment required by different groups. On the one end, some groups meet only weekly or even less frequently, while others consist of tightly knit groups that consume all or most of a member's free time. Some groups have only a minimum of rules governing behavior, while others demand strict and minute conformity to rules that govern every aspect of life. Everyone in the public is free to join or leave or change their religious affiliation, and there is constant movement between religious groups.

The experiment in religious freedom adopted by the country's founders has had it crises, but after more than two centuries it has become ingrained in the nation's life, and one can hardly conceive of any movement backward as continued testing of the boundaries continues. Because of its success, it has become a model for the world, and the religious freedom it pioneered has spread globally in the twentieth century as country after country has adapted the concept to its local conditions.

Bibliography

GENERAL SOURCES

Albanese, Catherine. *American Religion and Religions.* 2d ed. Belmont, CA: Wadsworth, 1992.

Bedell, George C., and Charles T. Wellborn. *Religion in America.* New York: Macmillan, 1997.

Dowdy, Thomas E., and Patrick J. McNamara. *Religion: North American Style.* New Brunswick, NJ: Rutgers University Press, 1997.

Hudson, Winthrop S. *Religion in America.* 6th ed. New York: Charles Scribner's Sons, 1998.

Marty, Martin E. *Pilgrims in Their Own Land.* Boston: Little, Brown & Co., 1984.

Melton, J. Gordon. *Encyclopedia of American Religions.* 6th ed. Detroit: Gale Research Company, 1999.

——. *Religious Leaders of America.* 2d ed. New York: Gale Research Company, 1999.

Murphy, Larry G., Jr., J. Gordon Melton, and Gary L. Ward, eds. *Encyclopedia of African American Religion.* New York: Garland, 1993.

Williams, Peter. *America's Religious Traditions and Culture.* New York: Macmillan, 1990.

I. THE FIRST AMERICAN RELIGIONS

Bowden, Henry Warner. *American Indians and Christian Missions: Studies in Cultural Conflict.* Chicago: University of Chicago Press, 1981.

Gill, Sam D. *Native American Religions: An Introduction.* Belmont, CA: Wadsworth, 1982.

——. *Native American Traditions: Sources and Interpretations.* The Religious Life of Man Series. Belmont, CA: Wadsworth, 1983.

Gill, Sam D., and Irene F. Sullivan. *Dictionary of Native American Mythology.* Santa Barbara, CA: ABC-CLIO, 1992.

Griffiths, Nicolas, and Fernando Cervantes. *Spiritual Encounters: Interactions between Christianity and Native Religions in Colonial America.* Lincoln: University of Nebraska Press, 1999.

Hall, Robert L. *An Archeology of the Soul: North American Indian Belief and Ritual*. Urbana: University of Illinois Press, 1997.

Klots, Steve, and Frank W. Porter. *Native Americans and Christianity*. New York: Chelsea House, 1997.

Tedlock, Dennis, and Barbara Tedlock, eds. *Teachings for the American Earth: Indian Religion and Philosophy*. New York: Liveright, 1975.

Treats, James, ed. *Native and Christian: Indigenous Voices on Religious Identity in the United States and Canada*. New York: Routledge, 1995.

Vecsey, Christopher. *Imagine Ourselves Richly: Mythic Narratives of North American Indians*. New York: Crossroad, 1988.

Weatherford, Jack. *Native Roots: How the Indian Enriched America*. New York: Crown, 1991.

2. PIONEERS AND THE COMING OF CHRISTIANITY

Davies, A. Mervyn. *Foundation of American Freedom*. New York: Abingdon Press, 1955.

Dolan, Jay P. *The American Catholic Experience: A History from Colonial Times to the Present*. Garden City, NY: Doubleday & Company, 1985.

Ellis, John Tracy. *American Catholicism*. Garden City, NY: Doubleday & Company, 1965.

Grimm, Harold John. *The Reformation Era, 1500–1620*. New York: Macmillan, 1973.

Knight, Janice. *Orthodoxies in Massachusetts: Rereading American Puritanism*. Cambridge: Harvard University Press, 1997.

Spurr, John. *English Puritanism, 1603–1689*. New York: St. Martin's Press, 1998.

3. THE COLONIAL CHURCH

Bonomi, Patricia U. *Under the Cope of Heaven: Religion, Society, and Politics in Colonial America*. New York: Oxford University Press, 1986.

Butler, Jon. *Awash in a Sea of Faith: Christianizing the American People*. Cambridge: Harvard University Press, 1990.

Durnbaugh, Donald F. *The Brethren in Colonial America*. Elgin, IL: The Brethren Press, 1967.

Hiemert, Alan, and Andrew Delbanco, eds. *The Puritans in America*. Cambridge: Harvard University Press, 1985.

Johnson, Paul E. *African American Christianity: Essays in History*. Berkeley: University of California Press, 1994.

Jones, Rufus. *The Quakers in the American Colonies*. New York: Norton & Co., 1967.

Morais, Herbert M. *Deism in Eighteenth Century America*. New York: Russell & Russell, 1976.

Pestana, Carla Gardina. *Liberty of Conscience and the Growth of Religious Diversity in Early America, 1636–1786*. Providence, RI: John Carter Brown Library, 1987.

Sweet, William Warren. *Religion in Colonial America*. New York: Charles Scribner's Sons, 1951.

Trinterud, Leonard J. *The Forming of an American Tradition*. Philadelphia: Westminster Press, 1949.

Wallace, Paul A. W. *The Muhlenbergs of Pennsylvania*. Philadelphia: University of Pennsylvania Press, 1950.

Woolverton, John Frederick. *Colonial Anglicanism in North America*. Detroit: Wayne State University Press, 1984.

4. DENOMINATIONALISM—BUILDING THE POST-REVOLUTION CHURCH

Arrington, Leonard J., and Davis Britton. *The Mormon Experience*. New York: Alfred A. Knopf, 1979.

Brown, Slater. *The Heyday of Spiritualism*. New York: Hawthorne Books, 1970.

George, Carol V. R. *Segregated Sabbaths: Richard Allen and the Rise of Independent Black Churches, 1760–1840*. New York: Oxford University Press, 1973.

Harrell, David Edwin. *The Social Sources of Division in the Disciples of Christ*. Athens, GA: Publishing Systems, 1973.

Hatch, Nathan O. *The Democratization of American Christianity*. New Haven: Yale University Press, 1989.

Johnson, Paul E., ed. *African American Christianity: Essays in History*. Berkeley: University of California Press, 1994.

McBeth, H. Leon. *The Baptist Heritage*. Nashville, TN: Broadman Press, 1987.

McLoughlin, William G., Jr. *Modern Revivalism: Charles Grandison Finney to Billy Graham*. New York: Ronald Press, 1959.

Manross, William W. *A History of the American Episcopal Church*. New York: Morehouse-Gorham, 1950.

Nelson, E. Clifford. *The Lutherans in North America*. Philadelphia: Fortress Press, 1980.

Norwood, Frederick A. *The Story of American Methodism*. Nashville, TN: Abingdon Press, 1974.

Richey, Russell E. *Early American Methodism: A Reconsideration*. Religion in North America. Bloomington: Indiana University Press, 1991.

5. URBANIZATION AND PLURALISM

Cunningham, Lawrence S. *The Catholic Experience: Space, Time, Silence, Prayer, Sacraments, Story, Persons, Catholicity, Community, and Expectations.* New York: Crossroad, 1987.

Dolan, Jay P. *The Immigrant Church.* Baltimore: Johns Hopkins University Press, 1975.

Dorn, Jacob H. *Socialism and Christianity in Early Twentieth Century America.* Westport, CT: Greenwood Publication Group, 1998.

Gottshalk, Stephen. *The Emergence of Christian Science in American Religious Life.* Berkeley: University of California Press, 1978.

Land, Gary, ed. *Adventism in America.* Grand Rapids, MI: Eerdmans, 1986.

Lincoln, C. Eric, and Lawrence H. Mamiya. *The Black Church in the African American Experience.* Durham, NC: Duke University Press, 1990.

Moore, R. Laurence. *In Search of White Crows: Spiritualism, Parapsychology and American Culture.* New York: Oxford University Press, 1977.

———. *Religious Outsiders and the Making of America.* New York: Oxford University Press, 1986.

Pitzer, Donald E. *America's Communal Utopias.* Chapel Hill: University of North Carolina Press, 1997.

Sarna, Jonathan D. *Minority Faiths and the American Protestant Mainstream.* Urbana: University of Illinois Press, 1998.

Stein, Stephen J. *The Shaker Experience in America: A History of the United Society of Believers.* New Haven: Yale University Press, 1992.

Washington, James Melvin. *Frustrated Fellowship: The Black Baptist Quest for Social Power.* Macon, GA: Mercer University Press, 1986.

White, Ronald C., and C. Howard Hopkins. *The Social Gospel: Religion and Reform in Changing America.* Philadelphia: Temple University Press, 1976.

6. FUNDAMENTALISM AND MODERNISM

Ellingsen, Mark. *The Evangelical Movement: Growth, Impact, Controversy, Dialog.* Minneapolis: Augsburg, 1988.

Gatewood, Willard B., Jr. *Controversy in the Twenties: Fundamentalism, Modernism, and Evolution.* Nashville, TN: Vanderbilt University Press, 1969.

Hutchinson, William R. *The Modernist Impulse in American Protestantism.* Oxford: Oxford University Press, 1976.

Numbers, Ronald. *The Creationists: The Evolution of Scientific Creationism.* Berkeley: University of California Press, 1993.

Roberts, John H. *Darwinism and the Divine in America: Protestant Intellectuals and Organic Evolution, 1859–1900.* Madison: University of Wisconsin Press, 1988.

Sandeen, Ernest R. *The Roots of Fundamentalism: British and American Millenarianism, 1800–1930.* Chicago: University of Chicago Press, 1970.

Sweet, Leonard I. *The Evangelical Tradition in America.* Macon, GA: Mercer University Press, 1984.

Weber, Timothy B. *Living in the Shadow of the Second Coming: American Premillennialism, 1875–1925.* New York: Oxford University Press, 1979.

White, Ronald C., Jr., and C. Howard Hopkins. *The Social Gospel: Religion and Reform in Changing America.* Philadelphia: Temple University Press, 1976.

7. RELIGION IN A SECULAR WORLD

Abbot, Walter, ed. *The Documents of Vatican II.* New York: Guild Press, 1966.

Braaten, Carl E., and Robert W. Jensen, eds. *A Map of Twentieth-Century Theology: Readings from Karl Barth to Radical Pluralism.* Philadelphia: Fortress Press, 1995.

Cavert, Samuel McCrea. *Church Cooperation and Unity in America: A Historical Review, 1900–1970.* New York: Association Press, 1970.

Deiter, Melvin Easterday. *The Holiness Revival of the Nineteenth Century.* Metuchen, NJ: Scarecrow Press, 1980.

Doyle, Dennis M. *The Church Emerging from Vatican II: A Popular Approach to Contemporary Catholicism.* Mystic, CT: Twenty Third Publications, 1992.

Ellwood, Robert S. *The 60s Spiritual Awakening: American Religion Moving from Modern to Postmodern.* New Brunswick, NJ: Rutgers University Press, 1994.

Hadden, Jeffrey K., and Charles E. Swann. *Prime-Time Preachers: The Rising Power of Televangelism.* Cambridge, MA: Addison-Wesley, 1981.

Hunter, James Davison. *American Evangelicalism: Conservative Religion and the Quandary of Modernity.* New Brunswick, NJ: Rutgers University Press, 1983.

Karp, Abraham J. *Haven and Hope: A History of the Jews in America.* New York: Schocken Books, 1985.

Kurtz, Paul. *The Humanist Alternative.* Buffalo, NY: Prometheus Press, 1979.

McSweeney, William. *Roman Catholicism: The Search for Relevance.* New York: St. Martin's Press, 1980.

Marty, Martin E. *Freethought and American Religion.* Cleveland: World Publishing Co., 1961.

———. *Modern American Religion.* 2 vols. Chicago: University of Chicago Press, 1986, 1991.

Powe, Karla O., ed. *Charismatic Christianity as a Global Culture.* Columbia: University of South Carolina Press, 1994.

Rosenthal, Gilbert S. *Contemporary Judaism: Patterns of Survival.* New York: Human Sciences Press, 1986.

Stein, Gordon. *The Encyclopedia of Unbelief.* Buffalo, NY: Prometheus Books, 1985.

Synan, Vinson. *The Twentieth Century Pentecostal Explosion.* Altamonte Springs, FL: Creation House, 1987.

8. CONTEMPORARY FAITHS

Adler, Margot. *Drawing Down the Moon.* Boston: Beacon Press, 1987.

Albanese, Catherine L. *Nature Religion in America: From the Algonkian Indians to the New Age.* Chicago: University of Chicago Press, 1990.

Campbell, Bruce F. *A History of the Theosophical Movement.* Berkeley: University of California Press, 1980.

Faivre, Antoine, and Jacob Needleman, eds. *Modern Esoteric Spirituality.* New York: Crossroad, 1992.

Fields, Rick. *How the Swans Came to the Lake.* Boulder, CO: Shambhala, 1986.

Haddad, Yvonne Yazbeck, ed. *The Muslims of America.* New York: Oxford University Press, 1991.

Hunter, Louise H. *Buddhism in Hawaii.* Honolulu: University of Hawaii Press, 1971.

Jackson, Carl T. *The Oriental Religions and American Thought.* Westport, CT: Greenwood Press, 1981.

Jenkins, Philip. *Mystics and Messiahs: Cults and New Religions in American History.* New York: Oxford University Press, 2000.

Lane, David Christopher. *The Radhasoami Tradition: A Critical History.* New York: Garland, 1992.

Melton, J. Gordon. *The Encyclopedia Handbook of Cults in America.* New York: Garland, 1992.

Miller, Timothy, ed. *America's Alternative Religions.* Albany: State University of New York Press, 1995.

Mullin, Robert Bruce, and Russell E. Richey. *Reimaging Denominationalism: Interpretive Essays.* New York: Oxford University Press, 1994.

Rawlinson, Andrew. *The Book of Enlightened Masters: Western Teachers and Eastern Traditions.* La Salle IL: Open Court, 1997.

Tarasar, Constance J., ed. *Orthodox America, 1794–1976.* Syosset, NY: Orthodox Church in America, Department of History and Archives, 1975.

Williams, Raymond Brady. *Religions of Immigrants from India and Pakistan: New Threads in the American Tapestry.* Cambridge: Cambridge University Press, 1988.

Illustration Credits

Page 12: John R. Swanton. *The Indians of the Southeastern United States.* Washington, DC: Government Printing Offices, 1946.

Page 13: John R. Swanton. *The Indians of the Southeastern United States.* Washington, DC: Government Printing Offices, 1946.

Page 15 (top): John R. Swanton. *The Indians of the Southeastern United States.* Washington, DC: Government Printing Offices, 1946.

Page 15 (bottom): John R. Swanton. *The Indians of the Southeastern United States.* Washington, DC: Government Printing Offices, 1946.

Page 17: Courtesy of Theodore B. Hetzel.

Page 19: James Mooney. *The Ghost Dance Religion.* In the *Fourteenth Annual Report of the American Bureau of Ethnography.* Washington, DC: Government Printing Office, 1896.

Page 20: John R. Swanton. *The Indians of the Southeastern United States.* Washington, DC: Government Printing Offices, 1946.

Page 21: James Mooney. *The Ghost Dance Religion.* In the *Fourteenth Annual Report of the American Bureau of Ethnography.* Washington, DC: Government Printing Office, 1896.

Page 22 (top): James Mooney. *The Ghost Dance Religion.* In the *Fourteenth Annual Report of the American Bureau of Ethnography.* Washington, DC: Government Printing Office, 1896.

Page 22 (bottom): James Mooney. *The Ghost Dance Religion.* In the *Fourteenth Annual Report of the American Bureau of Ethnography.* Washington, DC: Government Printing Office, 1896.

Page 24: James Mooney. *The Ghost Dance Religion.* In the *Fourteenth Annual Report of the American Bureau of Ethnography.* Washington, DC: Government Printing Office, 1896.

Page 25: James Mooney. *The Ghost Dance Religion.* In the *Fourteenth Annual Report of the American Bureau of Ethnography.* Washington, DC: Government Printing Office, 1896.

Page 28: Angie Debo. *A History of Indians in the United States.* Norman: University of Oklahoma Press, 1970.

Page 30: B. W. Arnett. *The Budget.* Philadelphia: the Author, 1884.

Page 31: National Portrait Gallery, Smithsonian Institute, Washington, DC.

Page 32: A. B. Hyde. *The Story of Methodism throughout the World.* Chicago: Johns Publishing House, 1887.

Page 34: John R. Swanton. *The Indians of the Southeastern United States.* Washington, DC: Government Printing Offices, 1946.

Page 35: Library of Congress

Page 36: AP Photo

Page 40: Institute for the Study of American Religion, Santa Barbara, CA

Page 42: Courtesy of Edwin Gaustad.

Page 45: Vincent L. Milner. *Religious Denominations of the World*. Philadelphia: Bradley Garretson, 1872.

Page 49: Library of Congress.

Page 53: Library of Congress.

Page 54: William Stevens Perry. *The History of the American Episcopal Church, 1587–1883*. Boston: James R. Osgood & Company, 1885.

Page 55: Philosophical Society.

Page 56: American Religion Collection.

Page 57: *The Illustrated Book of All Religions*. Chicago: Star Publishing Company, n.d.

Page 58: William Stevens Perry. *The History of the American Episcopal Church, 1587–1883*. Boston: James R. Osgood & Company, 1885.

Page 59: William Stevens Perry. *The History of the American Episcopal Church, 1587–1883*. Boston: James R. Osgood, 1885.

Page 60: Vincent L. Milner. *Religious Denominations of the World*. Philadelphia: Bradley Garretson, 1872.

Page 61: Library of Congress (engraving from *Harper's Monthly*, February 1901).

Page 62: John de Visser and Harold Kalmon. *Pioneer Churches*. New York: W. W. Norton, 1976.

Page 63: Edgar Franklin Romig. *The Tercentenary Year*. New York: Reformed Church in America, 1929.

Page 64 (top): William R. Shepherd. *The Story of New Amsterdam*. New York: Alfred A. Knopf, 1926.

Page 64 (bottom): Courtesy of John de Visser.

Page 66 (left): Elizabeth Emmitt. *The Story of Quakerism*. London: Headley Brothers, 1908.

Page 66 (right): Special Collections, Davidson Library, University of California–Santa Barbara

Page 67: C. Henry Smith. *The Mennonites*. Berne, IN: Mennonite Book Concern, 1920.

Page 68: *Seventh Day Baptists in Europe and America*. Plainfield, NJ: Seventh Day Baptist General Conference 1910.

Page 69: Vincent L. Milner. *Religious Denominations of the World*. Philadelphia: Bradley Garretson, 1872.

Page 70: Courtesy of John de Visser.

Page 75: William Stevens Perry. *The History of the American Episcopal Church, 1587–1883*. Boston: James R. Osgood & Company, 1885.

Page 76: William Stevens Perry. *The History of the American Episcopal Church, 1587-1883*. Boston: James R. Osgood & Company, 1885.

Page 77: William Stevens Perry. *The History of the American Episcopal Church, 1587-1883*. Boston: James R. Osgood & Company, 1885.

Page 78: Edgar Franklin Romig. *The Tercentenary Year.* New York: Reformed Church in America, 1929.

Page 80: Albert D. Belden. *George Whitefield—The Awakener.* London: Sapson, Low, Marston & Co., n.d.

Page 81: Special Collections, Davidson Library, University of California–Santa Barbara

Page 82 (left): *Seventh Day Baptists in Europe and America.* Plainfield, NJ: Seventh Day Baptist General Conference 1910.

Page 82 (right): *Seventh Day Baptists in Europe and America.* Plainfield, NJ: Seventh Day Baptist General Conference 1910.

Page 84: C. Henry Smith. *The Mennonites.* Berne, IN: Mennonite Book Concern, 1920.

Page 86: Courtesy of John de Visser.

Page 89 (top): *The Illustrated Book of All Religions.* Chicago: Star Publishing Company, n.d.

Page 89 (bottom): William Nelson Gemmill, *The Salem Witch Trials.* Chicago: A. C. McClurg & Co., 1924.

Page 90: *The Illustrated Book of All Religions.* Chicago: Star Publishing Company, n.d.

Page 93: Presbyterian Historical Society.

Page 95: Gordon Melton.

Page 97: Albert D. Belden. *George Whitefield—The Awakener.* London: Sapson, Low, Marston & Co., n.d.

Page 98: Presbyterian Historical Society.

Page 99 (left): *The Illustrated Book of All Religions.* Chicago: Star Publishing Company, n.d.

Page 99 (right): Matthew Simpson. *Cyclopedia of Methodism.* Philadelphia: Louis H. Everts, 1881.

Page 101 (top): *Presbyterian Reunion: A Memorial Volume. 1837-1871.* New York: De Witt C. Lent & Company, 1870.

Page 101 (bottom left): *The Illustrated Book of All Religions.* Chicago: Star Publishing Company, n.d.

Page 101 (bottom right): L. B. Fisher. *A Brief History of the Universalist Church.* Boston: Universalist Publishing House, 1912.

Page 103: American Religion Collection.

Page 104 (left): *History of all the Religious Denominations in the United States.* Harrisburg, PA: John Winebrunner, 1848.

Page 104 (right): J. B. Wakeley. *Lost Chapters Recovered from the Early History of American Methodism.* New York: Carlton and Porter, 1858.

Page 112 (top): George Wallingford Noyes, ed. *The Religious Experiences of John Humphrey Noyes.* New York: Macmillan Company, 1923.

Page 112 (bottom): William J. Finck. *Lutheran Landmarks and Pioneers in America.* Philadelphia: General Council Publication House, 1913.

Page 113: *The Illustrated Book of All Religions.* Chicago: Star Publishing Company, n.d.

Page 114 (left): George Wallingford Noyes, ed. *The Religious Experiences of John

Humphrey Noyes. New York: Macmillan Company, 1923.

Page 114 (right): *History of all the Religious Denominations in the United States.* Harrisburg, PA: John Winebrunner, 1848.

Page 115: *Fundamental Laws.* Allentown, PA: Philosophical Publishing Company, 1916.

Page 118: Library of Congress.

Page 121 (top): Gordon Melton.

Page 121 (bottom): Vincent L. Milner. *Religious Denominations of the World.* Philadelphia: Bradley Garretson, 1872.

Page 123: *Christian Advocate,* September 9, 1926

Page 124: Samuel Wilberforce. *A History of the Episcopal Church in America.* London: James Burnes, 1844.

Page 125: Gordon Melton.

Page 126: Matthew Simpson. *Cyclopedia of Methodism.* Philadelphia: Louis H. Everts, 1881.

Page 127 (top): Archive of the Central Illinois Methodist Conference of the United Methodist Church

Page 127 (bottom): A. B. Hyde. *The Story of Methodism throughout the World.* Chicago: Johns Publishing House, 1887.

Page 129: *Seventh Day Baptists in Europe and America.* Plainfield, NJ: Seventh Day Baptist General Conference 1910.

Page 131: C. L. Thompson. *Times of Refreshing.* Rockford, IL: Golden Censer, 1880.

Page 132: *The Illustrated Book of All Religions.* Chicago: Star Publishing Company, n.d.

Page 135: B. W. Arnett. *The Budget.* Philadelphia: the Author, 1884.

Page 136: B. W. Arnett. *The Budget.* Philadelphia: the Author, 1884.

Page 140: Corbis-Bettmann.

Page 141: Library of Congress.

Page 143: Jesse Lyman Hurlbut. *Sunday Half Hours with Great Preachers,* 1907.

Page 144: Philosophical Library.

Page 146: Philosophical Library.

Page 147 (top): Gary L. Bunker and Davis Bitton. *The Mormon Graphic Image, 1834-1914.* Salt Lake City: University of Utah Press, 1983.

Page 147 (bottom): Gary L. Bunker and Davis Bitton. *The Mormon Graphic Image, 1834-1914.* Salt Lake City: University of Utah Press, 1983.

Page 148: A. Leah Underhill. *The Missing Link in Modern Spiritualism.* New York: Thomas R. Knox & Co., 1885.

Page 149 (top): Andrew Jackson Davis. *The Great Harmonia.* Boston: Benjamin B. Mussey & Co., 1853.

Page 149 (bottom): Houdini. *A Magician among the Spirits.* New York: Harper & Brothers, 1924.

Page 150 (left): Cora Richmond. *The Soul.* The Author, 1888.

Page 150 (right): L. B. Fisher. *A Brief History of the Universalist Church.* Boston: Universalist Publishing House, 1912.

Page 151 (left): Charles T. Brooks. *William Ellery Channing.* Boston: Roberts Brothers,

1880.

Page 151 (right): *History of all the Religious Denominations in the United States.* Harrisburg, PA: John Winebrunner, 1848.

Page 156 (top): A. B. Hyde. *The Story of Methodism throughout the World.* Chicago: Johns Publishing House, 1887.

Page 156 (bottom): Matthew Simpson. *Cyclopedia of Methodism.* Philadelphia: Louis H. Everts, 1881.

Page 159: John Henry Barrows. *The World's Parliament of Religions.* Chicago: Parliament Publishing Company, 1893.

Page 160–161: J. Taylor Stanley. *A History of Black Congregational Christian Churches of the South.* New York: United Church Press, 1978.

Page 163: B. W. Arnett. *The Budget.* Philadelphia: the Author, 1884.

Page 165 (left): Reuben, Maury. *The Wars of the Godly.* New York: Robert M. McBride & Company, 1928.

Page 165 (right): Library of Congress.

Page 166: *History of all the Religious Denominations in the United States.* Harrisburg, PA: John Winebrunner, 1848.

Page 167: Albert E. Smith. *Cardinal Gibbons: Churchman and Citizen.* Baltimore: O'Donovan Brothers, 1921.

Page 170 (top): Walter Elliott. *The Life of Father Haecker.* New York: Columbus Press, 1894.

Page 170 (bottom): Reuben Maury. *The Wars of the Godly.* New York: Robert M. McBride & Company, 1928.

Page 173: Anna A. Gordon. *The Beautiful Life of Frances E. Willard.* Chicago: Woman's Temperance Publishing Association, 1898.

Page 175: Thomas Knox, *Life and Work of Henry Ward Beecher.* Hartford, CT: Hartford Publishing Company, 1887.

Page 177: J. N. Lenker. *Lutherans in All Lands.* Milwaukee, WI: Lutherans in All Lands Company, 1896.

Page 178: John Henry Barrows. *The World's Parliament of Religions.* Chicago: Parliament Publishing Company, 1893.

Page 179: Special Collections, Davidson Library, University of California–Santa Barbara

Page 180 (right): Matilda Erickson Andross. *Story of the Advent Message.* Takoma Park, MD: Review and Herald Publishing Association, 1926.

Page 180 (far right): Watch Tower Bible and Tract Society, Brooklyn, NY.

Page 180 (below): Philosophical Library.

Page 181: Matilda Erickson Andross. *Story of the Advent Message.* Takoma Park, MD: Review and Herald Publishing Association, 1926.

Page 182: New Hampshire Historical Society.

Page 183: Courtesy of Richard Southhall Grant.

Page 184: Elwood Worcester. *Life's Adventure.* New York: Charles Scribner's Sons, 1932.

Page 185: Courtesy of Gerald Poesnecker.

Page 186 (top): C. Henry Smith. *The Mennonites.* Berne, IN: Mennonite Book Concern, 1920.

Page 186 (bottom): Shaker Community, Inc.

Page 187: Shaker Community, Inc.

Page 188: Shaker Community, Inc.

Page 192: Jesse Lyman Hurlbut. *Sunday Half Hours with Great Preachers,* 1907.

Page 196 (left): Jesse Lyman Hurlbut. *Sunday Half Hours with Great Preachers,* 1907.

Page 196 (right): John Henry Barrows. *The World's Parliament of Religions.* Chicago: Parliament Publishing Company, 1893.

Page 197 (left): Jesse Lyman Hurlbut. *Sunday Half Hours with Great Preachers,* 1907.

Page 197 (right): Jesse Lyman Hurlbut. *Sunday Half Hours with Great Preachers,* 1907.

Page 199: Sam Jones. *Sam Jones' Own Book.* Cincinnati: Cranston & Stowe, 1886.

Page 200: Arthur Newcomb. *Dowie: Anointed of the Lord.* New York: Century Co., 1930.

Page 201: Charles H. Gabriel. *George C. Stebbins: Reminiscences and Gospel Hymn Stories.* New York: George H. Doran, 1924.

Page 202: William E. Moody. *The Life of Dwight L. Moody.* New York: Fleming H. Revell, 1900.

Page 203 (top): William E. Moody. *The Life of Dwight L. Moody.* New York: Fleming H. Revell, 1900.

Page 203 (bottom): Charles H. Gabriel. *George C. Stebbins: Reminiscences and Gospel Hymn Stories.* New York: George H. Doran, 1924.

Page 204: William T. Ellis. *Billy Sunday: The Man and His Message.* Philadelphia: John C. Winston Company, 1914.

Page 205: William T. Ellis. *Billy Sunday: The Man and His Message.* Philadelphia: John C. Winston Company, 1914

Page 206 (left): Harold Begbie. *The Life of General William Booth.* New York: Macmillan Company, 1920.

Page 206 (right): Harold Begbie. *The Life of General William Booth.* New York: Macmillan Company, 1920.

Page 207: George E. MacDonald. *Fifty Years of Freethought.* New York: Truth Seeker Company, 1929.

Page 208: George E. MacDonald. *Fifty Years of Freethought.* New York: Truth Seeker Company, 1929.

Page 210: Hy Pickering. *Chief Men among the Brethren.* London: Pickering & Inglis, n.d.

Page 214 (top): Bryan College Archives.

Page 214 (bottom): George E. MacDonald. *Fifty Years of Freethought.* New York: Truth Seeker Company, 1929.

Page 215: Courtesy of Charles E. Fuller.

Page 220: Gordon Melton.

Page 221: Thomas Paine. *The Age of Reason.* Middletown, NJ: George H. Evans, 1840.

Page 226: AP Photo, Ed Bailey.

Page 227 (upper left): *The Philosophical Forum,* Boston, 1954.

Page 227 (lower left): Meredith Corporation.

Page 227 Library of Congress.

Page 228: Special Collections, Davidson Library, University of California–Santa Barbara.

Page 230: Special Collections, Davidson Library, University of California–Santa Barbara.

Page 231: Special Collections, Davidson Library, University of California–Santa Barbara.

Page 232: The Peace Mission Movement.

Page 233: National Archives/New York Times.

Page 234: Archive Photos.

Page 235: Library of Congress.

Page 237: John Henry Barrows. *The World's Parliament of Religions.* Chicago: Parliament Publishing Company, 1893.

Page 238: AP Photo.

Page 239 (left): Special Collections, Davidson Library, University of California–Santa Barbara.

Page 239 (right): Reuben Maury. *The Wars of the Godly.* New York: Robert M. McBride & Company, 1928.

Page 241: E. A. Girvin. *Phineas F. Bresee: A Prince in Israel.* Kansas City, MO: Pentecostal Nazarene Publishing House.

Page 242: Bettmann/Corbis.

Page 243: Billy Graham Evangelistic Association.

Page 245: Mrs. Charles F. Parham. *The Life of Charles F. Parham, Founder of the Apostolic Faith Movement.* Joplin, MO: Hunter Printing Company, 1930.

Page 247: Aimee Semple McPherson. *This is That.* Los Angeles: Echo Park Evangelistic Association, 1923.

Page 249: Courtesy of David Edwin Harrell, Jr.

Page 250: David Philipson and Louis Grossman, eds. *Selected Writings of Isaac M. Wise.* Cincinnati: Robert Charles Company, 1900.

Page 253: John Henry Barrows. *The World's Parliament of Religions.* Chicago: Parliament Publishing Company, 1893.

Page 254: Special Collections, Davidson Library, University of California–Santa Barbara.

Page 262 (left): L. P. Mercer. *Review of the World's Religious Congresses.* Chicago: Rand McNally & Company, 1893.

Page 262 (right): William C. Hartmann. *Who's Who in Occultism, New Thought, Psychism and Spiritualism.* Jamaica, NY: Occult Press, 1927.

Page 264: Special Collections, Davidson Library, University of California–Santa Barbara.

Page 267 (top): Charles Mason Remey. *Observations of a Baha'i Traveller.* Privately Published, 1914.

Page 267 (bottom): L. P. Mercer. *Review of the World's Religious Congresses.* Chicago: Rand McNally & Company, 1893.

Page 268 (top): L. P. Mercer. *Review of the World's Religious Congresses.* Chicago: Rand McNally & Company, 1893.

Page 268 (bottom): John Henry Barrows. *The World's Parliament of Religions.* Chicago: Parliament Publishing Company, 1893.

Page 270 (top): Gordon Melton.

Page 270 (bottom): Gordon Melton.

Page 271 (left): Sister Devamata. *Swami Paramananda and His Work.* La Crescenta, CA: Ananda Ashrama, 1926.

Page 271 (upper right): William C. Hartmann, *Who's Who in Occultism, New Thought, Psychism and Spiritualism.* Jamaica, NY: Occult Press, 1927.

Page 271 (lower right): John Henry Barrows. *The World's Parliament of Religions.* Chicago: Parliament Publishing Company, 1893.

Page 272: Gordon Melton.

Page 274: Horatio W. Dresser. *Voices of Freedom.* New York: G. P. Putnam's Son's, 1906.

Page 275 (left): A. P. Sinnett. *Incidents in the Life of Madame Blavatsky.* London: Theosophical Publishing Society, 1913.

Page 275 (right): C. Jinajarasa. *Golden Book of the Theosophical Society.* Adyar, India: Theosophical Publishing House, 1925.

Page 276: C. W. Leadbeater. *The Masters and the Path.* Ayar, India; Theosophical Publishing House.

Page 277: Special Collections, Davidson Library, University of California–Santa Barbara.

Page 278: Bettmann/Corbis

Page 279: Special Collections, Davidson Library, University of California–Santa Barbara.

Page 281: Special Collections, Davidson Library, University of California–Santa Barbara.

Page 283 (right): Special Collections, Davidson Library, University of California–Santa Barbara.

Page 283 (left): Special Collections, Davidson Library, University of California–Santa Barbara.

Page 285 (top): Special Collections, Davidson Library, University of California–Santa Barbara.

Page 285 (bottom): Special Collections, Davidson Library, University of California–Santa Barbara.

Page 286: Special Collections, Davidson Library, University of California–Santa Barbara.

Page 288 (upper left): Archive Photos.

Page 288 (upper right): AP Photo.

Page 288 (bottom): Gordon Melton.

Index

Polish National Catholic Church, 165

Ponce de León, Juan, 12, 41–42

Pontiac, Chief, 18

Popé, 17–18, 30

Potter, Charles Francis, 222

The Power of Positive Thinking (Peale), 274

Prabhupada, A. C. Bhaktivedanta Swami, 282

Premillennialism, 210–211

Presbyterian Church (U.S.A.), 229

Presbyterians
    in colonial America, 79, 98–99, 102, 131
    and conservative theology, 209
    Cumberland, 198
    divisions among, 99, 102, 140, 171, 195
    and education, 131, 195
    on the frontier, 133
    and fundamentalism, 211, 213, 215
    as missionaries, 32, 34, 163
    and modernism, 195, 196, 211, 213, 244
    and revivalism, 133, 134, 171, 198
    in Scotland, 52–53
    on slavery, 140

Princeton University, 101 (illus.), 102, 131, 209

Progressive National Baptist Convention, 232

Protestant Episcopal Church, 120–122, 155. *See also* Episcopalians

Provost, Samuel, 122

Puritans, 51, 52–53, 58–59, 73, 79, 85, 88, 91

Quakers
    in colonial America, 59–60, 67, 70, 80–81, 81 (illus.)
    in England, 66
    and Pentecostalism, 246
    on Revolutionary War, 114–115
    on slavery, 103, 139

Quimby, Phineas Parkhurst, 183

Radical Reformers, 82

Raleigh, Sir Walter, 14

Raleigh Institute, 162

Ralston, Robert, 137

Randolph, Pascal Beverly, 185 (illus.)

Rationalism, 220

Reason the Only Oracle of Man (Allen), 220

Reconstructionist Judaism, 252

Reese, Curtis W., 222

Reform Judaism, 250–252

Reformation, 44, 47–48, 106

Reformed Church in America, 179

Reformed movement and churches, 32, 50, 63 (illus.), 65, 78–79, 91–92, 176, 178, 179

Religious Science movement, 184

Re-Thinking Missions (Hocking), 197–198, 240

Revivalism
    in colonial America, 92–93, 97–98, 99, 102
    and evangelism, 202–206
    on the frontier, 132–134, 171, 199
    as a means of conversion, 198–199, 201, 204, 206
    sentiment against, 245–246
    in urban areas, 201, 202, 204

Revivals of Religion (Finney), 134

Revolutionary War, U.S., 111, 113–115, 116

Rhode Island
    religions in, 59, 70 (illus.), 91

Rice, Luther, 128–129

Richmond, Cora, 150 (illus.)

Richmond Theological Seminary, 162

Riverside Church, New York, N.Y., 213

Roberts, Oral, 248, 249 (illus.)

Roberts, Richard, 248

Robertson, Pat, 248

Rodeheaver, Homer, 202

Roman Catholics
    in colonial Maryland, 62, 65, 73, 74
    in England, 50–52, 53–54, 60, 73
    in Europe, 44–46, 49
    as missionaries, 17, 29, 30, 34, 42, 44
    and revivalism, 201
    on the Revolutionary War, 113
    sentiment against, 52, 53, 73, 165–66, 170, 261
    in the United States, 164–169, 236, 240, 259
    and Vatican II, 235, 236, 238–240, 261
    on women's role, 235

Roncalli, Angelo Giuseppe, 238–239